Sexual Harassment

Teaching Texts in Law and Politics

David A. Schultz
General Editor

Vol. 12

PETER LANG
New York • Washington, D.C./Baltimore • Bern
Frankfurt am Main • Berlin • Brussels • Vienna • Oxford

Paul I. Weizer

Sexual Harassment

Cases, Case Studies, & Commentary

PETER LANG
New York • Washington, D.C./Baltimore • Bern
Frankfurt am Main • Berlin • Brussels • Vienna • Oxford

LIBRARY OF CONGRESS CATALOGING-IN-PUBLICATION DATA

Weizer, Paul I.
Sexual harassment: cases, case studies, and commentary / Paul I. Weizer.
p. cm. — (Teaching texts in law and politics; vol. 12)
Includes bibliographical references and index.
1. Sexual harassment—Law and legislation—United States. 2. Sex discrimination in employment—
Law and legislation—United States. I. Title. II. Series.
KF3467 .W448   344.7301'133—dc21   2001038819
ISBN 0-8204-5261-0
ISSN 1083-3447

DIE DEUTSCHE BIBLIOTHEK-CIP-EINHEITSAUFNAHME

Weizer, Paul I.:
Sexual harassment: cases, case studies, and commentary / Paul I. Weizer.
–New York; Washington, D.C./Baltimore; Bern; Frankfurt am Main;
Berlin; Brussels; Vienna; Oxford: Lang.
(Teaching texts in law and politics; Vol. 12)
ISBN 0-8204-5261-0

Cover design by Joni Holst

The paper in this book meets the guidelines for permanence and durability
of the Committee on Production Guidelines for Book Longevity
of the Council of Library Resources.

Printed in the United States of America

In memory of Diane Spiller

Table of Contents

Part 3. Commentary

Part 4. Appendix

Acknowledgments

I would like to thank several people for their encouragement and support during the writing process. Dr. Jim Heasley was the co-author of Taking the Science Out of Decision Making: Sexual Harassment Policy and Human Resource Management, one of the case studies contained in this book. He was also instrumental in providing encouragement as well as editing. Without his vital contributions, this book would not have been possible.

Among the friends and colleagues to whom I am grateful are Dr. Ellis Katz, Dr. Conrad Weiler, and Dr. Sean Goodlett. Your thoughtful comments and guidance are greatly appreciated.

I would also like to thank my series editor, Dr. David Schultz, for his valuable insight and thoughtful comments regarding my manuscript. I remain most appreciative.

Above all, to Randi and Jessica, for their support during the creation of this text, thank you.

Finally, grateful acknowledgment is hereby made to copyright holders for their permission to reprint from the following works:

Forell, Caroline A. and Donna M. Matthews. *A Law of Her Own: The Reasonable Woman as a Measure of Man.* New York: New York University Press, 1999, 23-33. Reprinted by permission of the publisher.

Oppenheimer, David B. "Workplace Harassment and the First Amendment: A Reply to Professor Volokh." *Berkeley Journal of Employment & Labor Law,* 17 (1996): 320-331. Reprinted by permission of the publisher.

Schultz, David. "From Reasonable Man to Unreasonable Victim." *Suffolk University Law Review*, 27 (1995): 717-748. Reprinted by permission of the publisher.

Volokh, Eugene. "What Speech Does "Hostile Work Environment" Harassment Law Restrict?" 85 *Georgetown Law Journal*, 85 (1997): 627- 653. Reprinted by permission of the author.

Introduction

It is not always clear what actually constitutes "sexual harassment" or how it differs from other types of discrimination based on gender. Often times, what is thought of as sexual harassment by one person might be considered simply rude or immature behavior by another. While sexual harassment is a major issue in America, there is no bona fide consensus as to what sexual harassment really is.

This book is designed to bring together material on an issue that is currently troubling most workplaces and schools in the United States: the problem of how to deal with a distressing increase in sexual harassment claims in all areas of American life. This subject is enormously complicated. The more one looks at the legal, practical, and moral context of the issue, the less amenable it appears to a simple solution. Many students seem to view the issue in black and white, in terms of right and wrong. Yet attempts to formulate rules to deal with the problem of harassment have proven to fall upon many shades of gray. There are many competing interests at stake in various situations of alleged harassment that do not fit easily into categories of absolutely right or absolutely wrong.

This book does not attempt to answer all of the questions of how best to prevent sexual harassment while preserving the rights of the accused. No book can provide such answers. This book is designed to provide readers a variety of material to begin the journey of discovering these answers for themselves. To this end, I have provided three types of material, all of which offer different perspectives on the problem at hand: leading judicial opinions, original case studies addressing some of the dilemmas involved in creating and enforcing harassment policies, and commentary from major authors of the field.

I have tried to provide a balanced approach to the issue throughout the book. While I admit to having strong feelings on the subject, I have tried to include a wide variety of competing viewpoints. I have endeavored to include court cases that represent all aspects of sexual harassment law. They are listed chronologically to show the evolution of the law in this area. Where court decisions have attracted dissenting points of view, I have included them. I have tried to find the most articulate and thorough representatives of the various positions on the issue of sexual harassment in the commentary section.

Finally, I have tried to make this book self-contained. This volume should provide the reader with the essentials necessary to understand the complexity of the problem of regulating sexual harassment. The solutions will not always come easily. However, I hope this will provide an academic and challenging introduction to the myriad of interests involved in dealing with an often sensationalized (and frequently trivialized) subject.

History

Most sexual harassment cases arise under Title VII of the Civil Rights Act of 1964. Its original purpose as a civil rights measure was to outlaw racial segregation. Sex, as a category, was added at the last minute as an amendment in a cynical attempt to defeat the bill altogether.[1] The amendment to include sex as a protected category was raised on February 8, 1964, just two days before final passage of the bill in the House of Representatives. House Rules Committee Chairman Howard Smith of Virginia (who was no champion of civil rights in any form) introduced the amendment but was hardly enthusiastic about it. He completed his speech on the amendment by concluding "this bill is so imperfect, what harm will this little amendment do?"[2]   Surprisingly, the amendment received support. Representative Martha W. Griffiths of Michigan argued that without the addition of sex as a separate category, black women (due to their race) would be protected by the bill, but white women would not.[3]   Though many Representatives ultimately opposed this amendment, there were no substantive arguments in opposition. Finally, the amendment was approved by a vote of 168—133.

Though an afterthought, sex-based criteria have developed into one of the most litigated parts of the civil rights agenda. According to the United States census bureau, it is estimated that there are slightly more than thirty-five million African Americans while there are more than one hundred and forty million women living in the United States.[4] Thus all of the protections of the Civil Rights Act provide equal employment opportunity protection to far more women than racial minorities.

Cases

Title VII does not specifically outlaw sexual harassment or sexual speech. Instead, its broad proclamation makes it illegal for an employer to discriminate "against any individual with respect to his compensation, terms, conditions, or privileges of employment, because of such individual's race, color, religion, sex, or national origin."[5]

Sexual harassment can take two separate and distinct forms. The first of these is called quid pro quo harassment. This entails something for something, such as an employer demanding sex in exchange for a job or promotion. This is clearly the classic type of harassment where the employment context is altered through the exploitation of an employee on the basis of sex or sexuality. In this type of situation, the harassment necessarily involves a hierarchical dynamic that is subjugated as an abuse of authority. As quid pro quo harassment can only exist though a supervisor exercising the power of his or her position, an employer will always be strictly liable for the actions of employees.

The second and more complicated form of sexual harassment is what is called hostile environment harassment. This occurs when the workplace is so polluted with discrimination that it makes the environment of the employment setting hostile or intimidating. In this instance, the existence of harassment is not dependent on the existence of a power relationship or on any tangible job benefit. The workplace atmosphere alone forms the basis of the proscribed behavior. Because this type of harassment is necessarily a more broadly defined category and can be caused by anyone (not just supervisory personnel exercising the power of their position), an employer may be liable for the environment in its workplace subject to an affirmative defense.

Courts first held that sexual harassment of employees was a violation of Title VII in the mid-1970s.[6] Prior to this, courts often allowed sex-based demands and requests to continue so long as they were not directly accompanied by employment consequences supported by company policies. Individual actions of supervisors were considered to be insufficient to state a claim under Title VII. As seen in *Corne v. Bausch and Lomb*, "personal urges" of supervisors were held to be separate and distinct from employment practices that fell under the protections of Title VII.

Tompkins v. PSE&G was one of the first decisions to recognize quid pro quo harassment as a form of employment discrimination. The court in *Tompkins* recognized that offers of benefits or threats of reprisal resulting from sexual propositions are a violation of federal civil rights laws, holding that "her employer, either knowingly or constructively, made acquiescence in her supervisor's sexual demands a necessary prerequisite to the continuation of, or advancement in, her job."[7] *Bundy v. Jackson* provides a classic example of the type of hostile environment which was all too common during this time period. Women who didn't play the "game" in the workplace were treated differently. As harassment law evolved, this began to change.

The Supreme Court first took up the issue of sexual harassment in the 1986 case of *Meritor Savings Bank v. Vinson*. The standards for sexual harassment in the workplace had been emerging through opinions of the lower federal courts and guidelines provided by the EEOC. In its first ruling on sexual harassment under Title VII, the Supreme Court unanimously approved of the path that was being taken. While not reaching the crucial issue of employer liability, the Supreme Court did recognize the existence of the "hostile environment" theory of harassment, thus making it the law of the land. It defined hostile environment sexual harassment as conduct that is "sufficiently severe or pervasive" as to "alter the conditions of employment and create an abusive working environment." The Court further held that the crux of any sexual harassment dispute would be whether the sexual advances were "unwelcome."[8]

Following the *Meritor* decision, it was left to the lower courts to determine the level of severity and pervasiveness needed to create a hostile environment as well as the degree of welcoming in sexual advances. Not surprisingly, different views of these standards emerged. Later in 1986, the Sixth Circuit Court of Appeals in *Rabidue v. Osceola Refining Co.*, found that vulgarity and obscene poster displays in the workplace, without more, was not enough to violate Title VII.

Five years later, in *Robinson v. Jacksonville Shipyards Inc.*, a United States District Court ruled that vulgarity and pornographic dislays can alter the dynamic of the workplace, thus changing the "terms and conditions" of employment. The *Robinson* court held that workplaces must accommodate men and women alike. "It is absurd to believe that Title VII opened the doors of such places in form and closed them in substance."[9]

During that same year, the Ninth Circuit Court of Appeals added a new dynamic to the method of interpretation used in sexual harassment cases. In *Ellison v. Brady*, the court adopted a reasonable woman standard (first mentioned in the *Rabidue* dissent), stating that "we believe that in evaluating the severity and pervasiveness of sexual harassment, we should focus on the perspective of the victim."[10]

While lower courts continued to differ in applying the Supreme Court's *Meritor* standard in the workplace, the High Court turned its attention to sexual harassment in the schools. In *Franklin v. Gwinnett County Public Schools*, the Supreme Court ruled for the first time that monetary damages were available for violations of Title IX and that schools could be liable for those violations. Title IX of the Educational Amendments of 1972, which prohibits sexual discrimination by educational institutions receiving federal funds, was one of the first major legal steps taken to eliminate sex discrimination from schools.[11] In *Franklin*, the Court ruled that Title IX damages could be awarded to individual victims of sexual harassment. This opens the door to suits by parents or students who can show that they have suffered harassment in school, that this conduct affected their educational opportunities, and that the school did not do enough to stop the harassing behavior. This landmark decision would be expanded upon several years later in *Davis v. Monroe County Board of Education*.

In 1993, the Supreme Court heard its second case on the issue of sexual harassment in the workplace. In *Harris v. Forklift Systems Inc.*, the Court was presented with another opportunity to clarify for the lower courts the standard of a hostile environment. In this decision, the Justices ruled that no tangible harm was needed to proceed with a sexual harassment complaint. It held that "Title VII comes into play before the harassing conduct leads to a nervous breakdown."[12] And that, "certainly Title VII bars conduct that would seriously affect a reasonable person's psychological well-being, but the statute is not limited to such conduct. So long as the environment would reasonably be perceived, and is perceived, as hostile or abusive, there is no need for it also to be psychologically injurious."[13]

Following *Harris*, it would take four years for the Supreme Court to decide another sexual harassment claim. In *Oncale v. Sundowner Offshore Services*, the Court for the first time confronted the issue of same-sex harassment. Settling a deep conflict among the lower courts, it ruled that sexual behavior is a violation of Title VII even if it is not motivated by sexual desire. [While recognizing that this was not the aim of the legislation, the Court held that sexual harassment in any form is a violation.] "As some courts have observed, male-on-male sexual harassment in the workplace was assuredly not the principal evil Congress was concerned with when it enacted Title VII. But statutory prohibitions often go beyond the principal evil to cover reasonably comparable evils."[14]

During the same term, the Supreme Court would also consider directly the issue of employer liability in hostile environment cases. In quid pro quo cases, an employer is always strictly liable for the actions of its personnel. However, it had previously declined to address the scope of liability when tangible job consequences were not at issue. In *Burlington Industries v. Ellerth*, the Court held that a private employer can be vicariously liable for the actions of its employees, subject to an affirmative defense by the employer. This decision greatly expanded the scope of potential liability for employers. A companion case, *Faragher v. Boca Raton*, extended this standard of liability to public employers as well.

Sexual harassment under Title IX was revisited in 1999. *Franklin* had allowed school districts to be held liable for sexual harassment in schools but had not set the level at which liability attached. In *Davis v. Monroe County Board of Education*, the Supreme Court ruled that a standard of deliberate indifference would be the bar to be cleared to claim liability. Noting the different intents between Title VII and Title IX, this is a much higher standard than the one set the year prior for workplace harassment.

Since the Supreme Court first addressed the issue of sexual harassment in *Meritor*, the challenge of defining what sexual harassment is and who is liable for it have become increasingly complex. Students will need to sort through the various opinions and determine for themselves the application of these precedents to new and multifaceted circumstances. Perhaps the major challenge in addressing sexual harassment today comes in trying to pinpoint a precise definition. Without one, the scope of the law remains an open question.

Case Studies

As the materials that follow make clear, sexual harassment is one of the most difficult legal problems facing the United States today.   Three case studies are included in this volume which examine the topic of sexual harassment from a variety of angles. "The Clarence Thomas Confirmation Hearings: The Awakening of America to the Issue of Sexual Harassment" takes an historical approach to the growth of awareness of this issue.   Many Americans had never considered the issue of sexual harassment before the allegations made by Anita Hill first surfaced during the process of evaluating Clarence Thomas for the Supreme Court. Since that time, the issue of sexual harassment has become the focus of ongoing national attention. The hearings were a watershed event in American history. This selection details the main arguments made during the hearings and looks at the lasting impact of this event on the American legal and social fabric.

The book examines the impact of sexual harassment law on public administration in "Taking the Science out of Decision Making: Sexual Harassment Policy and Human Resource Management."   By focusing on a specific encounter in Cambridge, Massachusetts, this selection scrutinizes the range of decisions managers face in dealing with vicarious liability for the actions of their employees. Owing to the scope of the law, and this potential for liability, the traditional theories of decision making are viewed in action.

Finally, "Sexual Harassment and Free Speech: The Lessons of the Campus Speech Code Controversies" applies the logic of recent court decisions regarding codes of behavior in comparison to the sexual harassment workplace decisions contained in this book. Considering that these codes of conduct, many of which have been ruled unconstitutional, closely mirror the language of Title VII, important questions must be raised. The similarities and differences between the speech codes and existing sexual harassment regulations are examined and debated to help the readers reach conclusions of their own.

Commentary

The final section of this book provides commentary that includes a range of competing perspectives on the issues raised in the previous sections. The first two readings are general overviews of the debate about free speech and the impact of harassment law on the First Amendment.

First, Eugene Volokh argues passionately that harassment law has wide-reaching implications beyond just limiting sexual harassment.[15] He contends that the broad scope of the law also sweeps up much protected speech and expression, thus presenting a major issue under the First Amendment. The chilling effect of these laws is to limit discourse in general, whether it would be protected or not.

In response, David Oppenheimer disputes this contention, claiming instead that there is no First Amendment issue involved in limiting sexist behavior.[16] He contends that the First Amendment does not apply in most workplace settings. In the alternative, Oppenheimer argues that not all speech is protected by the First Amendment, regardless of the setting, and that whatever is considered sexual harassment belongs alongside of obscenity, blackmail, and other forms of unprotected speech.

The final two selections move from the protection of the behavior that falls under the purview of sexual harassment to the liability for employers involved. Specifically, the authors debate the soundness of the "reasonable woman" standard.

Caroline A. Forell and Donna M. Matthews put forth the position that many actions are viewed differently through the eyes of men and women.[17] They contend that since women have habitually been the victims of sexual harassment, it is impossible for the traditional "reasonable person" standard to adequately express the disparity that women have traditionally held under the law.

David Schultz strongly disagrees. He argues that all current reasonableness standards are conceptually problematic. In their place, Schultz advocates a balancing of interests test as a better means to weigh the interests of free speech and the victim's sensitivity.[18]

There are no "right" answers to this complex problem. However, these selections provide thought-provoking insights into the difficulty of applying the current standard of sexual harassment.

1.   *Barnes v. Costle*, 561 F. 2D 983 (D.C. Cir.1977).

2.   Loevy, Robert D., *To End All Segregation* (Lanham, MD: University Press of America) 1990, p. 120.

3.   Ibid.

4.   More detailed statistical information is available at www.census.government.

5.   Title VII, Civil Rights Act of 1964, 42 U.S.C., section 2000e-2.

6.   *Barnes v. Costle*, 561 F. 2D 983 (D.C. Cir.1977).

7.   *Tompkins v. Public Service Electric and Gas Co.*, 568 F. 2d 1045 (1977).

8.   *Meritor Savings Bank v. Vinson*, 477 U.S. 57 (1986).

9.   *Robinson v. Jacksonville Shipyards Inc.*, 760 F. Supp. 1486 (1991).

10.   *Ellison v. Brady*, 924 F.2d 872 (1991).

11.   Title IX of the Educational Amendments of 1972, 20 U.S.C. Sec. 1681.

12.   *Harris v. Forklift Systems Inc.*, 510 U.S. 17 (1993).

13.   *Harris v. Forklift Systems Inc.*, 510 U.S. 17 (1993).

14.   *Oncale v. Sundowner Offshore Services*, 523 U.S. 75 (1998).

15.   Eugene Volokh, "What Speech Does 'Hostile Work Environment' Harassment Law Restrict?," 85 *Geo. L.J.* 627 (1997).

16.   Oppenheimer, David Benjamin, "Workplace Harassment and the First Amendment: A Reply to Professor Volokh," 17 *Berkeley Journal of Employment and Labor Law* 321 (1996).

17.   Caroline A. Forell and Donna M. Matthews, *A Law of Her Own*, (New York: New York University Press, 2000).

18.   David Schultz, "From Reasonable Man to Unreasonable Victim?", 27 *Suffolk University Law Review* 717 (1993).

Part 1
Cases

Corne v. Bausch and Lomb, Inc.

390 F. Supp. 161 (1975)
United States District Court for the District of Arizona
Opinion by: Frey, D.J.

Plaintiffs Jane Corne and Geneva DeVane filed the present complaint alleging a violation of civil rights based on sex discrimination. The suit was instituted pursuant to Section 706(f)(1) and (3) of Title VII of the Civil Rights Act of 1964 (Title 42, United States Code, Section 2000e et seq). It is alleged that at the time the discriminatory acts occurred, plaintiffs were employed by defendant Bausch and Lomb, and defendant Leon Price was in a supervisory capacity over plaintiffs....

The complaint further alleges the following: plaintiffs worked in a clerical capacity for defendants in the period before the filing of the EEOC complaints; plaintiffs' employment conditions became increasingly onerous in that they were repeatedly subjected to verbal and physical sexual advances from defendant Price; defendant Price's illegal activities were directed not only to plaintiffs but also to other female employees and thus constituted a condition of employment that discriminates by sex in violation of Title VII; cooperation with defendant Price's illegal activities resulted in favored employment that discriminates by sex in violation of Title VII; immediately before the filing of the complaint with the EEOC, defendant Price's activities directed to plaintiffs became so onerous that plaintiffs were forced to resign.

Defendant Bausch and Lomb has filed a Motion to Dismiss the complaint....

A hearing on the motions was held on January 20, 1975, and the matter is now deemed submitted. The main focus here is on the issue of whether a claim for relief is stated under Title VII.

Assuming that all allegations in the complaint are true, plaintiffs have failed to state a claim for relief under Title VII of the Civil Rights Act.

Title 42, United States Code, Section 2000e-2(a) provides in pertinent part:

> (a) Employers. It shall be an unlawful employment practice for an employer....
> (1) to fail or refuse to hire or to discharge any individual, or otherwise to discriminate against any individual with respect to his compensation, terms, conditions, or privileges of employment, because of such individual's race, color, religion, sex, or national origin; or
> (2) to limit, segregate, or classify his employees or applicants for employment in any way which would deprive or tend to deprive any individual of employment opportunities or otherwise adversely affect his status as an employee, because of such individual's race, color, religion, sex, or national origin.

Plaintiffs allege that they are females; that they were repeatedly subjected to verbal and physical sexual advances from defendant Price; and that due to such advances plaintiffs terminated their employment with Bausch and Lomb. Plaintiffs allege that putting a male in a supervisory position over female employees, where the male supervisor persistently takes unsolicited and unwelcome sexual liberties with the female employees is the creation of a sex discriminatory condition, and a limitation that tends to deprive the women of equal employment opportunities; the plaintiffs seek to hold the employer liable because its administrative personnel knew or should have known of defendant Price's conduct toward female employees.

There is little legislative history surrounding the addition of the word "sex" to the employment discrimination provisions of Title VII of the Civil Rights Act of 1964. In *Diaz v. Pan Am. Airways, Inc.*, 442 F.2d 385 (5th Cir. 1971), the Court stated:

The amendment adding the word "sex to race, color, religion and national origin" was adopted one day before House passage of the Civil Rights Act. It was added on the floor and engendered little relevant debate. In attempting to read Congress' intent in these circumstances, however, it is reasonable to assume, from a reading of the statute itself, that one of Congress' main goals was to provide equal access to the job market for both men and women....

With respect to unlawful employment practices by employers, it can be seen that in addition to the specific language in Title 42, United States Code, Section 2000e-2(a) making it unlawful for an employer to discriminate because of an individual's sex with respect to hiring, discharging, classification or compensation of individuals, it has been held an unlawful employment practice for an employer to discriminate against individuals with respect to job assignment or transfer, *Rosenfeld v. Southern Pacific Co.*, 444 F.2d 1219 (9th Cir. 1971); hours of employment, *Ridinger v. General Motors Corp.*, 325 F. Supp. 1089 (D. Ohio 1971); or "fringe benefits" such as retirement, pension, and death benefits, *Bartmess v. Drewrys U.S.A., Inc.*, 444 F.2d 1186 (7th Cir. 1971). Employers have been found to have discriminated against female employees because of their sex where they maintained policies which discriminated against females because they were married, *Jurinko v. Edwin L. Wiegand Co.*, 331 F. Supp. 1184 (D. Pa. 1971) or pregnant, *Schattman v. Texas Employment Co.*, 330 F. Supp. 328 (D. Tex. 1971). In addition, it has been held that an employer's rule which forbids or restricts the employment of married women and which is not applicable to married men is a discrimination based on sex prohibited by Title VII. *Sprogis v. United Air Lines, Inc.*, 444 F.2d 1194 (7th Cir. 1971).

In all of the above-mentioned cases the discriminatory conduct complained of, arose out of company policies. There was apparently some advantage to, or gain by, the employer from such discriminatory practices. Always such discriminatory practices were employer designed and oriented. In the present case, Mr. Price's conduct appears to be nothing more than a personal proclivity, peculiarity or mannerism. By his alleged sexual advances, Mr. Price was satisfying a personal urge. Certainly no employer policy is here involved; rather than the company being benefited in any way by the conduct of Price, it is obvious it can only be damaged by the very nature of the acts complained of.

Nothing in the complaint alleges nor can it be construed that the conduct complained of was company-directed policy which deprived women of employment opportunities. A reasonably intelligent reading of the statute demonstrates it can only mean that an unlawful employment practice must be discrimination on the part of the employer, Bausch and Lomb. Further, there is nothing in the Act which could reasonably be construed to have it apply to "verbal and physical sexual advances" by another employee, even though he be in a supervisory capacity where such complained-of acts or conduct had no relationship to the nature of the employment.

It would be ludicrous to hold that the sort of activity involved here was contemplated by the Act because to do so would mean that if the conduct complained of was directed equally to males there would be no basis for suit. Also, an outgrowth of holding such activity to be actionable under Title VII would be a potential federal lawsuit every time any employee made amorous or sexually oriented advances toward another. The only sure way an employer could avoid such charges would be to have employees who were asexual....

It Is Ordered that defendants' Motions to Dismiss, are granted and the complaint, is dismissed.

Discussion Questions

1) In what sense were the advances allegedly made toward Corne a "sex-based term or condition" of her employment?

2) Why did the court focus on Price's actions in a personal rather than managerial context?

3) Why did the court find that Price's actions "had no relationship to the nature of the employment"? Is this a fair reading of the law?

Tompkins v. Public Service Electric & Gas Co.

568 F.2d 1044 (1977)
United States Court of Appeals for the Third Circuit
Opinion of the Court: Aldisert, Circuit Judge

Taken as true, the facts set out in appellant's complaint demonstrate that Adrienne Tomkins was hired by PSE&G in April 1971 and progressed to positions of increasing responsibility from that time until August 1973, when she began working in a secretarial position under the direction of a named supervisor. On October 30, 1973, the supervisor told Tomkins that she should have lunch with him in a nearby restaurant in order to discuss his upcoming evaluation of her work as well as a possible job promotion. At lunch, he made advances toward her, indicating his desire to have sexual relations with her and stating that this would be necessary if they were to have a satisfactory working relationship. When Tomkins attempted to leave the restaurant, the supervisor responded first by threats of recrimination against Tomkins in her employment, then by threats of physical force, and ultimately by physically restraining Tomkins. During the incident, he told her that no one at PSE&G would help her should she lodge a complaint against him.

Tomkins' complaint alleges that PSE&G and certain of its agents knew or should have known that such incidents would occur and that they nevertheless "placed [Tomkins] in a position where she would be subjected to the aforesaid conduct of [the supervisor] and failed to take adequate supervisory measures to prevent such incidents from occurring." It further alleged that on the day following the lunch, Tomkins expressed her intention to leave PSE&G as a result of the incident. She agreed to continue work only after being promised a transfer to a comparable position elsewhere in the company. A comparable position did not become available, however, and Tomkins was instead placed in an inferior position in another department. There, she was subjected to false and adverse employment evaluations, disciplinary layoffs, and threats of demotion by various PSE&G employees. Tomkins maintains that as a result of the supervisor's conduct and the continued pattern of harassment by PSE&G personnel, she suffered physical and emotional distress, resulting in absenteeism and loss of income.

In January 1975, PSE&G fired Tomkins. Following her dismissal, she filed an employment discrimination complaint with the Equal Employment Opportunity Commission, which ultimately issued a Notice of Right to Sue. After Tomkins filed suit in district court, PSE&G moved to dismiss the complaint on various grounds, including failure to state a claim upon which relief may be granted. In addressing the motion, the district court bifurcated the issues raised in the complaint. The court denied the company's motion to dismiss Tomkins' claim of company retaliation against her for complaining about her supervisor's conduct. However, the company's motion to dismiss Tomkins' claim against PSE&G for his actions was granted for failure to state a claim. The latter judgment was determined final by the district court under Rule 54(b), Fed. R. Civ. P., and this appeal followed.

Section 703(a)(1) of Title VII, 42 U.S.C. § 2000e-2(a)(1), provides that "it shall be an unlawful employment practice for an employer...to discharge any individual...or otherwise to discriminate against any individual with respect to...terms, conditions, or privileges of employment because of such individual's...sex..." In order to state a claim under this provision, then, it is necessary that Tomkins establish both that the acts complained of constituted a condition of employment and that this condition was imposed by the employer on the basis of sex.

Tomkins claims that the sexual demands of her supervisor imposed a sex-based "term or condition" on her employment. She alleges that her promotion and favorable job evaluation were made conditional upon her granting sexual favors and that she suffered adverse job consequences as a result of this incident. In granting appellees' motion to dismiss, however, the district court characterized the supervisor's acts as "abuse of authority...for personal purposes." The court thus overlooked the major thrust of Tomkins' complaint, i.e., that her employer, either knowingly or constructively, made acquiescence in her supervisor's sexual demands a necessary prerequisite to the continuation of, or advancement in, her job.

The facts as alleged by appellant clearly demonstrate an incident with employment ramifications, one within the intended coverage of Title VII. The context within which the sexual advances occurred is itself strong evidence of a job-related condition: Tomkins was asked to lunch by her supervisor for the express purpose of discussing his upcoming evaluation of her work and possible recommendation of her for a promotion. But one need not infer the added condition from the setting alone. It is expressly alleged that the supervisor stated to Tomkins that her continued success and advancement at PSE&G were dependent upon her agreeing to his sexual demands. The demand thus amounted to a condition of employment, an additional duty or burden Tomkins was required by her supervisor to meet as a prerequisite to her continued employment.

Cases dealing with the issue presented in this appeal are scarce, and our research has produced no controlling precedent. Reference to certain of the cases is helpful, however, for a discernible pattern emerges from the decisions. The District of Columbia Circuit was presented with similar facts in *Barnes v. Costle*, 561 F.2d 983 (1977), a Title VII action in which appellant alleged that her job was abolished in retaliation for her refusal to engage in sexual relations with her male supervisor. Plaintiff claimed that in the course of her employment, the supervisor made a number of sexual advances and conditioned any enhancement of her job status on her acquiescing to his sexual demands. Noting appellant's assertion that "she became the target of her superior's sexual desires because she was a woman, and was asked to bow to his demands as the price for holding her job," the Court of Appeals determined that the alleged facts constituted a violation of Title VII and therefore reversed the district court's grant of summary judgment in favor of defendant.

Faced with claims that at first appear similar, two district courts reached different results. In *Corne v. Bausch and Lomb, Inc.*, 390 F. Supp. 161 (D. Ariz. 1975), it was held that verbal sexual advances by a male employee to female fellow employees did not constitute actionable sex discrimination under Title VII. *Corne* is distinguishable from the facts before us because plaintiff Corne did not allege that acquiescence in the sexual advances was required as a condition of her employment. Appellant Tomkins, by contrast, clearly alleged such an employment nexus. Also distinguishable from the current appeal is *Miller v. Bank of America*, 418 F. Supp. 233. Plaintiff Miller alleged that her male supervisor promised her job advancement in return for engaging in sexual relations with him and subsequently dismissed her when she refused to do so. Not only was it undisputed that defendant bank discouraged such employee misconduct, but plaintiff had failed to avail herself of a bank complaint procedure designed to resolve precisely this sort of complaint.

Although these cases are not dispositive of this appeal, they disclose a pattern of how sexual advances in the employment context do or do not constitute a Title VII violation. The courts have distinguished between complaints alleging sexual advances of an individual or personal nature and those alleging direct employment consequences flowing from the advances, finding Title VII violations in the latter category. This distinction recognizes two elements necessary to find a violation of Title VII: first, that a term or condition of employment has been imposed and second, that it has been imposed by the employer, either directly or vicariously, in a sexually discriminatory fashion. Applying these requirements to the present complaint, we conclude that Title VII is violated when a supervisor, with the actual or constructive knowledge of the employer, makes sexual advances or demands toward a subordinate employee and conditions that employee's job status—evaluation, continued employment, promotion, or other aspects of career development—on a favorable response to those advances or demands, and the employer does not take prompt and appropriate remedial action after acquiring such knowledge.

We do not agree with the district court that finding a Title VII violation on these facts will result in an unmanageable number of suits and a difficulty in differentiating between spurious and meritorious claims. The congressional mandate that the federal courts provide relief is strong; it must not be thwarted by concern for judicial economy. More significant, however, this decision in no way relieves the plaintiff of the burden of proving the facts alleged to establish the required elements of a Title VII violation. Although any theory of liability may be used in vexatious or bad faith suits, we are confident that traditional judicial mechanisms will separate the valid from the invalid complaints.

Discussion Questions

1) In what sense were the advances allegedly made toward Tompkins a "sex-based term or condition" of her employment?

2) Would the same logic have applied if no job-related consequences were promised or threatened? Had the supervisor suggested a sexual relationship without stating that it would be necessary for their working relationship, would Tompkins still prevail?

3) If the person who made the offending comments to Tompkins had been a co-worker rather than her supervisor, would she still have a claim of sexual harassment?

Barnes v. Costle

561 F.2d 983 (1977)
United States Court of Appeals for the
District of Columbia Circuit
Opinion: Robinson, Circuit Judge

This appeal launches a review of an order of the District Court awarding a summary judgment to appellee on the ground that Title VII of the Civil Rights Act of 1964, as amended by the Equal Employment Opportunity Act of 1972, does not offer redress for appellant's complaint that her job at the Environmental Protection Agency was abolished because she repulsed her male superior's sexual advances. We reverse.

Appellant, a black woman, was hired by the director of the Agency's equal employment opportunity division, who also is black, as his administrative assistant at grade GS-5. During a pre-employment interview, she asserts, he promised a promotion to grade GS-7 within ninety days. Shortly after commencement of the employment, she claims, the director initiated a quest for sexual favors by "(a) repeatedly soliciting [her] to join him for social activities after office hours, notwithstanding [her] repeated refusal to do so; (b) by making repeated remarks to [her] which were sexual in nature; (c) by repeatedly suggesting to [her] that if she cooperated with him in a sexual affair, her employment status would be enhanced." Appellant states that she "continually resisted [his] overture...and finally advised him that notwithstanding his stated belief that many executives 'have affairs with their personnel', she preferred that their relationship remain a strictly professional one." Thereafter, she charges, the director "alone and in concert with other agents of [appellee], began a conscious campaign to belittle [her], to harass her and to strip her of her job duties, all culminating in the decision of [appellee's] agent . . . to abolish [her] job in retaliation for [her] refusal to grant him sexual favors." These activities, appellant declares, "would not have occurred but for [her] sex."

After seeking unsuccessfully an informal resolution of the matter, appellant, acting pro se, filed a formal complaint alleging that the director sought to remove her from his office when she "refused to have an after hour affair with" him. The complaint charged discrimination based on race rather than gender, a circumstance which appellant attributes to erroneous advice by agency personnel. A hearing on the complaint was conducted by an appeals examiner, who excluded proffered evidence of sex discrimination and found no evidence of race discrimination. In its final decision, the Agency concurred in the examiner's finding....

Thereafter, appellant filed her complaint in the District Court, confining her theory, by allegations to which we have averted, to sex discrimination violative of Title VII and the Fifth Amendment. The court, limiting the inquiry to reexamination of the administrative record, granted appellee's motion for summary judgment in the view that "the alleged discriminatory practices are not encompassed by the Act." The "alleged retaliatory actions of [appellant's] supervisor taken because [appellant] refused his request for an 'after hour affair," the court held, "are not the type of discriminatory conduct contemplated by the 1972 Act." The court reasoned:

> The substance of [appellant's] complaint is that she was discriminated against, not because she was a woman, but because she refused to engage in a sexual affair with her supervisor. This is a controversy underpinned by the subtleties of an inharmonious personal relationship. Regardless of how inexcusable the conduct of [appellant's] supervisor might have been, it does not evidence an arbitrary barrier to continued employment based on [appellant's] sex.

The appeal to this court then followed.

By adoption of Title VII of the Civil Rights Act of 1964, Congress made it an unlawful employment practice for nongovernmental employers, with exceptions not presently relevant, "to...discriminate against any individual with respect to his...terms, conditions, or privileges of employment, because of such individual's...sex...." Unfortunately, the early history of that legislation lends no assistance to endeavors to define the scope of this prohibition more precisely, if indeed any elucidation were needed. It was offered as an addition to other proscriptions by opponents in a last-minute attempt to block the bill which became the Act, and the bill, with the amendment barring sex-discrimination, then quickly passed. Thus, for an eight-year period following its original enactment, there was no legislative history to refine the congressional language.

When, however, the 1964 Act was amended by the Equal Employment Opportunity Act of 1972, there was considerable discussion on the topic. Not surprisingly, it then became evident that Congress was deeply concerned about employment discrimination founded on gender and intended to combat it as vigorously as any other type of forbidden discrimination....

Not unexpectedly, then, during the thirteen years since enactment of Title VII it has become firmly established that the Act invalidates all "artificial, arbitrary and unnecessary barriers to employment when the barriers operate invidiously to discriminate on the basis of...impermissible classifications." Title VII has been invoked to strike down a wide variety of impediments to equal employment opportunity between the sexes, including insufficiently validated tests, discriminatory seniority systems, weight-lifting requirements, and height and weight standards solely for those of one gender. Congress could hardly have been more explicit in its command that there be no sex-based discrimination "against any individual with respect to his...terms, conditions, or privileges of employment...."

Title VII now requires, inter alia, that "all personnel actions affecting employees...in [federal] executive agencies...shall be made free from any discrimination based on...sex...." It is not argued, nor plausibly could it be, that elimination of appellant's then position within the Environmental Protection Agency was not a "personnel action" within the contemplation of this provision. Nor can it be doubted that the action effected a "discrimination"—a difference in treatment—against appellant vis-a-vis other employees of the Agency, since there is no indication that the position of any other employee of the agency was similarly eliminated. The question debated, and the issue pivotal on this appeal, is whether the discrimination, in the circumstances described by appellant, was as a matter of law "based on...sex...."

We start with the statute as written, and, so measured, we think the discrimination as portrayed was plainly based on appellant's gender. Her thesis, in substance, is that her supervisor retaliated by abolishing her job when she resisted his sexual advances. More particularly, she states that he repeatedly told her that indulgence in a sexual affair would enhance her employment status; that he endeavored affirmatively but futilely to consummate his proposition; and that, upon her refusal to accede, he campaigned against her continued employment in his department and succeeded eventually in liquidating her position. So it was, by her version, that retention of her job was conditioned upon submission to sexual relations—an exaction which the supervisor would not have sought from any male. It is much too late in the day to contend that Title VII does not outlaw terms of employment for women which differ appreciably from those set for men, and which are not genuinely and reasonably related to performance on the job.

The District Court felt, however, that appellant's suit amounted to no more than a claim "that she was discriminated against, not because she was a woman, but because she refused to engage in a sexual affair with her supervisor." In similar vein, appellee has argued that "appellant was allegedly denied employment enhancement not because she was a woman, but rather because she decided not to furnish the sexual consideration claimed to have been demanded." We cannot accept this analysis of the situation charged by appellant. But for her womanhood, from aught that appears, her participation in sexual activity would never have been solicited. To say, then, that she was victimized in her employment simply because she declined the invitation is to ignore the asserted fact that she was invited only because she was a woman subordinate to the inviter in the hierarchy of agency personnel. Put another way, she became the target of her superior's sexual desires because she was a woman, and was asked to bow to his demands as the price for holding her job. The circumstance imparting high visibility to the role of gender in the affair is that no male employee was susceptible to such an approach by appellant's supervisor. Thus gender cannot be eliminated from the formulation which appellant advocates, and that formulation advances a prima facie case of sex discrimination within the purview of Title VII.

It is clear that the statutory embargo on sex discrimination in employment is not confined to differentials founded wholly upon an employee's gender. On the contrary, it is enough that gender is a factor contributing to the discrimination in a substantial way. That this was the intent of Congress is readily apparent from a small but highly significant facet of the legislative history of Title VII. When the bill incorporating Title VII was under consideration in 1964, an amendment that would have expressly restricted the sex ban to discrimination based solely on gender was defeated on the floor of the House. Like the Fifth Circuit, we take this as an indication of congressional awareness of the debilitating effect that such a limitation would have had on any attempt to stamp out sex-based factors irrelevant to job competence.

Interpretations of the Act, both judicial and administrative, more than adequately reflect this understanding and appreciation of the legislative purpose. In *Phillips v. Martin Marietta Corporation*, 400 U.S. at 544, the Supreme Court held that a company's refusal of employment to mothers but not to fathers of pre-school-age children was prima facie sex discrimination within the meaning of Title VII. Not all women were excluded from the employment, but only those who had pre-school-age children. Nonetheless, since gender was a criterion in the determination of employability, a prima facie violation of Title VII was shown. Other courts, in analogous contexts, have similarly concluded that distinctions predicated only partly though firmly on gender are covered by Title VII's ban on sex discrimination. *Willingham v. Macon Tel. Publishing Co.*, 507 F.2d at 1089; *Sprogis v. United Air Lines, Inc.*, 444 F.2d 1194, 1198 (7th Cir.), cert. denied, 404 U.S. 991 (1971). See also *Gillin v. Federal Paper Bd., Co.*, 479 F.2d 97, 102 (2d Cir. 1973)....

In all of these situations, the objectionable employment condition embraced something more than the employee's gender, but the fact remained that gender was also involved to a significant degree. For while some but not all employees of one sex were subjected to the condition, no employee of the opposite sex was affected; and that is the picture here. It does not suffice to say, as the District Court did, that appellant's position was eliminated merely because she refused to respond to her supervisor's alleged call for sexual favors. Appellant's gender, just as much as her cooperation, was an indispensable factor in the job-retention condition of which she complains, absent a showing that the supervisor imposed a similar condition upon a male co-employee....

At no time during our intensive study of this case have we encountered anything to support the notion that employment conditions summoning sexual relations between employees and superiors are somehow exempted from the coverage of Title VII. The statute in explicit terms proscribes discrimination "because of...sex," with only narrowly defined exceptions completely foreign to the situation emerging here. The legislative history similarly discloses a congressional purpose to outlaw any and all sex-based discrimination, equally with any other form of discrimination which Title VII condemns. Beyond these considerations, the courts have consistently recognized that Title

VII must be construed liberally to achieve its objectives; as we ourselves recently noted, it "requires an interpretation animated by the broad humanitarian and remedial purposes underlying the federal proscription of employment discrimination." It would be pointless to speculate as to whether Congress envisioned the particular type of activity which the job-retention condition allegedly levied on appellant would have exacted. As Judge Goldberg of the Fifth Circuit has so well put it,

> Congress chose neither to enumerate specific discriminatory practices, nor to elucidate in extenso the parameter of such nefarious activities. Rather, it pursued the path of wisdom by being unconstrictive, knowing that constant change is the order of our day and that the seemingly unreasonable practices of the present can easily become the injustices of the morrow. *Rogers v. EEOC*, 454 F.2d 234, 238 (5th Cir. 1971), cert. denied, 406 U.S. 957 (1972).

Against this backdrop, we cannot doubt that Title VII intercepts the discriminatory practice charged here. The same result has been reached in the District Court. *Williams v. Saxbe*, 413 F. Supp. 654 (D.D.C. 1976). We are aware that other courts have reached the opposite conclusion. *Corne v. Bausch & Lomb, Inc.* 390 F. Supp. 161 (1975); *Miller v. Bank of America*, 418 F. Supp. 233 (1976); *Tomkins v. Public Serv. Elec. & Gas Co.*, 422 F. Supp. 553 (D.N.J. 1976). With the latter, we must respectfully disagree. The judgment appealed from is accordingly reversed, and the case is remanded to the District Court for further proceedings consistent with this opinion.

Reversed and remanded.

Discussion Questions

1) In what sense were the advances allegedly made toward Barnes a "sex-based term or condition" of her employment?

2) Why did this court disagree with the decision in *Corne v. Bausch and Lomb*?

3) The District Court felt that appellant's suit amounted to no more than a claim "that she was discriminated against, not because she was a woman, but because she refused to engage in a sexual affair with her supervisor." What reasons did this court give for rejecting this logic?

Bundy v. Jackson

641 F.2d 934 (1981)
United States Court of Appeals, District of Columbia Circuit
Opinion for the court filed by Chief Judge J. Skelly Wright

In *Barnes v. Costle*, 561 F.2d 983 (D.C. Cir.1977), we held that an employer who abolished a female employee's job to retaliate against the employee's resistance of his sexual advances violated Title VII of the Civil Rights Act of 1964. The appellant in this case asserts some claims encompassed by the *Barnes* decision, arguing that her rejection of unsolicited and offensive sexual advances from several supervisors in her agency caused those supervisors unjustifiably to delay and block promotions to which she was entitled. Equally important, however, appellant asks us to extend *Barnes* by holding that an employer violates Title VII merely by subjecting female employees to sexual harassment, even if the employee's resistance to that harassment does not cause the employer to deprive her of any tangible job benefits.

The District Court in this case made an express finding of fact that in appellant's agency "the making of improper sexual advances to female employees (was) standard operating procedure, a fact of life, a normal condition of employment," and that the director of the agency, to whom she complained of the harassment, failed to investigate her complaints or take them seriously, Nevertheless, the District Court refused to grant appellant any declaratory or injunctive relief, concluding that sexual harassment does not in itself represent discrimination "with respect to...terms, conditions, or privileges of employment" within the meaning of Title VII....

Appellant Sandra Bundy is now, and was at the time she filed her lawsuit, a Vocational Rehabilitation Specialist, level GS-9, with the District of Columbia Department of Corrections...In recent years Bundy's chief task has been to find jobs for former criminal offenders. The District Court's finding that sexual intimidation was a "normal condition of employment" in Bundy's agency finds ample support in the District Court's own chronology of Bundy's experiences there. Those experiences began in 1972 when Bundy, still a GS-5, received and rejected sexual propositions from Delbert Jackson, then a fellow employee at the agency but now its Director and the named defendant in this lawsuit in his official capacity. It was two years later, however, that the sexual intimidation Bundy suffered began to intertwine directly with her employment, when she received propositions from two of her supervisors, Arthur Burton and James Gainey. Burton became Bundy's supervisor when Bundy became an Employment Development Specialist in 1974. Shortly thereafter Gainey became her first-line supervisor and Burton her second-line supervisor, although Burton retained control of Bundy's employment status. Burton began sexually harassing Bundy in June 1974, continually calling her into his office to request that she spend the workday afternoon with him at his apartment and to question her about her sexual proclivities. Shortly after becoming her first-line supervisor Gainey also began making sexual advances to Bundy, asking her to join him at a motel and on a trip to the Bahamas. Bundy complained about these advances to Lawrence Swain, who supervised both Burton and Gainey. Swain casually dismissed Bundy's complaints, telling her that "any man in his right mind would want to rape you," and then proceeding himself to request that she begin a sexual relationship with him in his apartment. Bundy rejected his request.

In denying Bundy any relief, the District Court found that Bundy's supervisors did not take the "g˙ ˌne" of sexually propositioning female employees "seriously and that Bundy's rejection of their advances did not evoke in them any motive to take any action against her. The record, however, contains nothing to support this view, and indeed some evidence directly belies it. For example, after Bundy complained to Swain, Burton began to derogate her for alleged malingering and poor work performance, though she had not previously received any such criticism...The District Court appeared to find that even Bundy took a casual attitude toward the pattern of unsolicited sexual advances in the agency, thereby implying that these advances by themselves did no harm to female employees....

We thus readily conclude that Bundy's employer discriminated against her on the basis of sex. What remains is the novel question whether the sexual harassment of the sort Bundy suffered amounted by itself to sex discrimination with respect to the "terms, conditions, or privileges of employment." Though no court has as yet so held, we believe that an affirmative answer follows ineluctably from numerous cases finding Title VII violations where an employer created or condoned a substantially discriminatory work environment, regardless of whether the complaining employees lost any tangible job benefits as a result of the discrimination.

Bundy's claim on this score is essentially that "conditions of employment" include the psychological and emotional work environment that the sexually stereotyped insults and demeaning propositions to which she was indisputably subjected and which caused her anxiety and debilitation, illegally poisoned that environment....

The relevance of these "discriminatory environment" cases to sexual harassment is beyond serious dispute. Racial or ethnic discrimination against a company's minority clients may reflect no intent to discriminate directly against the company's minority employees, but in poisoning the atmosphere of employment it violates Title VII. Sexual stereotyping through discriminatory dress requirements may be benign in intent and may offend women only in a general, atmospheric manner, yet it violates Title VII. Racial slurs, though intentional and directed at individuals, may still be just verbal insults, yet they too may create Title VII liability. How then can sexual harassment, which injects the most demeaning sexual stereotypes into the general work environment and which always represents an intentional assault on an individual's innermost privacy, not be illegal?

Thus, unless we extend the Barnes holding, an employer could sexually harass a female employee with impunity by carefully stopping short of firing the employee or taking any other tangible actions against her in response to her resistance, thereby creating the impression the one received by the District Court in this case that the employer did not take the ritual of harassment and resistance "seriously." Indeed, so long as women remain inferiors in the employment hierarchy, they may have little recourse against harassment beyond the legal recourse Bundy seeks in this case. The law may allow a woman to prove that her resistance to the harassment cost her her job or some economic benefit, but this will do her no good if the employer never takes such tangible actions against her...It may even be pointless to require the employee to prove that she "resisted" the harassment at all. So long as the employer never literally forces sexual relations on the employee, "resistance" may be a meaningless alternative for her. If the employer demands no response to his verbal or physical gestures other than good-natured tolerance, the woman has no means of communicating her rejection. She neither accepts nor rejects the advances; she simply endures them. She might be able to contrive proof of rejection by objecting to the employer's advances in some very visible and dramatic way, but she would do so only at the risk of making her life on the job even more miserable. It hardly helps that the remote prospect of legal relief under Barnes remains available if she objects so powerfully that she provokes the employer into firing her.

The employer can thus implicitly and effectively make the employee's endurance of sexual intimidation a "condition" of her employment. The woman then faces a "cruel trilemma." She can endure the harassment. She can attempt to oppose it, with little hope of success, either legal or practical, but with every prospect of making the job even less tolerable for her. Or she can leave her job, with little hope of legal relief and the likely prospect of another job where she will face harassment anew.

Bundy proved that she was the victim of a practice of sexual harassment and a discriminatory work environment permitted by her employer. Her rights under Title VII were therefore violated. We thus reverse the District Court's holding on this issue and remand it to that court so it can fashion appropriate injunctive relief.

Discussion Questions

1) In what sense were the advances allegedly made toward Bundy a "sex-based term or condition" of her employment?

2) Why did the court hold that it was not necessary to suffer tangible harm, such as a firing or lack of promotion, in order to succeed in a claim of sexual harassment?

3) How does this ruling affect the "cruel trilemma" facing women that the court alludes to in this opinion?

Meritor Savings Bank v. Vinson

477 U.S. 57 (1986)
Supreme Court of the United States
Opinion by: Justice Rehnquist

This case presents important questions concerning claims of workplace "sexual harassment" brought under Title VII of the Civil Rights Act of 1964.

In 1974, Mechelle Vinson met Sidney Taylor, a vice president of Meritor Savings Bank and manager of one of its branch offices. With Taylor as her supervisor, respondent started as a teller-trainee, and thereafter was promoted to teller, head teller, and assistant branch manager. She worked at the same branch for four years, and it is undisputed that her advancement there was based on merit alone. In September 1978, respondent notified Taylor that she was taking sick leave for an indefinite period. On November 1, 1978, the bank discharged her for excessive use of that leave.

Respondent brought this action against Taylor and the bank, claiming that during her four years at the bank she had "constantly been subjected to sexual harassment" by Taylor in violation of Title VII. At the 11-day bench trial, the parties presented conflicting testimony about Taylor's behavior during respondent's employment. Respondent testified that during her probationary period as a teller-trainee, Taylor treated her in a fatherly way and made no sexual advances. Shortly thereafter, however, he invited her out to dinner and, during the course of the meal, suggested that they go to a motel to have sexual relations. At first she refused, but out of what she described as fear of losing her job she eventually agreed. According to respondent, Taylor thereafter made repeated demands upon her for sexual favors, usually at the branch, both during and after business hours; she estimated that over the next several years she had intercourse with him some 40 or 50 times. In addition, respondent testified that Taylor fondled her in front of other employees, followed her into the women's restroom when she went there alone, exposed himself to her, and even forcibly raped her on several occasions. These activities ceased after 1977, respondent stated, when she started going with a steady boyfriend. Finally, respondent testified that because she was afraid of Taylor she never reported his harassment to any of his supervisors and never attempted to use the bank's complaint procedure.

Taylor denied respondent's allegations of sexual activity, testifying that he never fondled her, never made suggestive remarks to her, never engaged in sexual intercourse with her, and never asked her to do so. He contended instead that respondent made her accusations in response to a business-related dispute. The bank also denied respondent's allegations and asserted that any sexual harassment by Taylor was unknown to the bank and engaged in without its consent or approval.

The District Court denied relief, but did not resolve the conflicting testimony about the existence of a sexual relationship between respondent and Taylor. It found instead that:

> [if] [respondent] and Taylor did engage in an intimate or sexual relationship during the time of [respondent's] employment with [the bank], that relationship was a voluntary one having nothing to do with her continued employment or her advancement or promotions at that institution." The court ultimately found that respondent "was not the victim of sexual harassment and was not the victim of sexual discrimination" while employed at the bank.

Although it concluded that respondent had not proved a violation of Title VII, the District Court nevertheless went on to address the bank's liability. After noting the bank's express policy against discrimination, and finding that neither respondent nor any other employee had ever lodged a complaint about sexual harassment by Taylor, the court ultimately concluded that "the bank was without notice and cannot be held liable for the alleged actions of Taylor."

The Court of Appeals for the District of Columbia Circuit reversed. The court stated that a violation of Title VII may be predicated on either of two types of sexual harassment: harassment that involves the conditioning of concrete employment benefits on sexual favors, and harassment that, while not affecting economic benefits, creates a hostile or offensive working environment. The court drew additional support for this position from the Equal Employment Opportunity Commission's Guidelines on Discrimination Because of Sex which set out these two types of sexual harassment claims. Believing that "Vinson's grievance was clearly of the [hostile environment] type," and that the District Court had not considered whether a violation of this type had occurred, the court concluded that a remand was necessary.

The court further concluded that the District Court's finding that any sexual relationship between respondent and Taylor "was a voluntary one" did not obviate the need for a remand. "[Uncertain] as to precisely what the [district] court meant" by this finding, the Court of Appeals held that if the evidence otherwise showed that "Taylor made Vinson's toleration of sexual harassment a condition of her employment," her voluntariness "had no materiality whatsoever."

As to the bank's liability, the Court of Appeals held that an employer is absolutely liable for sexual harassment practiced by supervisory personnel, whether or not the employer knew or should have known about the misconduct. The court relied chiefly on Title VII's definition of "employer" to include "any agent of such a person," as well as on the EEOC Guidelines. The court held that a supervisor is an "agent" of his employer for Title VII purposes, even if he lacks authority to hire, fire, or promote, since "the mere existence—or even the appearance—of a significant degree of influence in vital job decisions gives any supervisor the opportunity to impose on employees."

In accordance with the foregoing, the Court of Appeals reversed the judgment of the District Court and remanded the case for further proceedings. We granted certiorari and now affirm, but for different reasons.

Title VII of the Civil Rights Act of 1964 makes it "an unlawful employment practice for an employer...to discriminate against any individual with respect to his compensation, terms, conditions, or privileges of employment, because of such individual's race, color, religion, sex, or national origin." Respondent argues, and the Court of Appeals held, that unwelcome sexual advances that create an offensive or hostile working environment violate Title VII. Without question, when a supervisor sexually harasses a subordinate because of the subordinate's sex, that supervisor "discriminate[s]" on the basis of sex. Petitioner apparently does not challenge this proposition. It contends instead that in prohibiting discrimination with respect to "compensation, terms, conditions, or privileges" of employment, Congress was concerned with what petitioner describes as "tangible loss" of "an economic character," not "purely psychological aspects of the workplace environment." In support of this claim petitioner observes that in both the legislative history of Title VII and this Court's Title VII decisions, the focus has been on tangible, economic barriers erected by discrimination.

We reject petitioner's view. First, the language of Title VII is not limited to "economic" or "tangible" discrimination. The phrase "terms, conditions, or privileges of employment" evinces a congressional intent "'to strike at the entire spectrum of disparate treatment of men and women'" in employment.

Second, in 1980 the EEOC issued Guidelines specifying that "sexual harassment," as there defined, is a form of sex discrimination prohibited by Title VII. The EEOC Guidelines fully support the view that harassment leading to noneconomic injury can violate Title VII. In defining "sexual harassment," the Guidelines first describe the kinds of workplace conduct that may be actionable under Title VII. These include "[unwelcome] sexual advances, requests for sexual favors, and other verbal or physical conduct of a sexual nature." Relevant to the charges at issue in this case, the Guidelines provide that such sexual misconduct constitutes prohibited "sexual harassment," whether or not it is directly linked to the grant or denial of an economic quid pro quo, where "such conduct has the purpose or effect of unreasonably interfering with an individual's work performance or creating an intimidating, hostile, or offensive working environment."

In concluding that so-called "hostile environment" (i.e., non quid pro quo) harassment violates Title VII, the EEOC drew upon a substantial body of judicial decisions and EEOC precedent holding that Title VII affords employees the right to work in an environment free from discriminatory intimidation, ridicule, and insult.

[The] phrase "terms, conditions or privileges of employment" in [Title VII] is an expansive concept which sweeps within its protective ambit the practice of creating a working environment heavily charged with ethnic or racial discrimination...One can readily envision working environments so heavily polluted with discrimination as to destroy completely the emotional and psychological stability of minority group workers.

Of course, not all workplace conduct that may be described as "harassment" affects a "term, condition, or privilege" of employment within the meaning of Title VII. Mere utterance of an ethnic or racial epithet which engenders offensive feelings in an employee would not affect the conditions of employment to sufficiently significant degree to violate Title VII. For sexual harassment to be actionable, it must be sufficiently severe or pervasive "to alter the conditions of [the victim's] employment and create an abusive working environment." Respondent's allegations in this case—which include not only pervasive harassment but also criminal conduct of the most serious nature—are plainly sufficient to state a claim for "hostile environment" sexual harassment.

The question remains, however, whether the District Court's ultimate finding that respondent "was not the victim of sexual harassment," effectively disposed of respondent's claim. The

Court of Appeals recognized, we think correctly, that this ultimate finding was likely based on one or both of two erroneous views of the law. First, the District Court apparently believed that a claim for sexual harassment will not lie absent an economic effect on the complainant's employment. Since it appears that the District Court made its findings without ever considering the "hostile environment" theory of sexual harassment, the Court of Appeals' decision to remand was correct. Second, the District Court's conclusion that no actionable harassment occurred might have rested on its earlier "finding" that "[if] [respondent] and Taylor did engage in an intimate or sexual relationship...that relationship was a voluntary one." But the fact that sex-related conduct was "voluntary," in the sense that the complainant was not forced to participate against her will, is not a defense to a sexual harassment suit brought under Title VII. The gravamen of any sexual harassment claim is that the alleged sexual advances were "unwelcome." While the question whether particular conduct was indeed unwelcome presents difficult problems of proof and turns largely on credibility determinations committed to the trier of fact, the District Court in this case erroneously focused on the "voluntariness" of respondent's participation in the claimed sexual episodes. The correct inquiry is whether respondent by her conduct indicated that the alleged sexual advances were unwelcome, not whether her actual participation in sexual intercourse was voluntary.

Although the District Court concluded that respondent had not proved a violation of Title VII, it nevertheless went on to consider the question of the bank's liability. Finding that "the bank was without notice" of Taylor's alleged conduct, and that notice to Taylor was not the equivalent of notice to the bank, the court concluded that the bank therefore could not be held liable for Taylor's alleged actions. The Court of Appeals took the opposite view, holding that an employer is strictly liable for a hostile environment created by a supervisor's sexual advances, even though the employer neither knew nor reasonably could have known of the alleged misconduct. The court held that a supervisor, whether or not he possesses the authority to hire, fire, or promote, is necessarily an "agent" of his employer for all Title VII purposes, since "even the appearance" of such authority may enable him to impose himself on his subordinates.

This debate over the appropriate standard for employer liability has a rather abstract quality about it given the state of the record in this case. We do not know at this stage whether Taylor made any sexual advances toward respondent at all, let alone whether those advances were unwelcome, whether they were sufficiently pervasive to constitute a condition of employment, or whether they were "so pervasive and so long continuing…that the employer must have become conscious of [them]."

We therefore decline the parties' invitation to issue a definitive rule on employer liability, but we do agree with the EEOC that Congress wanted courts to look to agency principles for guidance in this area. While such common-law principles may not be transferable in all their particulars to Title VII, Congress' decision to define "employer" to include any "agent" of an employer surely evinces an intent to place some limits on the acts of employees for which employers under Title VII are to be held responsible. For this reason, we hold that the Court of Appeals erred in concluding that employers are always automatically liable for sexual harassment by their supervisors. For the same reason, absence of notice to an employer does not necessarily insulate that employer from liability. Finally, we reject petitioner's view that the mere existence of a grievance procedure and a policy against discrimination, coupled with respondent's failure to invoke that procedure, must insulate petitioner from liability. While those facts are plainly relevant, the situation before us demonstrates why they are not necessarily dispositive. The bank's grievance procedure apparently required an employee to complain first to her supervisor, in this case Taylor. Since Taylor was the alleged perpetrator, it is not altogether surprising that respondent failed to invoke the procedure and report her grievance to him. Petitioner's contention that respondent's failure should insulate it from liability might be substantially stronger if its procedures were better calculated to encourage victims of harassment to come forward.

In sum, we hold that a claim of "hostile environment" sex discrimination is actionable under Title VII. As to employer liability, we conclude that the Court of Appeals was wrong to entirely disregard agency principles and impose absolute liability on employers for the acts of their supervisors, regardless of the circumstances of a particular case. It is so ordered.

Discussion Questions

1) What distinction does the Court recognize between quid pro quo harassment and hostile environment sexual harassment?

2) If the person who made the sexual advances to Vinson had been a co-worker rather than her supervisor, would she still have a claim of sexual harassment?

3) Why did the Court reject "voluntariness" as a valid defense in sexual harassment claims?

4) What standard of employer liability did the Court accept in this decision? How does this differ from the strict liability imposed in *Tompkins*? Should there be a difference in employer liability depending upon which form of harassment was found to exist?

Rabidue v. Osceola Refining Company

805 F.2d 611 (1986)
United States Court of Appeals for the Sixth Circuit
Opinion: Krupansky, Circuit Judge

The plaintiff initially occupied the job classification of executive secretary. In that position, she performed a variety of duties, which included attending the telephone, typing, and a limited amount of bookkeeping. In 1973, the plaintiff was promoted to the position of administrative assistant. In her new position, the plaintiff was responsible for, among other duties, purchasing office supplies, monitoring and/or distributing incoming governmental regulations, and contacting customers. Subsequently, she was assigned additional duties as credit manager and office manager. Included in the plaintiff's new responsibilities was the authority to assign work to a number of other Osceola employees.

The plaintiff was a capable, independent, ambitious, aggressive, intractable, and opinionated individual. The plaintiff's supervisors and co-employees with whom plaintiff interacted almost uniformly found her to be an abrasive, rude, antagonistic, extremely willful, uncooperative, and irascible personality. She consistently argued with co-workers and company customers in defiance of supervisory direction and jeopardized Osceola's business relationships with major oil companies. She disregarded supervisory instruction and company policy whenever such direction conflicted with her personal reasoning and conclusions. In sum, the plaintiff was a troublesome employee.

The plaintiff's charged sexual harassment arose primarily as a result of her unfortunate acrimonious working relationship with Douglas Henry. Henry was a supervisor of the company's key punch and computer section. Occasionally, the plaintiff's duties required coordination with Henry's department and personnel, although Henry exercised no supervisory authority over the plaintiff nor the plaintiff over him. Henry was an extremely vulgar and crude individual who customarily made obscene comments about women generally, and, on occasion, directed such obscenities to the plaintiff. Management was aware of Henry's vulgarity, but had been unsuccessful in curbing his offensive personality traits during the time encompassed by this controversy. The plaintiff and Henry, on the occasions when their duties exposed them to each other, were constantly in a confrontational posture. The plaintiff, as well as other female employees, were annoyed by Henry's vulgarity. In addition to Henry's obscenities, other male employees from time to time displayed pictures of nude or scantily clad women in their offices and/or work areas, to which the plaintiff and other women employees were exposed.

The plaintiff was formally discharged from her employment at the company on January 14, 1977, as a result of her many job-related problems, including her irascible and opinionated personality and her inability to work harmoniously with co-workers and customers. Subsequent to her discharge, the plaintiff applied for unemployment benefits, payment of which the company opposed. The plaintiff also filed charges of discrimination against her former employer with the EEOC and thereafter commenced the instant action in the district court.

This court has examined the trial court's disposition of the plaintiff's Title VII. In arriving at its decision, the district court viewed the plaintiff's disparate treatment sex discrimination charge as alleging continuing sex-based discriminatory conduct on the part of the defendant culminating in the plaintiff's discharge. A review of the record disclosed that the trial court's findings, namely, that the company's predischarge actions toward the plaintiff did not evince an anti-female animus, were not clearly erroneous. Consequently, the trial court's conclusion that the plaintiff failed to establish violations of Title VII in this regard is affirmed.

The plaintiff's claim of sexual harassment derives from Title VII's proscription that "it shall be an unlawful employment practice for an employer...to discriminate against any individual with respect to his...terms, conditions or privileges of employment, because of such individual's... sex...." 42 U.S.C. § 2000e-2(a)(1) (§ 703(a)(1) of Title VII). The case law in this area has recognized two basic variants of sexual harassment: "harassment that creates an offensive environment ('condition of work') and harassment in which a supervisor demands sexual consideration in exchange for job benefits ('quid pro quo')."

This circuit has entertained cases involving a spectrum of sexual harassment issues; however, it has not directly addressed a claim asserting a violation of Title VII based upon an alleged sexually discriminatory work environment which had not resulted in a tangible job detriment as joined by the issues of the plaintiff's charges herein. Although the quid pro quo category of sexual harassment appears to have given rise to the greatest proliferation of case law to date, other circuits have recognized that an offensive work environment could, under appropriate circumstances, constitute Title VII sexual harassment without the necessity of asserting or proving tangible job detriment by the harassed employee, which proof underlies the quid pro quo variant of sexual harassment. Moreover, the Supreme Court has recently permitted a plaintiff to pursue a Title VII cause of action arising as a result of discrimination based upon sexually hostile or abusive work environment. *Meritor Savings Bank v. Vinson*, 477 U.S. 57 (1986). In addressing the issues presented by such a sexual harassment charge, this court's attention is initially directed to the guidelines issued by the Equal Employment Opportunity Commission (EEOC) as an informed source of instruction to assist its efforts to probe the parameters of Title VII sexual harassment. Those guidelines define sexual harassment in the following terms:

Harassment on the basis of sex is a violation of Sec. 703 of Title VII. Unwelcome sexual advances, requests for sexual favors, and other verbal or physical conduct of a sexual nature constitute sexual harassment when submission to such conduct is made either explicitly or implicitly a term or condition of an individual's employment, submission to or rejection of such conduct by an individual is used as the basis for employment decisions affecting such individual, or such conduct has the purpose or effect of unreasonably interfering with an individual's work performance or creating an intimidating, hostile, or offensive working environment.

After having considered the EEOC guidelines and after having canvassed existing legal precedent that has discussed the issue, this court concludes that a plaintiff, to prevail in a Title VII offensive work environment sexual harassment action, must assert and prove that: (1) the employee was a member of a protected class; (2) the employee was subjected to unwelcomed sexual harassment in the form of sexual advances, requests for sexual favors, or other verbal or physical conduct of a sexual nature; (3) the harassment complained of was based upon sex; (4) the charged sexual harassment had the effect of unreasonably interfering with the plaintiff's work performance and creating an intimidating, hostile, or offensive working environment that affected seriously the psychological well-being of the plaintiff; and (5) the existence of respondeat superior liability.

Thus, to prove a claim of abusive work environment premised upon sexual harassment, a plaintiff must demonstrate that she would not have been the object of harassment but for her sex. It is of significance to note that instances of complained-of sexual conduct that prove equally offensive to male and female workers would not support a Title VII sexual harassment charge because both men and women were accorded like treatment. Unlike quid pro quo sexual harassment which may evolve from a single incident, sexually hostile or intimidating environments are characterized by multiple and varied combinations and frequencies of offensive exposures, which characteristics would dictate an order of proof that placed the burden upon the plaintiff to demonstrate that injury resulted not from a single or isolated offensive incident, comment, or conduct, but from incidents, comments, or conduct that occurred with some frequency. To accord appropriate protection to both plaintiffs and defendants in a hostile and/or abusive work environment sexual harassment case, the trier of fact, when judging the totality of the circumstances impacting upon the asserted abusive and hostile environment placed in issue by the plaintiff's charges, must adopt the perspective of a reasonable person's reaction to a similar environment under essentially like or similar circumstances. Thus, in the absence of conduct which would interfere with that hypothetical reasonable individual's work performance and affect seriously the psychological well-being of that reasonable person under like circumstances, a plaintiff may not prevail on asserted charges of sexual harassment anchored in an alleged hostile and/or abusive work environment regardless of whether the plaintiff was actually offended by the defendant's conduct. Assuming that the plaintiff has successfully satisfied the burden of proving that the defendant's conduct would have interfered with a reasonable individual's work performance and would have affected seriously the psychological well-being of a reasonable employee, the particular plaintiff would nevertheless also be required to demonstrate that she was actually offended by the defendant's conduct and that she suffered some degree of injury as a result of the abusive and hostile work environment.

Accordingly, a proper assessment or evaluation of an employment environment that gives rise to a sexual harassment claim would invite consideration of such objective and subjective factors as the nature of the alleged harassment, the background and experience of the plaintiff, her co-workers, and supervisors, the totality of the physical environment of the plaintiff's work area, the lexicon of obscenity that pervaded the environment of the workplace both before and after the plaintiff's introduction into its environs, coupled with the reasonable expectation of the plaintiff upon voluntarily entering that environment. Thus, the presence of actionable sexual harassment would be different depending upon the personality of the plaintiff and the prevailing work environment and must be considered and evaluated upon an ad hoc basis. As Judge Newblatt aptly stated in his opinion in the district court:

> Indeed, it cannot seriously be disputed that in some work environments, humor and language are rough hewn and vulgar. Sexual jokes, sexual conversations and girlie magazines may abound. Title VII was not meant to—or can—change this. It must never be forgotten that Title VII is the federal court mainstay in the struggle for equal employment opportunity for the female workers of America. But it is quite different to claim that Title VII was designed to bring about a magical transformation in the social mores of American workers. Clearly, the Court's qualification is necessary to enable 29 C.F.R. § 1604.11(a)(3) to function as a workable judicial standard.

To prevail in an action that asserts a charge of offensive work environment sexual harassment, the ultimate burden of proof is upon the plaintiff to additionally demonstrate respondeat superior liability by proving that the employer, through its agents or supervisory personnel, knew or should have known of the charged sexual harassment and failed to implement prompt and appropriate corrective action. This court emphasizes that the instant case does not involve alleged acts of sexual harassment by a supervisor. Henry exercised no supervisory authority over the plaintiff nor the plaintiff over him, but rather the two parties were peers at Osceola.

A review of the Title VII sexual harassment issue in this matter prompts this court to conclude that the plaintiff neither asserted nor proved a claim of "sexual advances," "sexual favors," or "physical conduct," or sexual harassment implicating those elements typically at issue in a case of quid pro quo sexual harassment. Thus, the plaintiff to have prevailed in her cause of action against the defendant on this record must have proved that she had been subjected to unwelcomed verbal conduct and poster displays of a sexual nature which had unreasonably interfered with her work performance and created an intimidating, hostile, or offensive working environment that affected seriously her psychological well-being.

The record effectively disclosed that Henry's obscenities, although annoying, were not so startling as to have affected seriously the psyches of the plaintiff or other female employees. The evidence did not demonstrate that this single employee's vulgarity substantially affected the totality of the workplace. The sexually oriented poster displays had a de minimis effect on the plaintiff's work environment when considered in the context of a society that condones and publicly features and commercially exploits open displays of written and pictorial erotica at the newsstands, on prime-time television, at the cinema, and in other public places. In sum, Henry's vulgar language, coupled with the sexually oriented posters, did not result in a working environment that could be considered intimidating, hostile, or offensive.

Dissent: Keith, Circuit Judge

I dissent for several reasons. First, after review of the entire record I am firmly convinced, that although supporting evidence exists, the court is mistaken in affirming the findings that defendant's treatment of plaintiff evinced no anti-female animus and that gender-based discrimination played no role in her discharge. The overall circumstances of plaintiff's workplace evince an anti-female environment. For seven years plaintiff worked at Osceola as the sole woman in a salaried management position. In common work areas plaintiff and other female employees were exposed daily to displays of nude or partially clad women belonging to a number of male employees at Osceola. One poster, which remained on the wall for eight years, showed a prone woman who had a golf ball on her breasts with a man standing over her, golf club in hand, yelling "Fore." And one desk plaque declared "Even male chauvinist pigs need love." Plaintiff testified the posters offended her and her female co-workers.

In addition, Computer Division Supervisor Doug Henry regularly spewed anti-female obscenity. Henry routinely referred to women as "whores," "cunt," "pussy," and "tits." Of plaintiff, Henry specifically remarked "All that bitch needs is a good lay" and called her "fat ass." Plaintiff arranged at least one meeting of female employees to discuss Henry and repeatedly filed written complaints on behalf of herself and other female employees who feared losing their jobs if they complained directly. Osceola Vice President Charles Muetzel stated he knew that employees were "greatly disturbed" by Henry's language. However, because Osceola needed Henry's computer expertise, Muetzel did not reprimand or fire Henry. In response to subsequent complaints about Henry, a later supervisor, Charles Shoemaker, testified that he gave Henry "a little fatherly advice" about Henry's prospects if he learned to become "an executive type person."

In contrast to the supervisors' reluctance to address Henry's outrageous behavior, plaintiff was frequently told to tone down and discouraged from executing procedures she felt were needed to correct waste and improve efficiency as her job required. Not only did plaintiff receive minimal support, but she was repeatedly undermined. For example, supervisor Doug Henry once directed his employees to ignore plaintiff's procedures for logging time and invoices, a particularly damaging directive given plaintiff's responsibility of coordinating the work of Henry's computer staff. In another example, plaintiff returned from her vacation to find that none of the check-depositing procedures agreed upon had been implemented and that some of her duties had been permanently transferred to the male who filled in during her vacation. In contrast to the fatherly advice and the praise for potential which Henry received, plaintiff was informed she had set her goals too high. After dismissal, but prior to final notice, plaintiff received instructions not to return to the refinery. In contrast, male employees fired for embezzlement were allowed to return to clean out their desks.

The record establishes plaintiff possessed negative personal traits. These traits did not, however, justify the sex-based disparate treatment recounted above. Whatever undesirable behavior plaintiff exhibited, it was clearly no worse than Henry's. I conclude the misogynous language and decorative displays tolerated at the refinery, the primitive views of working women expressed by Osceola supervisors and defendant's treatment of plaintiff as the only female salaried employee clearly evince anti-female animus.

Nor do I agree with the majority holding that a court considering hostile environment claims should adopt the perspective of the reasonable person's reaction to a similar environment. In my view, the reasonable person perspective fails to account for the wide divergence between most women's views of appropriate sexual conduct and those of men. I would have courts adopt the perspective of the reasonable victim which simultaneously allows courts to consider salient sociological differences as well as shield employers from the neurotic complainant. Moreover, unless the outlook of the reasonable woman is adopted, the defendants as well as the courts are permitted to sustain ingrained notions of reasonable behavior fashioned by the offenders, in this case, men.

Indeed, it cannot seriously be disputed that in some work environments, humor and language are rough hewn and vulgar. Sexual jokes, sexual conversations and girlie magazines may abound. Title VII was not meant to—or can—change this. It must never be forgotten that Title VII is the federal court mainstay in the struggle for equal employment opportunity for the female workers of America. But it is quite different to claim that Title VII was designed to bring about a magical transformation in the social mores of American workers. (quoting the district court opinion, *Osceola v. Rabidue*, 584 F. Supp. at 430.)

In my view, Title VII's precise purpose is to prevent such behavior and attitudes from poisoning the work environment of classes protected under the Act. To condone the majority's notion of the "prevailing workplace" I would also have to agree that if an employer maintains an anti-semitic workforce and tolerates a workplace in which "kike" jokes, displays of Nazi literature and anti-Jewish conversation "may abound," a Jewish employee assumes the risk of working there, and a court must consider such a work environment as "prevailing." I cannot. As I see it, job relatedness is the only additional factor which legitimately bears on the inquiry of plaintiff's reasonableness in finding her work environment offensive. In other words, the only additional question I would find relevant is whether the behavior complained of is required to perform the work. For example, depending on their job descriptions, employees of soft pornography publishers or other sex-related industries should reasonably expect exposure to nudity, sexually explicit language or even simulated sex as inherent aspects of working in that field. However, when that exposure goes beyond what is required professionally, even sex industry employees are protected under the Act from non-job related sexual demands, language or other offensive behavior by supervisors or co-workers. As I believe no woman should be subjected to an environment where her sexual dignity and reasonable sensibilities are visually, verbally or physically assaulted as a matter of prevailing male prerogative, I dissent.

Discussion Questions

1) What is the standard that the court held need be satisfied to claim a hostile environment?

2) The court held "to prove a claim of abusive work environment premised upon sexual harassment, a plaintiff must demonstrate that she would not have been the object of harassment but for her sex." Does this mean that an employer who openly harasses both men and women could not create a hostile environment?

3) Would "a magical transformation in the social mores of American workers" be necessary to eliminate sexual harassment from most workplaces?

4) The majority and the dissent sharply disagree as to whether the person who created the hostile environment being a co-worker rather than a supervisor should be a factor in the outcome of a sexual harassment claim. Which side is right?

5) Why does the dissent feel that decisions should not rest on a "reasonable person's" reaction to a similar environment?

Robinson v. Jacksonville Shipyards Inc.

760 F. Supp. 1486 (1991)
United States District Court for the Middle District of Florida
Opinion by: Howell W. Melton, United States District Judge

Findings of Fact

This action was commenced by plaintiff Lois Robinson pursuant to Title VII of the Civil Rights Act of 1964. Plaintiff asserts defendants created and encouraged a sexually hostile, intimidating work environment. Her claim centers around the presence in the workplace of pictures of women in various stages of undress and in sexually suggestive or submissive poses, as well as remarks by male employees and supervisors which demean women.

JSI is, in the words of its employees, "a boys club," and "more or less a man's world." Women craftworkers are an extreme rarity. The company reports that women form less than 5 percent of the skilled crafts. Robinson testified that she was the only woman in a crowd of men on occasions when she was sexually harassed at JSI. JSI has never employed a woman as a leaderman, quarterman, assistant foreman, foreman, superintendent, or coordinator. Nor has any woman ever held a position of Vice-President or President of JSI.

Robinson credibly testified to the extensive, pervasive posting of pictures depicting nude women, partially nude women, or sexual conduct and to the occurrence of other forms of harassing behavior perpetrated by her male coworkers and supervisors. Robinson's testimony provides a vivid description of a visual assault on the sensibilities of female workers at JSI that did not relent during working hours. She credibly testified that the pervasiveness of the pictures left her unable to recount every example, but those pictures which she did describe illustrate the extent of this aspect of the work environment at JSI. She testified to seeing in the period prior to April 4, 1984, the three hundredth day prior to the filing of her EEOC charge:

> (a) a picture of a woman, breasts and pubic area exposed, inside a drydock area.
> (b) a picture of a nude black woman, pubic area exposed to reveal her labia, seen in the public locker room.
> (c) drawings and graffiti on the walls, including a drawing depicting a frontal view of a nude female torso with the words "USDA Choice" written on it, at the Commercial Yard in an area where Robinson was assigned to work.
> (d) a picture of a woman's pubic area with a meat spatula pressed on it, observed on a wall next to the sheetmetal shop.
> (e) centerfold-style pictures in the Mayport Yard toolroom trailer, which Robinson saw daily in the necessary course of her work....

Robinson's testimony concerning visual harassment includes a picture of a nude woman with long blonde hair wearing high heels and holding a whip, waved around by a coworker in an enclosed area where Robinson and approximately six men were working. Robinson testified she felt particularly targeted by this action because she has long blonde hair and works with a welding tool known as a whip....

Robinson also testified about comments of a sexual nature she recalled hearing at JSI from coworkers. In some instances these comments were made while she also was in the presence of the pictures of nude or partially nude women. Among the remarks Robinson recalled are: "Hey pussycat, come here and give me a whiff," "The more you lick it, the harder it gets," "I'd like to get in bed with that," "I'd like to have some of that," "Black women taste like sardines," and "You rate about an 8 or a 9 on a scale of 10." She recalled one occasion on which a welder told her he wished her shirt would blow over her head so he could look, another occasion on which a fitter told her he wished her shirt was tighter (because he thought it would be sexier), an occasion on which a foreman candidate asked her to "come sit" on his lap, and innumerable occasions on which a coworker or supervisor called her "honey," "dear," "baby," "sugar," "sugar-booger," and "momma" instead of calling her by her name.

Robinson testified concerning the presence of abusive language written on the walls in her working areas in 1987 and 1988. Among this graffiti were the phrases "lick me you whore dog bitch," "eat me," and "pussy." This first phrase appeared on the wall over a spot where Robinson had left her jacket. The second phrase was freshly painted in Robinson's work area when she observed it. The third phrase appeared during a break after she left her work area to get a drink of water.

Conclusions of Law

Five elements comprise a claim of sexual discrimination based on the existence of a hostile work environment: (1) plaintiff belongs to a protected category; (2) plaintiff was subject to unwelcome sexual harassment; (3) the harassment complained of was based upon sex; (4) the harassment complained of affected a term, condition or privilege of employment; and (5) defendants knew or should have known of the harassment and failed to take prompt, effective remedial action.

To affect a "term, condition, or privilege" of employment within the meaning of Title VII, the harassment "must be sufficiently severe or pervasive 'to alter the conditions of the victim's employment and create an abusive working environment.'"

The question is whether Robinson has shown she is an "affected individual," that is, she is at least as affected as the reasonable person under like circumstances. The evidence reflects the great upset that Robinson felt when confronted with individual episodes of harassment and the workplace as a whole. Further, the impact on her work performance is plain....

The objective standard asks whether a reasonable person of Robinson's sex, that is, a reasonable woman, would perceive that an abusive working environment has been created. The severity and pervasiveness aspects form a structure to test this hypothesis....

A reasonable woman would find that the working environment at JSI was abusive. This conclusion reaches the totality of the circumstances, including the sexual remarks, the sexual jokes, the sexually-oriented pictures of women, and the nonsexual rejection of women by coworkers. The testimony by Dr. Fiske and Ms. Wagner [expert witnesses for the plaintiff] provides a reliable basis upon which to conclude that the cumulative, corrosive effect of this work environment over time affects the psychological well-being of a reasonable woman placed in these conditions. This corollary conclusion holds true whether the concept of psychological well-being is measured by the impact of the work environment on a reasonable woman's work performance or more broadly by the impact of the stress inflicted on her by the continuing presence of the harassing behavior. The fact that some female employees did not complain of the work environment or find some behaviors objectionable does not affect this conclusion concerning the objective offensiveness of the work environment as a whole.

The Court recognizes the existence of authority supporting defendants' contention that sexually-oriented pictures and sexual remarks standing alone cannot form the basis for Title VII liability. The Court concludes that the reasoning of these cases is not consistent with Eleventh Circuit precedent and is otherwise unsound.

For example, the Sixth Circuit in *Rabidue* quoted with approval the conclusion of the district court that:

> it cannot seriously be disputed that in some work environments, humor and language are rough hewn and vulgar. Sexual jokes, sexual conversations and girlie magazines may abound. Title VII

was not meant to—or can—change this. It must never be forgotten that Title VII is the federal court mainstay in the struggle for equal employment opportunity for the female workers of America. But it is quite different to claim that Title VII was designed to bring about a magical transformation in the social mores of American workers.

This conclusion buttressed the appellate court's belief that "a proper assessment or evaluation of an employment environment" in a sexual harassment suit includes "the lexicon of obscenity that pervaded the environment of the workplace both before and after the plaintiff's introduction into its environs, coupled with the reasonable expectation of the plaintiff upon voluntarily entering that environment." The *Rabidue* court further expounded on the social context argument:

The sexually oriented poster displays had a de minimis effect on the plaintiff's work environment when considered in the context of a society that condones and publicly features and commercially exploits open displays of written and pictorial erotica at the newsstands, on prime-time television, at the cinema, and in other public places.

These propositions, however, cannot be squared with the Eleventh Circuit's holdings...The "social context" argument also lacks a sound analytical basis. Professor Kathryn Abrams has written an insightful critique of this argument:

The *Rabidue* court's proposed standard is wholly inappropriate for several reasons. Not only did the court overestimate the public consensus on the question of pornography, but the fact that many forms of objectionable speech and conduct may be protected against interference by public authorities in the world at large does not mean that pornography should be accepted as appropriate in the workplace. Pornography in the workplace may be far more threatening to women workers than it is to the world at large. Outside the workplace, pornography can be protested or substantially avoided—options that may not be available to women disinclined to challenge their employers or obliged to enter certain offices. Moreover, while publicly disseminated pornography may influence all viewers, it remains the expression of the editors of *Penthouse* or *Hustler* or the directors of *Deep Throat*. On the wall of an office, it becomes the expression of a coworker or supervisor as well.

In this context the effect of pornography on workplace equality is obvious. Pornography on an employer's wall or desk communicates a message about the way he views women, a view strikingly at odds with the way women wish to be viewed in the workplace. Depending upon the material in question, it may communicate that women should be the objects of sexual aggression, that they are submissive slaves to male desires, or that their most salient and desirable attributes are sexual. Any of these images may communicate to male coworkers that it is acceptable to view women in a predominately sexual way. All of the views to some extent detract from the image most women in the workplace would like to project: that of the professional, credible coworker.

The "social context" argument cannot be squared with Title VII's promise to open the workplace to women. When the pre-existing state of the work environment receives weight in evaluating its hostility to women, only those women who are willing to and can accept the level of abuse inherent in a given workplace—a place that may have historically been all male or historically excluded women intentionally—will apply to and continue to work there. It is absurd to believe that Title VII opened the doors of such places in form and closed them in substance. A pre-existing atmosphere that deters women from entering or continuing in a profession or job is no less destructive to and offensive to workplace equality than a sign declaring "Men Only."

JSI is liable for the hostile work environment to which Robinson was subjected.

Discussion Questions

1) What is the standard that the court held need be satisfied to claim a hostile environment?

2) How does the opinion in this case react to the decision of the Sixth Circuit in *Rabidue*? What are its reasons for disagreement?

3) Would a "reasonable person" have found the conditions here to be sexual harassment? Was it necessary to change the standard to reach the result desired by this court?

Ellison v. Brady

924 F.2d 872 (1991)
United States Court of Appeals for the Ninth Circuit
Opinion: Beezer, Circuit Judge

Kerry Ellison appeals the district court's order granting summary judgment to the Secretary of the Treasury on her sexual harassment action brought under Title VII of the Civil Rights Act of 1964. This appeal presents two important issues: (1) what test should be applied to determine whether conduct is sufficiently severe or pervasive to alter the conditions of employment and create a hostile working environment, and (2) what remedial actions can shield employers from liability for sexual harassment by co-workers. The district court held that Ellison did not state a prima facie case of hostile environment sexual harassment. We reverse and remand.

Kerry Ellison worked as a revenue agent for the Internal Revenue Service in San Mateo, California. During her initial training in 1984 she met Sterling Gray, another trainee, who was also assigned to the San Mateo office. The two co-workers never became friends, and they did not work closely together.

Gray's desk was twenty feet from Ellison's desk. Revenue agents in the San Mateo office often went to lunch in groups. In June of 1986 when no one else was in the office, Gray asked Ellison to lunch. She accepted. Gray had to pick up his son's forgotten lunch, so they stopped by Gray's house. He gave Ellison a tour of his house.

Ellison alleges that after the June lunch Gray started to pester her with unnecessary questions and hang around her desk. On October 9, 1986, Gray asked Ellison out for a drink after work. She declined, but she suggested that they have lunch the following week. She did not want to have lunch alone with him, and she tried to stay away from the office during lunchtime. One day during the following week, Gray uncharacteristically dressed in a three-piece suit and asked Ellison out for lunch. Again, she did not accept.

On October 22, 1986 Gray handed Ellison a note he wrote on a telephone message slip which read:

> I cried over you last night and I'm totally drained today. I have never been in such constant term oil (sic). Thank you for talking with me. I could not stand to feel your hatred for another day.

When Ellison realized that Gray wrote the note, she became shocked and frightened and left the room. Gray followed her into the hallway and demanded that she talk to him, but she left the building.

Ellison later showed the note to Bonnie Miller, who supervised both Ellison and Gray. Miller said "this is sexual harassment." Ellison asked Miller not to do anything about it. She wanted to try to handle it herself. Ellison asked a male co-worker to talk to Gray, to tell him that she was not interested in him and to leave her alone. The next day, Thursday, Gray called in sick.

Ellison did not work on Friday, and on the following Monday, she started four weeks of training in St. Louis, Missouri. Gray mailed her a card and a typed, single-spaced, three-page letter. She describes this letter as "twenty times, a hundred times weirder" than the prior note. Gray wrote, in part:

> I know that you are worth knowing with or without sex...Leaving aside the hassles and disasters of recent weeks. I have enjoyed you so much over these past few months. Watching you. Experiencing you from O so far away. Admiring your style and élan...Don't you think it odd that two people who have never even talked together, alone, are striking off such intense sparks...I will [write] another letter in the near future.

She immediately telephoned Miller. Ellison told her supervisor that she was frightened and really upset. She requested that Miller transfer either her or Gray because she would not be comfortable working in the same office with him. Miller then telephoned her supervisor, Joe Benton, and discussed the problem. That same day she had a counseling session with Gray. She informed him that he was entitled to union representation. During this meeting, she told Gray to leave Ellison alone.

At Benton's request, Miller apprised the labor relations department of the situation. She also reminded Gray many times over the next few weeks that he must not contact Ellison in any way. Gray subsequently transferred to the San Francisco office on November 24, 1986. Ellison returned from St. Louis in late November and did not discuss the matter further with Miller.

After three weeks in San Francisco, Gray filed union grievances requesting a return to the San Mateo office. The IRS and the union settled the grievances in Gray's favor, agreeing to allow him to transfer back to the San Mateo office provided that he spend four more months in San Francisco and promise not to bother Ellison. On January 28, 1987, Ellison first learned of Gray's request in a letter from Miller explaining that Gray would return to the San Mateo office. The letter indicated that management decided to resolve Ellison's problem with a six-month separation, and that it would take additional action if the problem recurred.

After receiving the letter, Ellison was "frantic." She filed a formal complaint alleging sexual harassment on January 30, 1987, with the IRS. She also obtained permission to transfer to San Francisco temporarily when Gray returned.

The IRS employee investigating the allegation agreed with Ellison's supervisor that Gray's conduct constituted sexual harassment. In its final decision, however, the Treasury Department rejected Ellison's complaint because it believed that the complaint did not describe a pattern or practice of sexual harassment covered by the EEOC regulations. After an appeal, the EEOC affirmed the Treasury Department's decision on a different ground. It concluded that the agency took adequate action to prevent the repetition of Gray's conduct.

Ellison filed a complaint in September of 1987 in federal district court. The court granted the government's motion for summary judgment on the ground that Ellison had failed to state a prima facie case of sexual harassment due to a hostile working environment. Ellison appeals.

Congress added the word "sex" to Title VII of the Civil Rights Act of 1964 n3 at the last minute on the floor of the House of Representatives. 110 Cong. Rec. 2,577-2,584 (1964). Virtually no legislative history provides guidance to courts interpreting the prohibition of sex discrimination. In *Meritor Savings Bank v. Vinson*, the Supreme Court held that sexual harassment constitutes sex discrimination in violation of Title VII.

The Supreme Court in *Meritor* held that Mechelle Vinson's working conditions constituted a hostile environment in violation of Title VII's prohibition of sex discrimination. Vinson's supervisor made repeated demands for sexual favors, usually at work, both during and after business hours. Vinson initially refused her employer's sexual advances, but eventually acceded because she feared losing her job. They had intercourse over forty times. She additionally testified that he "fondled her in front of other employees, followed her into the women's restroom when she went there alone, exposed himself to her, and even forcibly raped her on several occasions." The Court had no difficulty finding this environment hostile.

Since *Meritor*, we have not often reached the merits of a hostile environment sexual harassment claim. In *Jordan v. Clark*, 847 F.2d 1368, 1373 (9th Cir. 1988 (1989), we explained that a hostile environment exists when an employee can show (1) that he or she was subjected to sexual advances, requests for sexual favors, or other verbal or physical conduct of a sexual nature, (2) that this conduct was unwelcome, and (3) that the conduct was sufficiently severe or pervasive to alter the conditions of the victim's employment and create an abusive working environment.

The parties ask us to determine if Gray's conduct, as alleged by Ellison, was sufficiently severe or pervasive to alter the conditions of Ellison's employment and create an abusive working environment. The district court, with little Ninth Circuit case law to look to for guidance, held that Ellison did not state a prima facie case of sexual harassment due to a hostile working environment. It believed that Gray's conduct was "isolated and genuinely trivial." We disagree.

We begin our analysis of the third part of the framework we set forth in *Jordan* with a closer look at *Meritor*. The Supreme Court in *Meritor* explained that courts may properly look to guidelines issued by the Equal Employment Opportunity Commission (EEOC) for guidance when examining hostile environment claims of sexual harassment. The EEOC guidelines describe hostile environment harassment as "conduct [which] has the purpose or effect of unreasonably interfering with an individual's work performance or creating an intimidating, hostile, or offensive working environment." The EEOC, in accord with a substantial body of judicial decisions, has concluded that "Title VII affords employees the right to work in an environment free from discriminatory intimidation, ridicule, and insult."

The Supreme Court cautioned, however, that not all harassment affects a "term, condition, or privilege" of employment within the meaning of Title VII. For example, the "mere utterance of an ethnic or racial epithet which engenders offensive feelings in an employee" is not, by itself, actionable under Title VII. To state a claim under Title VII, sexual harassment "must be sufficiently severe or pervasive to alter the conditions of the victim's employment and create an abusive working environment."

Although *Meritor* and our previous cases establish the framework for the resolution of hostile environment cases, they do not dictate the outcome of this case. Gray's conduct falls somewhere between forcible rape and the mere utterance of an epithet.

The government asks us to apply the reasoning of other courts which have declined to find Title VII violations on more egregious facts. In *Scott v. Sears, Roebuck & Co.*, 798 F.2d 210, 212 (7th Cir. 1986), the Seventh Circuit analyzed a female employee's working conditions for sexual harassment. It noted that she was repeatedly propositioned and winked at by her supervisor. When she asked for assistance, he asked "what will I get for it?" Co-workers slapped her buttocks and commented that she must moan and groan during sex. The court examined the evidence to see if "the demeaning conduct and sexual stereotyping caused such anxiety and debilitation to the plaintiff that working conditions were 'poisoned' within the meaning of Title VII." The court did not consider the environment sufficiently hostile.

Similarly, in *Rabidue v. Osceola Refining Co.*, the Sixth Circuit refused to find a hostile environment where the workplace contained posters of naked and partially dressed women, and where a male employee customarily called women "whores," "cunt," "pussy," and "tits," referred to plaintiff as "fat ass," and specifically stated, "All that bitch needs is a good lay." Over a strong dissent, the majority held that the sexist remarks and the pin-up posters had only a de minimis effect and did not seriously affect the plaintiff's psychological well-being.

We do not agree with the standards set forth in *Scott* and *Rabidue*, and we choose not to follow those decisions. Neither *Scott's* search for "anxiety and debilitation" sufficient to "poison" a working environment nor *Rabidue's* requirement that a plaintiff's psychological well-being be "seriously affected" follows directly from language in *Meritor*. It is the harasser's conduct which must be pervasive or severe, not the alteration in the conditions of employment. Surely, employees need not endure sexual harassment until their psychological well-being is seriously affected to the extent that they suffer anxiety and debilitation. Although an isolated epithet by itself fails to support a cause of action for a hostile environment, Title VII's protection of employees from sex discrimination comes into play long before the point where victims of sexual harassment require psychiatric assistance.

We have closely examined *Meritor* and our previous cases, and we believe that Gray's conduct was sufficiently severe and pervasive to alter the conditions of Ellison's employment and create an abusive working environment. We first note that the required showing of severity or seriousness of the harassing conduct varies inversely with the pervasiveness or frequency of the conduct.

Next, we believe that in evaluating the severity and pervasiveness of sexual harassment, we should focus on the perspective of the victim. If we only examined whether a reasonable person would engage in allegedly harassing conduct, we would run the risk of reinforcing the prevailing level of discrimination. Harassers could continue to harass merely because a particular discriminatory practice was common, and victims of harassment would have no remedy.

We therefore prefer to analyze harassment from the victim's perspective. A complete understanding of the victim's view requires, among other things, an analysis of the different perspectives of men and women. Conduct that many men consider unobjectionable may offend many women.

We realize that there is a broad range of viewpoints among women as a group, but we believe that many women share common concerns which men do not necessarily share. For example, because women are disproportionately victims of rape and sexual assault, women have a stronger incentive to be concerned with sexual behavior. Women who are victims of mild forms of sexual harassment may understandably worry whether a harasser's conduct is merely a prelude to violent sexual assault. Men, who are rarely victims of sexual assault, may view sexual conduct in a vacuum without a full appreciation of the social setting or the underlying threat of violence that a woman may perceive.

In order to shield employers from having to accommodate the idiosyncratic concerns of the rare hyper-sensitive employee, we hold that a female plaintiff states a prima facie case of hostile environment sexual harassment when she alleges conduct which a reasonable woman would consider sufficiently severe or pervasive to alter the conditions of employment and create an abusive working environment. Of course, where male employees allege that co-workers engage in conduct which creates a hostile environment, the appropriate victim's perspective would be that of a reasonable man.

We realize that the reasonable woman standard will not address conduct which some women find offensive. Conduct considered harmless by many today may be considered discriminatory in the future. Fortunately, the reasonableness inquiry which we adopt today is not static. As the views of reasonable women change, so too does the Title VII standard of acceptable behavior.

We adopt the perspective of a reasonable woman primarily because we believe that a sex-blind reasonable person standard tends to be male-biased and tends to systematically ignore the experiences of women. The reasonable woman standard does not establish a higher level of protection for women than men. Instead, a gender-conscious examination of sexual harassment enables women to participate in the workplace on an equal footing with men. By acknowledging and not trivializing the effects of sexual harassment on reasonable women, courts can work towards ensuring that neither men nor women will have to "run a gauntlet of sexual abuse in return for the privilege of being allowed to work and make a living."

We note that the reasonable victim standard we adopt today classifies conduct as unlawful sexual harassment even when harassers do not realize that their conduct creates a hostile working environment. Well-intentioned compliments by co-workers or supervisors can form the basis of a sexual harassment cause of action if a reasonable victim of the same sex as the plaintiff would consider the comments sufficiently severe or pervasive to alter a condition of employment and create an abusive working environment. That is because Title VII is not a fault-based tort scheme." Title VII is aimed at the consequences or effects of an employment practice and not at the...motivation" of co-workers or employers. To avoid liability under Title VII, employers may have to educate and sensitize their workforce to eliminate conduct which a reasonable victim would consider unlawful sexual harassment.

The facts of this case illustrate the importance of considering the victim's perspective. Analyzing the facts from the alleged harasser's viewpoint, Gray could be portrayed as a modern-day Cyrano de Bergerac wishing no more than to woo Ellison with his words. There is no evidence that Gray harbored ill will toward Ellison. He even offered in his "love letter" to leave her alone if she wished. Examined in this light, it is not difficult to see why the district court characterized Gray's conduct as isolated and trivial.

Ellison, however, did not consider the acts to be trivial. Gray's first note shocked and frightened her. After receiving the three-page letter, she became really upset and frightened again. She immediately requested that she or Gray be transferred. Her supervisor's prompt response suggests that she too did not consider the conduct trivial. When Ellison learned that Gray arranged to return to San Mateo, she immediately asked to transfer, and she immediately filed an official complaint.

We cannot say as a matter of law that Ellison's reaction was idiosyncratic or hyper-sensitive. We believe that a reasonable woman could have had a similar reaction. After receiving the first bizarre note from Gray, a person she barely knew, Ellison asked a co-worker to tell Gray to leave her alone. Despite her request, Gray sent her a long, passionate, disturbing letter. He told her he had been "watching" and "experiencing" her; he made repeated references to sex; he said he would write again. Ellison had no way of knowing what Gray would do next. A reasonable woman could consider Gray's conduct, as alleged by Ellison, sufficiently severe and pervasive to alter a condition of employment and create an abusive working environment.

Sexual harassment is a major problem in the workplace. Adopting the victim's perspective ensures that courts will not "sustain ingrained notions of reasonable behavior fashioned by the offenders." Congress did not enact Title VII to codify prevailing sexist prejudices. To the contrary, "Congress designed Title VII to prevent the perpetuation of stereotypes and a sense of degradation which serve to close or discourage employment opportunities for women." We hope that over time both men and women will learn what conduct offends reasonable members of the other sex. When employers and employees internalize the standard of workplace conduct we establish today, the current gap in perception between the sexes will be bridged.

Dissent: Stephens, District Judge

I refer to the majority's use of the term "reasonable woman," a term I find ambiguous and therefore inadequate.

Nowhere in section 2000e of Title VII, the section under which the plaintiff in this case brought suit, is there any indication that Congress intended to provide for any other than equal treatment in the area of civil rights. The legislation is designed to achieve a balanced and generally gender neutral and harmonious workplace which would improve production and the quality of the employees' lives. In fact, the Supreme Court has shown a preference against systems that are not gender or race neutral, such as hiring quotas. While women may be the most frequent targets of this type of conduct that is at issue in this case, they are not the only targets. I believe that it is incumbent upon the court in this case to use terminology that will meet the needs of all who seek recourse under this section of Title VII. Possible alternatives that are more in line with a gender neutral approach include "victim," "target," or "person."

The term "reasonable man" as it is used in the law of torts, traditionally refers to the average adult person, regardless of gender, and the conduct that can reasonably be expected of him or her. For the purposes of the legal issues that are being addressed, such a term assumes that it is applicable to all persons. Section 2000e of Title VII presupposes the use of a legal term that can apply to all persons and the impossibility of a more individually tailored standard. It is clear that the authors of the majority opinion intend a difference between the "reasonable woman" and the "reasonable man" in Title VII cases on the assumption that men do not have the same sensibilities as women. This is not necessarily true. A man's response to circumstances faced by women and their effect upon women can be and in given circumstances may be expected to be understood by men.

It takes no stretch of the imagination to envision two complaints emanating from the same workplace regarding the same conditions, one brought by a woman and the other by a man. Application of the "new standard" presents a puzzlement which is born of the assumption that men's eyes do not see what a woman sees through her eyes. I find it surprising that the majority finds no need for evidence on any of these subjects. I am not sure whether the majority also concludes that the woman and the man in question are also reasonable without evidence on this subject. I am irresistibly drawn to the view that the conditions of the workplace itself should be examined as affected, among other things, by the conduct of those working there as to whether the workplace as existing is conducive to fulfilling the goals of Title VII.

The focus on the victim of the sexually discriminatory conduct has its parallel in rape trials in the focus put by the defense on the victim's conduct rather than on the unlawful conduct of the person accused. Modern feminists have pointed out that concentration by the defense upon evidence concerning the background, appearance and conduct of women claiming to have been raped must be carefully controlled by the court to avoid effectively shifting the burden of proof to the victim. It is the accused, not the victim, that should be subjected to scrutiny.

The circumstances existing in the workplace where only men are employed are different than they are where there are both male and female employees. The existence of the differences is readily recognizable and the conduct of employees can be changed appropriately. This is what Title VII requires. Whether a man or a woman has sensibilities peculiar to the person and what they are is not necessarily known. Until they become known by manifesting themselves in an obvious way, they do not become part of the circumstances of the workplace. Consequently, the governing element in the equation is the workplace itself, not concepts or viewpoints of individual employees. This does not conflict with existing legal concepts.

The creation of the proposed "new standard" which applies only to women will not necessarily come to the aid of all potential victims of the type of misconduct that is at issue in this case. I believe that a gender neutral standard would greatly contribute to the clarity of this and future cases in the same area.

Discussion Questions

1) What is the standard that the court held need be satisfied to claim a hostile environment?

2) Would a "reasonable person" have found the conditions here to constitute sexual harassment? Was it necessary to change the standard to reach the result desired by this court?

3) Assuming that the majority is correct in the view that men and women view sexual harassment differently, why not use the perspective of the accused to determine if a "reasonable person" would have found his actions to be reasonable?

4) Why does the dissent prefer a gender neutral alternative to the approach taken by this court? Are its concerns justified?

Franklin v. Gwinnett County Public Schools

503 U.S. 60 (1992)
Supreme Court of the United States
Opinion by: Justice White

This case presents the question whether the implied right of action under Title IX of the Education Amendments of 1972, 20 U. S. C. §§ 1681-1688 (Title IX) supports a claim for monetary damages.

Petitioner Christine Franklin was a student at North Gwinnett High School in Gwinnett County, Georgia, between September 1985 and August 1989. Respondent Gwinnett County School District operates the high school and receives federal funds. According to the complaint filed on December 29, 1988, in the United States District Court for the Northern District of Georgia, Franklin was subjected to continual sexual harassment beginning in the autumn of her tenth grade year (1986) from Andrew Hill, a sports coach and teacher employed by the district. Among other allegations, Franklin avers that Hill engaged her in sexually oriented conversations in which he asked about her sexual experiences with her boyfriend and whether she would consider having sexual intercourse with an older man, that Hill forcibly kissed her on the mouth in the school parking lot, that he telephoned her at her home and asked if she would meet him socially, and that, on three occasions in her junior year, Hill interrupted a class, requested that the teacher excuse Franklin, and took her to a private office where he subjected her to coercive intercourse. The complaint further alleges that though they became aware of and investigated Hill's sexual harassment of Franklin and other female students, teachers and administrators took no action to halt it and discouraged Franklin from pressing charges against Hill. On April 14, 1988, Hill resigned on the condition that all matters pending against him be dropped. The school thereupon closed its investigation.

In this action, the District Court dismissed the complaint on the ground that Title IX does not authorize an award of damages. The Court of Appeals affirmed 911 F.2d 617 (CA11 1990). As a basis for its holding that monetary damages were unavailable, the court reasoned that Title IX was enacted under Congress' Spending Clause powers and that "under such statutes, relief may frequently be limited to that which is equitable in nature, with the recipient of federal funds thus retaining the option of terminating such receipt in order to rid itself of an injunction." The court closed by observing it would "proceed with extreme care" to afford compensatory relief absent express provision by Congress or clear direction from this Court. Accordingly, it held that an action for monetary damages could not be sustained for an alleged intentional violation of Title IX, and affirmed the District Court's ruling to that effect. Because this opinion conflicts with a decision of the Court of Appeals for the Third Circuit, we granted certiorari. We reverse.

In this case we must decide what remedies are available in a suit brought pursuant to this implied right. As we have often stated, the question of what remedies are available under a statute that provides a private right of action is "analytically distinct" from the issue of whether such a right exists in the first place. Thus, although we examine the text and history of a statute to determine whether Congress intended to create a right of action, we presume the availability of all appropriate remedies unless Congress has expressly indicated otherwise.

"Where legal rights have been invaded, and a federal statute provides for a general right to sue for such invasion, federal courts may use any available remedy to make good the wrong done." *Bell v. Hood*, 327 U.S. 678, 684 (1946). The Court explained this longstanding rule as jurisdictional and upheld the exercise of the federal courts' power to award appropriate relief so long as a cause of action existed under the Constitution or laws of the United States.

The *Bell* Court's reliance on this rule was hardly revolutionary. From the earliest years of the Republic, the Court has recognized the power of the Judiciary to award appropriate remedies to redress injuries actionable in federal court. In *Marbury v. Madison*, for example, Chief Justice Marshall observed that our Government "has been emphatically termed a government of laws, and not of men. It will certainly cease to deserve this high appellation, if the laws furnish no remedy for the violation of a vested legal right." This principle originated in the English common law, and Blackstone described it as "a general and indisputable rule, that where there is a legal right, there is also a legal remedy, by suit or action at law, whenever that right is invaded."

Respondents and the United States as amicus curiae, however, maintain that whatever the traditional presumption may have been when the Court decided *Bell v. Hood*, it has disappeared in succeeding decades. We do not agree...That a statute does not authorize the remedy at issue "in so many words is no more significant than the fact that it does not in terms authorize execution to issue on a judgment."

The United States contends that the traditional presumption in favor of all appropriate relief was abandoned by the Court...The Government's position, however, mirrors the very misunderstanding over the difference between a cause of action and the relief afforded under it that sparked the confusion we attempted to clarify. Whether Congress may limit the class of persons who have a right of action under Title IX is irrelevant to the issue in this lawsuit. To reiterate, "the question whether a litigant has a 'cause of action' is analytically distinct and prior to the question of what relief, if any, a litigant may be entitled to receive."

The general rule, therefore, is that absent clear direction to the contrary by Congress, the federal courts have the power to award any appropriate relief in a cognizable cause of action brought pursuant to a federal statute.

We now address whether Congress intended to limit application of this general principle in the enforcement of Title IX. Because the cause of action was inferred by the Court in *Cannon*, the usual recourse to statutory text and legislative history in the period prior to that decision necessarily will not enlighten our analysis...In the years before and after Congress enacted this statute, the Court "followed a common-law tradition [and] regarded the denial of a remedy as the exception rather than the rule."

In the years after the announcement of *Cannon*, on the other hand, a more traditional method of statutory analysis is possible, because Congress was legislating with full cognizance of that decision. Our reading of the two amendments to Title IX enacted after *Cannon* leads us to conclude that Congress did not intend to limit the remedies available in a suit brought under Title IX.

Respondents and the United States nevertheless suggest three reasons why we should not apply the traditional presumption in favor of appropriate relief in this case.

First, respondents argue that an award of damages violates separation of powers principles because it unduly expands the federal courts' power into a sphere properly reserved to the Executive and Legislative Branches. In making this argument, respondents misconceive the difference between a cause of action and a remedy. Unlike the finding of a cause of action, which authorizes a court to hear a case or controversy, the discretion to award appropriate relief involves no such increase in judicial power. Federal courts cannot reach out to award remedies when the Constitution or laws of the United States do not support a cause of action. Indeed, properly understood, respondents' position invites us to abdicate our historic judicial authority to award appropriate relief in cases brought in our court system. It is well to recall that such authority historically has been thought necessary to provide an important safeguard against abuses of Legislative and Executive power, as well as to ensure an independent Judiciary.

Next, consistent with the Court of Appeals' reasoning, respondents and the United States contend that the normal presumption in favor of all appropriate remedies should not apply because Title IX was enacted pursuant to Congress' Spending Clause power. In *Pennhurst State School and Hospital v. Halderman*, 451 U.S. 1 (1981), the Court observed that remedies were limited under such Spending Clause statutes when the alleged violation was unintentional. Respondents and the United States maintain that this presumption should apply equally to intentional violations. We disagree. The point of not permitting monetary damages for an unintentional violation is that the receiving entity of federal funds lacks notice that it will be liable for a monetary award. This notice problem does not arise in a case such as this, in which intentional discrimination is alleged. Unquestionably, Title IX placed on the Gwinnett County Public Schools the duty not to discriminate on the basis of sex, and "when a supervisor sexually harasses a subordinate because of the subordinate's sex, that supervisor 'discriminate[s]' on the basis of sex." *Meritor Sav. Bank, FSB v. Vinson*, 477 U.S. 57 (1986). We believe the same rule should apply when a teacher sexually harasses and abuses a student. Congress surely did not intend for federal moneys to be expended to support the intentional actions it sought by statute to proscribe.

Finally, the United States asserts that the remedies permissible under Title IX should nevertheless be limited to backpay and prospective relief. In addition to diverging from our traditional approach to deciding what remedies are available for violation of a federal right, this position conflicts with sound logic. First, both remedies are equitable in nature, and it is axiomatic that a court should determine the adequacy of a remedy in law before resorting to equitable relief. Under the ordinary convention, the proper inquiry would be whether monetary damages provided an adequate remedy, and if not, whether equitable relief would be appropriate. Moreover, in this case the equitable remedies suggested by respondent and the Federal Government are clearly inadequate. Backpay does nothing for petitioner, because she was a student when the alleged discrimination occurred. Similarly, because Hill—the person she claims subjected her to sexual harassment—no longer teaches at the school and she herself no longer attends a school in the Gwinnett system, prospective relief accords her no remedy at all. The Government's answer that administrative action helps other similarly situated students in effect acknowledges that its approach would leave petitioner remediless.

In sum, we conclude that a damages remedy is available for an action brought to enforce Title IX. The judgment of the Court of Appeals, therefore, is reversed, and the case is remanded for further proceedings consistent with this opinion.

Discussion Questions

1) What is the standard that the court held need be satisfied to claim a Title IX violation?

2) How does Title IX differ from Title VII as far as liability?

3) Does the Court appear to place any limits on Title IX damages? If the harassment had been from a staff member or fellow student, rather than a teacher, would the district still face liability?

Teresa Harris v. Forklift Systems, Inc.

510 U.S. 17 (1993)
Supreme Court of the United States
Opinion by: Justice O'Connor

In this case we consider the definition of a discriminatorily "abusive work environment" (also known as a "hostile work environment") under Title VII of the Civil Rights Act of 1964, 78 Stat. 253, as amended, 42 U.S.C. § 2000e.

Teresa Harris worked as a manager at Forklift Systems, Inc., an equipment rental company, from April 1985 until October 1987. Charles Hardy was Forklift's president.

The Magistrate found that, throughout Harris' time at Forklift, Hardy often insulted her because of her gender and often made her the target of unwanted sexual innuendos. Hardy told Harris on several occasions, in the presence of other employees, "You're a woman, what do you know" and "We need a man as the rental manager"; at least once, he told her she was "a dumb ass woman." Again in front of others, he suggested that the two of them "go to the Holiday Inn to negotiate [Harris'] raise." Hardy occasionally asked Harris and other female employees to get coins from his front pants pocket. He threw objects on the ground in front of Harris and other women, and asked them to pick the objects up. He made sexual innuendos about Harris' and other women's clothing.

In mid-August 1987, Harris complained to Hardy about his conduct. Hardy said he was surprised that Harris was offended, claimed he was only joking, and apologized. He also promised he would stop, and based on this assurance Harris stayed on the job.

But in early September, Hardy began anew: While Harris was arranging a deal with one of Forklift's customers, he asked her, again in front of other employees, "What did you do, promise the guy...some [sex] Saturday night?" On October 1, Harris collected her paycheck and quit.

Harris then sued Forklift, claiming that Hardy's conduct had created an abusive work environment for her because of her gender. The United States District Court for the Middle District of Tennessee, adopting the report and recommendation of the Magistrate, found this to be "a close case," but held that Hardy's conduct did not create an abusive environment. The court found that some of Hardy's comments "offended [Harris], and would offend the reasonable woman," but that they were not "so severe as to be expected to seriously affect [Harris'] psychological well-being." A reasonable woman manager under like circumstances would have been offended by Hardy, but his conduct would not have risen to the level of interfering with that person's work performance. "Neither do I believe that [Harris] was subjectively so offended that she suffered injury....Although Hardy may at times have genuinely offended [Harris], I do not believe that he created a working environment so poisoned as to be intimidating or abusive to [Harris]." In focusing on the employee's psychological well-being, the District Court was following Circuit precedent. See *Rabidue v. Osceola Refining Co.*, 805 F.2d 611. The United States Court of Appeals for the Sixth Circuit affirmed in a brief unpublished decision.

We granted certiorari to resolve a conflict among the Circuits on whether conduct, to be actionable as "abusive work environment" harassment (no quid pro quo harassment issue is present here), must "seriously affect [an employee's] psychological well-being" or lead the plaintiff to "suffer injury."

Title VII of the Civil Rights Act of 1964 makes it "an unlawful employment practice for an employer...to discriminate against any individual with respect to his compensation, terms, conditions, or privileges of employment, because of such individual's race, color, religion, sex, or national origin." 42 U.S.C.

§ 2000e-2(a)(1). As we made clear in *Meritor Savings Bank, FSB v. Vinson*, 477 U.S. 57, (1986), this language "is not limited to 'economic' or 'tangible' discrimination. The phrase 'terms, conditions, or privileges of employment' evinces a congressional intent 'to strike at the entire spectrum of disparate treatment of men and women' in employment," which includes requiring people to work in a discriminatorily hostile or abusive environment. When the workplace is permeated with "discriminatory intimidation, ridicule, and insult," that is "sufficiently severe or pervasive to alter the conditions of the victim's employment and create an abusive working environment," Title VII is violated.

This standard, which we reaffirm today, takes a middle path between making actionable any conduct that is merely offensive and requiring the conduct to cause a tangible psychological injury. As we pointed out in *Meritor*, "mere utterance of an...epithet which engenders offensive feelings in a employee," does not sufficiently affect the conditions of employment to implicate Title VII. Conduct that is not severe or pervasive enough to create an objectively hostile or abusive work environment—an environment that a reasonable person would find hostile or abusive—is beyond Title VII's purview. Likewise, if the victim does not subjectively perceive the environment to be abusive, the conduct has not actually altered conditions of the victim's employment, and there is no Title VII violation.

But Title VII comes into play before the harassing conduct leads to a nervous breakdown. A discriminatorily abusive work environment, even one that does not seriously affect employees' psychological well-being, can and often will detract from employees' job performance, discourage employees from remaining on the job, or keep them from advancing in their careers.

Moreover, even without regard to these tangible effects, the very fact that the discriminatory conduct was so severe or pervasive that it created a work environment abusive to employees because of their race, gender, religion, or national origin offends Title VII's broad rule of workplace equality. The appalling conduct alleged in *Meritor*, and the reference in that case to environments "'so heavily polluted with discrimination as to destroy completely the emotional and psychological stability of minority group workers,'" merely present some especially egregious examples of harassment. They do not mark the boundary of what is actionable. We therefore believe the District Court erred in relying on whether the conduct "seriously affected plaintiff's psychological well-being" or led her to "suffer injury." Such an inquiry may needlessly focus the factfinder's attention on concrete psychological harm, an element Title VII does not require. Certainly Title VII bars conduct that would seriously affect a reasonable person's psychological well-being, but the statute is not limited to such conduct. So long as the environment would reasonably be perceived, and is perceived, as hostile or abusive, there is no need for it also to be psychologically injurious. This is not, and by its nature cannot be, a mathematically precise test. We need not answer today all the potential questions it raises, nor specifically address the Equal Employment Opportunity Commission's new regulations on this subject. But we can say that whether an environment is "hostile" or "abusive" can be determined only by looking at all the circumstances. These may include the frequency of the discriminatory conduct; its severity; whether it is physically threatening or humiliating, or a mere offensive utterance; and whether it unreasonably interferes with an employee's work performance. The effect on the employee's psychological well-being is, of course, relevant to determining whether the plaintiff actually found the environment abusive. But while psychological harm, like any other relevant factor, may be taken into account, no single factor is required.

Justice Scalia, Concurring

Meritor Savings Bank, FSB v. Vinson, 477 U.S. 57 (1986), held that Title VII prohibits sexual harassment that takes the form of a hostile work environment. The Court stated that sexual harassment is actionable if it is "sufficiently severe or pervasive 'to alter the conditions of [the victim's] employment and create an abusive working environment.'" Today's opinion elaborates that the challenged conduct must be severe or pervasive enough "to create an objectively hostile or abusive work environment—an environment that a reasonable person would find hostile or abusive."

"Abusive" (or "hostile," which in this context I take to mean the same thing) does not seem to me a very clear standard—and I do not think clarity is at all increased by adding the adverb "objectively" or by appealing to a "reasonable person['s]" notion of what the vague word means. Today's opinion does list a number of factors that contribute to abusiveness, but since it neither says how much of each is necessary (an impossible task) nor identifies any single factor as determinative, it thereby adds little certitude. As a practical matter, today's holding lets virtually unguided juries decide whether sex-related conduct engaged in (or permitted by) an employer is egregious enough to warrant an award of damages. One might say that what constitutes "negligence" (a traditional jury question) is not much more clear and certain than what constitutes "abusiveness." Perhaps so. But the class of plaintiffs seeking to recover for negligence is limited to those who have suffered harm, whereas under this statute "abusiveness" is to be the test of whether legal harm has been suffered, opening more expansive vistas of litigation.

Be that as it may, I know of no alternative to the course the Court today has taken. One of the factors mentioned in the Court's nonexhaustive list—whether the conduct unreasonably interferes with an employee's work performance—would, if it were made an absolute test, provide greater guidance to juries and employers. But I see no basis for such a limitation in the language of the statute. Accepting *Meritor's* interpretation of the term "conditions of employment" as the law, the test is not whether work has been impaired, but whether working conditions have been discriminatorily altered. I know of no test more faithful to the inherently vague statutory language than the one the Court today adopts. For these reasons, I join the opinion of the Court.

Discussion Questions

1) What is the standard that the court held need be satisfied to claim a hostile environment?

2) The majority held that "Title VII comes into play before the harassing conduct leads to a nervous breakdown." At exactly what point does Title VII come into play?

3) According to the majority, what type of circumstances would likely be present in a hostile environment sexual harassment claim?

4) Justice Scalia contends that "As a practical matter, today's holding lets virtually unguided juries decide whether sex-related conduct engaged in (or permitted by) an employer is egregious enough to warrant an award of damages." Is he correct? What more could be done to limit this danger?

5) Scalia contends that the tort of negligence is equally hard to define, yet is a traditional jury question. How does the finding of a hostile environment differ from a finding of negligence for a jury?

Oncale v. Sundowner Offshore Services

523 U.S. 75 (1998)
Supreme Court of the United States
Opinion by: Justice Scalia

This case presents the question whether workplace harassment can violate Title VII's prohibition against "discrimination… because of…sex," when the harasser and the harassed employee are of the same sex.

The precise details are irrelevant to the legal point we must decide, and in the interest of both brevity and dignity we shall describe them only generally. In late October 1991, Oncale was working for respondent Sundowner Offshore Services on a Chevron U.S.A., Inc., oil platform in the Gulf of Mexico. He was employed as a roust-about on an eight-man crew which included respondents John Lyons, Danny Pippen, and Brandon Johnson. Lyons, the crane operator, and Pippen, the driller, had supervisory authority. On several occasions, Oncale was forcibly subjected to sex-related, humiliating actions against him by Lyons, Pippen and Johnson in the presence of the rest of the crew. Pippen and Lyons also physically assaulted Oncale in a sexual manner, and Lyons threatened him with rape.

Oncale's complaints to supervisory personnel produced no remedial action; in fact, the company's Safety Compliance Clerk told Oncale that Lyons and Pippen "picked [on] him all the time too," and called him a name suggesting homosexuality. Oncale eventually quit—asking that his pink slip reflect that he "voluntarily left due to sexual harassment and verbal abuse." When asked at his deposition why he left Sundowner, Oncale stated "I felt that if I didn't leave my job, that I would be raped or forced to have sex."

Oncale filed a complaint against Sundowner in the United States District Court for the Eastern District of Louisiana, alleging that he was discriminated against in his employment because of his sex. Relying on the Fifth Circuit's decision in *Garcia v. Elf Atochem North America*, 28 F.3d 446, 451-452 (CA5 1994), the district court held that "Mr. Oncale, a male, has no cause of action under Title VII for harassment by male co-workers." On appeal, a panel of the Fifth affirmed. We granted certiorari.

Title VII of the Civil Rights Act of 1964 provides, in relevant part, that "it shall be an unlawful employment practice for an employer...to discriminate against any individual with respect to his compensation, terms, conditions, or privileges of employment, because of such individual's race, color, religion, sex, or national origin. We have held that this not only covers "terms" and "conditions" in the narrow contractual sense, but "evinces a congressional intent to strike at the entire spectrum of disparate treatment of men and women in employment." "When the workplace is permeated with discriminatory intimidation, ridicule, and insult that is sufficiently severe or pervasive to alter the conditions of the victim's employment and create an abusive working environment, Title VII is violated."

Title VII's prohibition of discrimination "because of...sex" protects men as well as women, and in the related context of racial discrimination in the workplace we have rejected any conclusive presumption that an employer will not discriminate against members of his own race. "Because of the many facets of human motivation, it would be unwise to presume as a matter of law that human beings of one definable group will not discriminate against other members of that group." In *Johnson v. Transportation Agency, Santa Clara Cty.*, 480 U.S. 616 (1987), a male employee claimed that his employer discriminated against him because of his sex when it preferred a female employee for promotion. Although we ultimately rejected the claim on other grounds, we did not consider it significant that the supervisor who made that decision was also a man. If our precedents leave any doubt on the question, we hold today that nothing in Title VII necessarily bars a claim of discrimination "because of...sex" merely because the plaintiff and the defendant (or the person charged with acting on behalf of the defendant) are of the same sex.

Courts have had little trouble with that principle in cases like *Johnson*, where an employee claims to have been passed over for a job or promotion. But when the issue arises in the context of a "hostile environment" sexual harassment claim, the state and federal courts have taken a bewildering variety of stances. Some, like the Fifth Circuit in this case, have held that same-sex sexual harassment claims are never cognizable under Title VII. See also, e.g., *Goluszek v. H. P. Smith*, 697 F. Supp. 1452 (ND Ill. 1988). Other decisions say that such claims are actionable only if the plaintiff can prove that the harasser is homosexual (and thus presumably motivated by sexual desire). Compare *McWilliams v. Fairfax County Board of Supervisors*, 72 F.3d 1191 (CA4 1996), with *Wrightson v. Pizza Hut of America*, 99 F.3d 138 (CA4 1996). Still others suggest that workplace harassment that is sexual in content is always actionable, regardless of the harasser's sex, sexual orientation, or motivations. See *Doe v. Belleville*, 119 F.3d 563 (CA7 1997).

We see no justification in the statutory language or our precedents for a categorical rule excluding same-sex harassment claims from the coverage of Title VII. As some courts have observed, male-on-male sexual harassment in the workplace was assuredly not the principal evil Congress was concerned with when it enacted Title VII. But statutory prohibitions often go beyond the principal evil to cover reasonably comparable evils, and it is ultimately the provisions of our laws rather than the principal concerns of our legislators by which we are governed. Title VII prohibits "discrimination...because of...sex" in the "terms" or "conditions" of employment. Our holding that this includes sexual harassment must extend to sexual harassment of any kind that meets the statutory requirements.

Respondents and their amici contend that recognizing liability for same-sex harassment will transform Title VII into a general civility code for the American workplace. But that risk is no greater for same-sex than for opposite-sex harassment, and is adequately met by careful attention to the requirements of the statute. Title VII does not prohibit all verbal or physical harassment in the workplace; it is directed only at "discrimination...because of...sex." We have never held that workplace harassment, even harassment between men and women, is automatically discrimination because of sex merely because the words used have sexual content or connotations. "The critical issue, Title VII's text indicates, is whether members of one sex are exposed to disadvantageous terms or conditions of employment to which members of the other sex are not exposed."

Courts and juries have found the inference of discrimination easy to draw in most male-female sexual harassment situations, because the challenged conduct typically involves explicit or implicit proposals of sexual activity; it is reasonable to assume those proposals would not have been made to someone of the same sex. The same chain of inference would be available to a plaintiff alleging same-sex harassment, if there were credible evidence that the harasser was homosexual. But harassing conduct need not be motivated by sexual desire to support an inference of discrimination on the basis of sex. A trier of fact might reasonably find such discrimination, for example, if a female victim is harassed in such sex-specific and derogatory terms by another woman as to make it clear that the harasser is motivated by general hostility to the presence of women in the workplace. A same-sex harassment plaintiff may also, of course, offer direct comparative evidence about how the alleged harasser treated members of both sexes in a mixed-sex workplace. Whatever evidentiary route the plaintiff chooses to follow, he or she must always prove that the conduct at issue was not merely tinged with offensive sexual connotations, but actually constituted "discrimination...because of...sex."

And there is another requirement that prevents Title VII from expanding into a general civility code: As we emphasized in *Meritor* and *Harris*, the statute does not reach genuine but innocuous differences in the ways men and women routinely interact with members of the same sex and of the opposite sex. The prohibition of harassment on the basis of sex requires neither asexuality nor androgyny in the workplace; it forbids only behavior so objectively offensive as to alter the "conditions" of the victim's employment. "Conduct that is not severe or pervasive enough to create an objectively hostile or abusive work environment—an environment that a reasonable person would find hostile or abusive—is beyond Title VII's purview. We have always regarded that requirement as crucial, and as sufficient to ensure that courts and juries do not mistake ordinary socializing in the workplace—such as male-on-male horseplay or intersexual flirtation—for discriminatory "conditions of employment."

We have emphasized, moreover, that the objective severity of harassment should be judged from the perspective of a reasonable person in the plaintiff's position, considering "all the circumstances." In same-sex (as in all) harassment cases, that inquiry requires careful consideration of the social context in which particular behavior occurs and is experienced by its target. A professional football player's working environment is not severely or pervasively abusive, for example, if the coach smacks him on the buttocks as he heads onto the field-even if the same behavior would reasonably be experienced as abusive by the coach's secretary (male or female) back at the office. The real social impact of workplace behavior often depends on a constellation of surrounding circumstances, expectations, and relationships which are not fully captured by a simple recitation of the words used or the physical acts performed. Common sense, and an appropriate sensitivity to social context, will enable courts and juries to distinguish between simple teasing or roughhousing among members of the same sex, and conduct which a reasonable person in the plaintiff's position would find severely hostile or abusive.

Because we conclude that sex discrimination consisting of same-sex sexual harassment is actionable under Title VII, the judgment of the Court of Appeals for the Fifth Circuit is reversed, and the case is remanded for further proceedings consistent with this opinion. It is so ordered.

Justice Thomas, Concurring

I concur because the Court stresses that in every sexual harassment case, the plaintiff must plead and ultimately prove Title VII's statutory requirement that there be discrimination "because of...sex."

Discussion Questions

1) What is the standard that the court held need be satisfied to claim a hostile environment in same-sex harassment cases?

2) Justice Scalia wrote that in dealing with this issue, "the state and federal courts have taken a bewildering variety of stances." What views had been expressed by the lower courts when confronting the question of same-sex harassment?

3) What does Justice Thomas' brief concurrence clarify in this decision?

4) Respondents and their amici contend that recognizing liability for same-sex harassment will transform Title VII into a general civility code for the American workplace. Is there any validity to this point of view?

Burlington Industries v. Kimberly B. Ellerth

524 U.S. 742 (1998)
Supreme Court of the United States
Opinion by: Justice Kennedy

We decide whether, under Title VII of the Civil Rights Act of 1964, an employee who refuses the unwelcome and threatening sexual advances of a supervisor, yet suffers no adverse, tangible job consequences, can recover against the employer without showing the employer is negligent or otherwise at fault for the supervisor's actions. The employer is Burlington Industries, the petitioner. The employee is Kimberly Ellerth, the respondent. From March 1993 until May 1994, Ellerth worked as a salesperson in one of Burlington's divisions in Chicago, Illinois. During her employment, she alleges, she was subjected to constant sexual harassment by her supervisor, one Ted Slowik.

In the hierarchy of Burlington's management structure, Slowik was a mid-level manager. Burlington has eight divisions, employing more than 22,000 people in some 50 plants around the United States. Slowik was a vice president in one of five business units within one of the divisions. He had authority to make hiring and promotion decisions subject to the approval of his supervisor, who signed the paperwork. According to Slowik's supervisor, his position was "not considered an upper-level management position," and he was "not amongst the decision-making or policy-making hierarchy." Slowik was not Ellerth's immediate supervisor. Ellerth worked in a two-person office in Chicago, and she answered to her office colleague, who in turn answered to Slowik in New York.

Against a background of repeated boorish and offensive remarks and gestures which Slowik allegedly made, Ellerth places particular emphasis on three alleged incidents where Slowik's comments could be construed as threats to deny her tangible job benefits. In the summer of 1993, while on a business trip, Slowik invited Ellerth to the hotel lounge, an invitation Ellerth felt compelled to accept because Slowik was her boss. When Ellerth gave no encouragement to remarks Slowik made about her breasts, he told her to "loosen up" and warned, "you know, Kim, I could make your life very hard or very easy at Burlington." In March 1994, when Ellerth was being considered for a promotion, Slowik expressed reservations during the promotion interview because she was not "loose enough." The comment was followed by his reaching over and rubbing her knee. Ellerth did receive the promotion; but when Slowik called to announce it, he told Ellerth, "you're gonna be out there with men who work in factories, and they certainly like women with pretty butts/legs."

In May 1994, Ellerth called Slowik, asking permission to insert a customer's logo into a fabric sample. Slowik responded, "I don't have time for you right now, Kim—unless you want to tell me what you're wearing." Ellerth told Slowik she had to go and ended the call. A day or two later, Ellerth called Slowik to ask permission again. This time he denied her request, but added something along the lines of, "are you wearing shorter skirts yet, Kim, because it would make your job a whole heck of a lot easier."

A short time later, Ellerth's immediate supervisor cautioned her about returning telephone calls to customers in a prompt fashion. In response, Ellerth quit. She faxed a letter giving reasons unrelated to the alleged sexual harassment we have described. About three weeks later, however, she sent a letter explaining she quit because of Slowik's behavior.

During her tenure at Burlington, Ellerth did not inform anyone in authority about Slowik's conduct, despite knowing Burlington had a policy against sexual harassment. In fact, she chose not to inform her immediate supervisor (not Slowik) because "'it would be his duty as my supervisor to report any incidents of sexual harassment.'" On one occasion, she told Slowik a comment he made was inappropriate.

In October 1994, after receiving a right-to-sue letter from the Equal Employment Opportunity Commission (EEOC), Ellerth filed suit in the United States District Court for the Northern District of Illinois, alleging Burlington engaged in sexual harassment and forced her constructive discharge, in violation of Title VII. The District Court granted summary judgment to Burlington. The Court found Slowik's behavior, as described by Ellerth, severe and pervasive enough to create a hostile work environment, but found Burlington neither knew nor should have known about the conduct. There was no triable issue of fact on the latter point, and the Court noted Ellerth had not used Burlington's internal complaint procedures. Although Ellerth's claim was framed as a hostile work environment complaint, the District Court observed there was a quid pro quo "component" to the hostile environment. Proceeding from the premise that an employer faces vicarious liability for quid pro quo harassment, the District Court thought it necessary to apply a negligence standard because the quid pro quo merely contributed to the hostile work environment. The District Court also dismissed Ellerth's constructive discharge claim.

The Court of Appeals en banc reversed in a decision which produced eight separate opinions and no consensus for a controlling rationale. The judges were able to agree on the problem they confronted: Vicarious liability, not failure to comply with a duty of care, was the essence of Ellerth's case against Burlington on appeal. The judges seemed to agree Ellerth could recover if Slowik's unfulfilled threats to deny her tangible job benefits was sufficient to impose vicarious liability on Burlington.

At the outset, we assume an important proposition yet to be established before a trier of fact. It is a premise assumed as well, in explicit or implicit terms, in the various opinions by the judges of the Court of Appeals. The premise is: a trier of fact could find in Slowik's remarks numerous threats to retaliate against Ellerth if she denied some sexual liberties. The threats, however, were not carried out or fulfilled. Cases based on threats which are carried out are referred to often as quid pro quo cases, as distinct from bothersome attentions or sexual remarks that are sufficiently severe or pervasive to create a hostile work environment. The terms quid pro quo and hostile work environment are helpful, perhaps, in making a rough demarcation between cases in which threats are carried out and those where they are not or are absent altogether, but beyond this are of limited utility.

Section 703(a) of Title VII forbids an employer:

> (1) to fail or refuse to hire or to discharge any individual, or otherwise to discriminate against any individual with respect to his compensation, terms, conditions or privileges of employment, because of such individual's...sex." 42 U.S.C. § 2000e-2(a)(1).

"Quid pro quo" and "hostile work environment" do not appear in the statutory text. The terms appeared first in the academic literature, see C. MacKinnon, *Sexual Harassment of Working Women* (1979); found their way into decisions of the Courts of Appeals and were mentioned in this Court's decision in *Meritor Savings Bank, v. Vinson*, 477 U.S. 57. In *Meritor*, the terms served a specific and limited purpose. There we considered whether the conduct in question constituted discrimination in the terms or conditions of employment in violation of Title VII. We assumed, and with adequate reason, that if an employer demanded sexual favors from an employee in return for a job benefit, discrimination with respect to terms or conditions of employment was explicit. Less obvious was whether an employer's sexually demeaning behavior altered terms or conditions of employment in violation of Title VII. We distinguished between quid pro quo claims and hostile environment claims, and said both were cognizable under Title VII, though the latter requires harassment that is severe or pervasive. The principal significance of the distinction is to instruct that Title VII is violated by either explicit or constructive alterations in the terms or conditions of employment and to explain the latter must be severe or pervasive. The distinction was not discussed for its bearing upon an employer's liability for an employee's discrimination. On this question *Meritor* held, with no further specifics, that agency principles controlled.

Nevertheless, as use of the terms grew in the wake of *Meritor*, they acquired their own significance. The standard of employer responsibility turned on which type of harassment occurred. If the plaintiff established a quid pro quo claim, the Courts of Appeals held, the employer was subject to vicarious liability.

Because Ellerth's claim involves only unfulfilled threats, it should be categorized as a hostile work environment claim which requires a showing of severe or pervasive conduct.

An employer may be liable for both negligent and intentional torts committed by an employee within the scope of his or her employment. Sexual harassment under Title VII presupposes intentional conduct. In order to accommodate the agency principles of vicarious liability for harm caused by misuse of supervisory authority, as well as Title VII's equally basic policies of encouraging forethought by employers and saving action by objecting employees, we adopt the following holding in this case and in *Faragher v. Boca Raton*, post, also decided today. An employer is subject to vicarious liability to a victimized employee for an actionable hostile environment created by a supervisor with immediate (or successively higher) authority over the employee. When no tangible employment action is taken, a defending employer may raise an affirmative defense to liability or damages, subject to proof by a preponderance of the evidence. The defense comprises two necessary elements: (a) that the employer exercised reasonable care to prevent and correct promptly any sexually harassing behavior, and (b) that the plaintiff employee unreasonably failed to take advantage of any preventive or corrective opportunities provided by the employer or to avoid harm otherwise. While proof that an employer had promulgated an anti-harassment policy with complaint procedure is not necessary in every instance as a matter of law, the need for a stated policy suitable to the employment circumstances may appropriately be addressed in any case when litigating the first element of the defense. And while proof that an employee failed to fulfill the corresponding obligation of reasonable care to avoid harm is not limited to showing any unreasonable failure to use any complaint procedure provided by the employer, a demonstration of such failure will normally suffice to satisfy the employer's burden under the second element of the defense. No affirmative defense is available, however, when the supervisor's harassment culminates in a tangible employment action, such as discharge, demotion, or undesirable reassignment.

Although Ellerth has not alleged she suffered a tangible employment action at the hands of Slowik, which would deprive Burlington of the availability of the affirmative defense, this is not dispositive. In light of our decision, Burlington is still subject to vicarious liability for Slowik's activity, but Burlington should have an opportunity to assert and prove the affirmative defense to liability.

For these reasons, we will affirm the judgment of the Court of Appeals, reversing the grant of summary judgment against Ellerth. On remand, the District Court will have the opportunity to decide whether it would be appropriate to allow Ellerth to amend her pleading or supplement her discovery.

Justice Thomas, with whom Justice Scalia joins, Dissenting

The Court today manufactures a rule that employers are vicariously liable if supervisors create a sexually hostile work environment, subject to an affirmative defense that the Court barely attempts to define. This rule applies even if the employer has a policy against sexual harassment, the employee knows about that policy, and the employee never informs anyone in a position of authority about the supervisor's conduct. As a result, employer liability under Title VII is judged by different standards depending upon whether a sexually or racially hostile work environment is alleged. The standard of employer liability should be the same in both instances: An employer should be liable if, and only if, the plaintiff proves that the employer was negligent in permitting the supervisor's conduct to occur.

Years before sexual harassment was recognized as "discrimination...because of...sex," 42 U.S.C. § 2000e-2(a)(1), the Courts of Appeals considered whether, and when, a racially hostile work environment could violate Title VII. In the landmark case *Rogers v. EEOC*, 454 F.2d 234 (1971), cert. denied, the Court of Appeals for the Fifth Circuit held that the practice of racially segregating patients in a doctor's office could amount to discrimination in "'the terms, conditions, or privileges'" of employment, thereby violating Title VII. Id., at 238 (quoting 42 U.S.C. § 2000e-2(a)(1)). The principal opinion in the case concluded that employment discrimination was not limited to the "isolated and distinguishable events" of "hiring, firing, and promoting." Rather, Title VII could also be violated by a work environment "heavily polluted with discrimination," because of the deleterious effects of such an atmosphere on an employee's well-being. In race discrimination cases, employer liability has turned on whether the plaintiff has alleged an adverse employment consequence, such as firing or demotion, or a hostile work environment. If a supervisor takes an adverse employment action because of race, causing the employee a tangible job detriment, the employer is vicariously liable for resulting damages. This is because such actions are company acts that can be performed only by the exercise of specific authority granted by the employer, and thus the supervisor acts as the employer. If, on the other hand, the employee alleges a racially hostile work environment, the employer is liable only for negligence: that is, only if the employer knew, or in the exercise of reasonable care should have known, about the harassment and failed to take remedial action. Liability has thus been imposed only if the employer is blameworthy in some way.

If a supervisor creates a hostile work environment, however, he does not act for the employer. As the Court concedes, a supervisor's creation of a hostile work environment is neither within the scope of his employment, nor part of his apparent authority. Indeed, a hostile work environment is antithetical to the interest of the employer. In such circumstances, an employer should be liable only if it has been negligent. That is, liability should attach only if the employer either knew, or in the exercise of reasonable care should have known, about the hostile work environment and failed to take remedial action.

Sexual harassment is simply not something that employers can wholly prevent without taking extraordinary measures—constant video and audio surveillance, for example--that would revolutionize the workplace in a manner incompatible with a free society. Indeed, such measures could not even detect incidents of harassment such as the comments Slowik allegedly made to respondent in a hotel bar. The most that employers can be charged with, therefore, is a duty to act reasonably under the circumstances. As one court recognized in addressing an early racial harassment claim:

Under a negligence standard, Burlington cannot be held liable for Slowik's conduct. Although respondent alleged a hostile work environment, she never contended that Burlington had been negligent in permitting the harassment to occur, and there is no question that Burlington acted reasonably under the circumstances. The company had a policy against sexual harassment, and respondent admitted that she was aware of the policy but nonetheless failed to tell anyone with authority over Slowik about his behavior. Burlington therefore cannot be charged with knowledge of Slowik's alleged harassment or with a failure to exercise reasonable care in not knowing about it.

Rejecting a negligence standard, the Court instead imposes a rule of vicarious employer liability, subject to a vague affirmative defense, for the acts of supervisors who wield no delegated authority in creating a hostile work environment. This rule is a whole-cloth creation that draws no support from the legal principles on which the Court claims it is based. Compounding its error, the Court fails to explain how employers can rely upon the affirmative defense, thus ensuring a continuing reign of confusion in this important area of the law. What these statements mean for district courts ruling on motions for summary judgment—the critical question for employers now subject to the vicarious liability rule—remains a mystery. Moreover, employers will be liable notwithstanding the affirmative defense, even though they acted reasonably, so long as the plaintiff in question fulfilled her duty of reasonable care to avoid harm. In practice, therefore, employer liability very well may be the rule. But as the Court acknowledges, this is the one result that it is clear Congress did not intend.

The Court's holding does guarantee one result: There will be more and more litigation to clarify applicable legal rules in an area in which both practitioners and the courts have long been begging for guidance. It thus truly boggles the mind that the Court can claim that its holding will effect "Congress' intention to promote conciliation rather than litigation in the Title VII context." All in all, today's decision is an ironic result for a case that generated eight separate opinions in the Court of Appeals on a fundamental question, and in which we granted certiorari "to assist in defining the relevant standards of employer liability."

Popular misconceptions notwithstanding, sexual harassment is not a freestanding federal tort, but a form of employment discrimination. As such, it should be treated no differently (and certainly no better) than the other forms of harassment that are illegal under Title VII. I would restore parallel treatment of employer liability for racial and sexual harassment and hold an employer liable for a hostile work environment only if the employer is truly at fault. I therefore respectfully dissent.

Discussion Questions

1) What is the standard that the court held need be satisfied to claim employer liability for a hostile environment?

2) How can an employer defend itself against a claim of vicarious liability?

3) How does the standard differ for employer liability between quid pro quo cases and hostile environment cases?

4) In dissent, Justice Thomas contends that "In race discrimination cases, employer liability has turned on whether the plaintiff has alleged an adverse employment consequence." How do sex discrimination cases, under the standard set in this case, operate differently?

5) What alternative solution to the question of employer liability does the dissent offer? Is this a practical alternative?

Davis v. Monroe County Board of Education

526 U.S. 629 (1999)
Supreme Court of the United States
Opinion by: Justice O'Connor

Petitioner brought suit against the Monroe County Board of Education and other defendants, alleging that her fifth-grade daughter had been the victim of sexual harassment by another student in her class. Among petitioner's claims was a claim for monetary and injunctive relief under Title IX of the Education Amendments of 1972. We consider here whether a private damages action may lie against the school board in cases of student-on-student harassment. We conclude that it may, but only where the funding recipient acts with deliberate indifference to known acts of harassment in its programs or activities. Moreover, we conclude that such an action will lie only for harassment that is so severe, pervasive, and objectively offensive that it effectively bars the victim's access to an educational opportunity or benefit.

Petitioner's minor daughter, LaShonda, was allegedly the victim of a prolonged pattern of sexual harassment by one of her fifth-grade classmates at Hubbard Elementary School, a public school in Monroe County, Georgia. According to petitioner's complaint, the harassment began in December 1992, when the classmate, G. F., attempted to touch LaShonda's breasts and genital area and made vulgar statements such as "I want to get in bed with you" and "I want to feel your boobs." Similar conduct allegedly occurred on or about January 4 and January 20, 1993. LaShonda reported each of these incidents to her mother and to her classroom teacher, Diane Fort. Petitioner, in turn, also contacted Fort, who allegedly assured petitioner that the school principal, Bill Querry, had been informed of the incidents. Petitioner contends that, notwithstanding these reports, no disciplinary action was taken against G. F.

G. F.'s conduct allegedly continued for many months. In early February, G. F. purportedly placed a door stop in his pants and proceeded to act in a sexually suggestive manner toward LaShonda during physical education class. LaShonda reported G. F.'s behavior to her physical education teacher, Whit Maples. Approximately one week later, G. F. again allegedly engaged in harassing behavior, this time while under the supervision of another classroom teacher, Joyce Pippin.   Again, LaShonda allegedly reported the incident to the teacher, and again petitioner contacted the teacher to follow up.

The string of incidents finally ended in mid-May, when G. F. was charged with, and pleaded guilty to, sexual battery for his misconduct. The complaint alleges that LaShonda had suffered during the months of harassment, however; specifically, her previously high grades allegedly dropped as she became unable to concentrate on her studies, and, in April 1993, her father discovered that she had written a suicide note. The complaint further alleges that, at one point, LaShonda told petitioner that she "didn't know how much longer she could keep [G. F.] off her."

Nor was LaShonda G. F.'s only victim; it is alleged that other girls in the class fell prey to G. F.'s conduct. At one point, in fact, a group composed of LaShonda and other female students tried to speak with Principal Querry about G. F.'s behavior. According to the complaint, however, a teacher denied the students' request with the statement,   "If [Querry] wants you, he'll call you." Petitioner alleges that no disciplinary action was taken in response to G. F.'s behavior toward LaShonda.   In addition to her conversations with Fort and Pippen, petitioner alleges that she spoke with Principal Querry in mid-May 1993. When petitioner inquired as to what action the school intended to take against G. F., Querry simply stated, "I guess I'll have to threaten him a little bit harder." Yet, petitioner alleges, at no point during the many months of his reported misconduct was G. F. disciplined for harassment. Indeed, Querry allegedly asked petitioner why LaShonda "was the only one complaining."

Nor, according to the complaint, was any effort made to separate G. F. and LaShonda. On the contrary, notwithstanding LaShonda's frequent complaints, only after more than three months of reported harassment was she even permitted to change her classroom seat so that she was no longer seated next to G. F. Moreover, petitioner alleges that, at the time of the events in question, the Monroe County Board of Education had not instructed its personnel on how to respond to peer sexual harassment and had not established a policy on the issue.

On May 4, 1994, petitioner filed suit in the United States District Court for the Middle District of Georgia against the Board. The complaint alleged that the Board is a recipient of federal funding for purposes of Title IX, that "the persistent sexual advances and harassment by the student G. F. upon [LaShonda] interfered with her ability to attend school and perform her studies and activities," and that "the deliberate indifference by Defendants to the unwelcome sexual advances of a student upon LaShonda created an intimidating, hostile, offensive and abusive school environment in violation of Title IX." The complaint sought compensatory and punitive damages, attorney's fees, and injunctive relief.

The defendants moved to dismiss petitioner's complaint under Federal Rule of Civil Procedure 12(b)(6) for failure to state a claim upon which relief could be granted, and the District Court granted respondents' motion. With regard to petitioner's claims under Title IX, the court concluded that Title IX provided no basis for liability absent an allegation "that the Board or an employee of the Board had any role in the harassment."

Petitioner appealed the District Court's decision dismissing her Title IX claim against the Board, and a panel of the Court of Appeals for the Eleventh Circuit reversed. Borrowing from Title VII law, a majority of the panel determined that student-on-student harassment stated a cause of action against the Board under Title IX: "We conclude that as Title VII encompasses a claim for damages due to a sexually hostile working environment created by co-workers and tolerated by the employer, Title IX encompasses a claim for damages due to a sexually hostile educational environment created by a fellow student or students when the supervising authorities knowingly fail to act to eliminate the harassment." The Eleventh Circuit panel recognized that petitioner sought to state a claim based on school "officials' failure to take action to stop the offensive acts of those over whom the officials exercised control," and the court concluded that petitioner had alleged facts sufficient to support a claim for hostile environment sexual harassment on this theory.

The Eleventh Circuit granted the Board's motion for rehearing en banc, and affirmed the District Court's decision to dismiss petitioner's Title IX claim against the Board. The en banc court relied, primarily, on the theory that Title IX was passed pursuant to Congress' legislative authority under the Constitution's Spending Clause, U.S. Const., Art I, § 8, cl. 1, and that the statute therefore must provide potential recipients of federal education funding with "unambiguous notice of the conditions they are assuming when they accept" it. Title IX, the court reasoned, provides recipients with notice that they must stop their employees from engaging in discriminatory conduct, but the statute fails to provide a recipient with sufficient notice of a duty to prevent student-on-student harassment. We now reverse.

Title IX provides, with certain exceptions not at issue here, that:

> no person in the United States shall, on the basis of sex, be excluded from participation in, be denied the benefits of, or be subjected to discrimination under any education program or activity receiving Federal financial assistance. 20 U.S.C. § 1681(a)

We agree with respondents that a recipient of federal funds may be liable in damages under Title IX only for its own misconduct. The recipient itself must "exclude [persons] from participation in...deny [persons] the benefits of, or...subject [persons] to discrimination under" its "programs or activities" in order to be liable under Title IX. The Government's enforcement power may only be exercised against the funding recipient, and we have not extended damages liability under Title IX to parties outside the scope of this power. We disagree with respondents' assertion, however, that petitioner seeks to hold the Board liable for G. F.'s actions instead of its own. Here, petitioner attempts to hold the Board liable for its own decision to remain idle in the face of known student-on-student harassment in its schools. In *Gebser*, we concluded that a recipient of federal education funds may be liable in damages under Title IX where it is deliberately indifferent to known acts of sexual harassment by a teacher. In that case, a teacher had entered into a sexual relationship with an eighth grade student, and the student sought damages under Title IX for the teacher's misconduct.

Accordingly, we rejected the use of agency principles to impute liability to the district for the misconduct of its teachers. Likewise, we declined the invitation to impose liability under what amounted to a negligence standard—holding the district liable for its failure to react to teacher-student harassment of which it knew or should have known. Rather, we concluded that the district could be liable for damages only where the district itself intentionally acted in clear violation of Title IX by remaining deliberately indifferent to acts of teacher-student harassment of which it had actual knowledge. Contrary to the dissent's suggestion, the misconduct of the teacher in *Gebser* was not "treated as the grant recipient's actions." Liability arose, rather, from "an official decision by the recipient not to remedy the violation."

By employing the "deliberate indifference" theory already used to establish municipal liability we concluded in *Gebser* that recipients could be liable in damages only where their own deliberate indifference effectively "caused" the discrimination. The high standard imposed in *Gebser* sought to eliminate any "risk that the recipient would be liable in damages not for its own official decision but instead for its employees' independent actions."

Gebser thus established that a recipient intentionally violates Title IX, and is subject to a private damages action, where the recipient is deliberately indifferent to known acts of teacher-student discrimination. Indeed, whether viewed as "discrimination" or "subjecting" students to discrimination, Title IX "unquestionably...placed on [the Board] the duty not" to permit teacher-student harassment in its schools and recipients violate Title IX's plain terms when they remain deliberately indifferent to this form of misconduct. We consider here whether the misconduct identified in *Gebser*—deliberate indifference to known acts of harassment—amounts to an intentional violation of Title IX, capable of supporting a private damages action, when the harasser is a student rather than a teacher. We conclude that, in certain limited circumstances, it does.

This is not to say that the identity of the harasser is irrelevant. On the contrary, both the "deliberate indifference" standard and the language of Title IX narrowly circumscribe the set of parties whose known acts of sexual harassment can trigger some duty to respond on the part of funding recipients. Deliberate indifference makes sense as a theory of direct liability under Title IX only where the funding recipient has some control over the alleged harassment. A recipient cannot be directly liable for its indifference where it lacks the authority to take remedial action. Where, as here, the misconduct occurs during school hours and on school grounds—the bulk of G. F.'s misconduct, in fact, took place in the classroom—the misconduct is taking place "under" an "operation" of the funding recipient.

Whether gender-oriented conduct rises to the level of actionable "harassment" thus "depends on a constellation of surrounding circumstances, expectations, and relationships," including, but not limited to, the ages of the harasser and the victim and the number of individuals involved. Courts, moreover, must bear in mind that schools are unlike the adult workplace and that children may regularly interact in a manner that would be unacceptable among adults. Indeed, at least early on, students are still learning how to interact appropriately with their peers. It is thus understandable that, in the school setting, students often engage in insults, banter, teasing, shoving, pushing, and gender-specific conduct that is upsetting to the students subjected to it. Damages are not available for simple acts of teasing and name-calling among school children, however, even where these comments target differences in gender. Rather, in the context of student-on-student harassment, damages are available only where the behavior is so severe, pervasive, and objectively offensive that it denies its victims the equal access to education that Title IX is designed to protect.

Justice Kennedy, with whom the Chief Justice, Justice Scalia, and Justice Thomas join, Dissenting

The majority contends that a school's deliberate indifference to known student harassment "subjects" students to harassment—that is, "causes [students] to undergo" harassment. The majority recognizes, however, that there must be some limitation on the third-party conduct that the school can fairly be said to cause. In search of a principle, the majority asserts, without much elaboration, that one causes discrimination when one has some "degree of control" over the discrimination and fails to remedy it. To state the majority's test is to understand that it is little more than an exercise in arbitrary line-drawing. The majority does not explain how we are to determine what degree of control is sufficient—or, more to the point, how the States were on clear notice that the Court would draw the line to encompass students. The majority nonetheless appears to see no need to justify drawing the "enough control" line to encompass students.

In truth, however, a school's control over its students is much more complicated and limited than the majority acknowledges. A public school does not control its students in the way it controls its teachers or those with whom it contracts. Most public schools do not screen or select students, and their power to discipline students is far from unfettered. Public schools are generally obligated by law to educate all students who live within defined geographic boundaries. Indeed, the Constitution of almost every State in the country guarantees the State's students a free primary and secondary public education.

The practical obstacles schools encounter in ensuring that thousands of immature students conform their conduct to acceptable norms may be even more significant than the legal obstacles. School districts cannot exercise the same measure of control over thousands of students that they do over a few hundred adult employees. The limited resources of our schools must be conserved for basic educational services. Some schools lack the resources even to deal with serious problems of violence and are already overwhelmed with disciplinary problems of all kinds.

Perhaps even more startling than its broad assumptions about school control over primary and secondary school students is the majority's failure to grapple in any meaningful way with the distinction between elementary and secondary schools, on the one hand, and universities on the other. The majority bolsters its argument that schools can control their students' actions by quoting our decision in *Vernonia School Dist. 47J v. Acton*, 515 U.S. 646, (1995), for the proposition that "the nature of [the State's] power [over public school children] is custodial and tutelary, permitting a degree of supervision and control that could not be exercised over free adults." Yet the majority's holding would appear to apply with equal force to universities, which do not exercise custodial and tutelary power over their adult students.

The law recognizes that children—particularly young children—are not fully accountable for their actions because they lack the capacity to exercise mature judgment. It should surprise no one, then, that the schools that are the primary locus of most children's social development are rife with inappropriate behavior by children who are just learning to interact with their peers. The amici on the front lines of our schools describe the situation best:

Unlike adults in the workplace, juveniles have limited life experiences or familial influences upon which to establish an understanding of appropriate behavior. The real world of school discipline is a rough-and-tumble place where students practice newly learned vulgarities, erupt with anger, tease and embarrass each other, share offensive notes, flirt, push and shove in the halls, grab and offend. Brief for National School Boards Association et al. as Amici Curiae.

No one contests that much of this "dizzying array of immature or uncontrollable behaviors by students," is inappropriate, even "objectively offensive" at times, and that parents and schools have a moral and ethical responsibility to help students learn to interact with their peers in an appropriate manner. It is doubtless the case, moreover, that much of this inappropriate behavior is directed toward members of the opposite sex, as children in the throes of adolescence struggle to express their emerging sexual identities. It is a far different question, however, whether it is either proper or useful to label this immature, childish behavior gender discrimination. Nothing in Title IX suggests that Congress even contemplated this question, much less answered it in the affirmative in unambiguous terms. The majority, nevertheless, has no problem labeling the conduct of fifth graders "sexual harassment" and "gender discrimination."

Analogies to Title VII hostile environment harassment are inapposite, because schools are not workplaces and children are not adults. The norms of the adult workplace that have defined hostile environment sexual harassment are not easily translated to peer relationships in schools, where teenage romantic relationships and dating are a part of everyday life. Analogies to Title IX teacher sexual harassment of students are similarly flawed. A teacher's sexual overtures toward a student are always inappropriate; a teenager's romantic overtures to a classmate (even when persistent and unwelcome) are an inescapable part of adolescence.

The majority admits that, under its approach, "whether gender-oriented conduct rises to the level of actionable 'harassment' 'depends on a constellation of surrounding circumstances, expectations, and relationships, including, but not limited to, the ages of the harasser and the victim and the number of individuals involved." The majority does not explain how a school is supposed to discern from this mishmash of factors what is actionable discrimination.

The difficulties schools will encounter in identifying peer sexual harassment are already evident in teachers' manuals designed to give guidance on the subject. For example, one teachers' manual on peer sexual harassment suggests that sexual harassment in kindergarten through third grade includes a boy being "put down" on the playground "because he wants to play house with the girls" or a girl being "put down because she shoots baskets better than the boys." Yet another manual suggests that one student saying to another, "You look nice" could be sexual harassment, depending on the "tone of voice," how the student looks at the other, and "who else is around." Blowing a kiss is also suspect. This confusion will likely be compounded once the sexual-harassment label is invested with the force of federal law, backed up by private damages suits.

The only guidance the majority gives schools in distinguishing between the "simple acts of teasing and name-calling among school children," said not to be a basis for suit even when they "target differences in gender," and actionable peer sexual harassment is, in reality, no guidance at all. The majority proclaims that "in the context of student-on-student harassment, damages are available only in the situation where the behavior is so serious, pervasive, and objectively offensive that it denies its victims the equal access to education that Title IX is designed to protect." The majority does not even purport to explain, however, what constitutes an actionable denial of "equal access to education." Is equal access denied when a girl who tires of being chased by the boys at recess refuses to go outside? When she cannot concentrate during class because she is worried about the recess activities? When she pretends to be sick one day so she can stay home from school? It appears the majority is content to let juries decide.

The majority's inability to provide any workable definition of actionable peer harassment simply underscores the myriad ways in which an opinion that purports to be narrow is, in fact, so broad that it will support untold numbers of lawyers who will prove adept at presenting cases that will withstand the defendant school districts' pretrial motions. Each of the barriers to run-away litigation the majority offers us crumbles under the weight of even casual scrutiny.

For example, the majority establishes what sounds like a relatively high threshold for liability—"denial of equal access" to education—and, almost in the same breath, makes clear that alleging a decline in grades is enough to survive and, it follows, to state a winning claim. The majority seems oblivious to the fact that almost every child, at some point, has trouble in school because he or she is being teased by his or her peers. The girl who wants to skip recess because she is teased by the boys is no different from the overweight child who skips gym class because the other children tease her about her size in the locker room; or the child who risks flunking out because he refuses to wear glasses to avoid the taunts of "four-eyes"; or the child who refuses to go to school because the school bully calls him a "scaredy-cat" at recess. Most children respond to teasing in ways that detract from their ability to learn. The majority's test for actionable harassment will, as a result, sweep in almost all of the more innocuous conduct it acknowledges as a ubiquitous part of school life.

The string of adjectives the majority attaches to the word "harassment—severe," pervasive, and objectively offensive"— likewise fails to narrow the class of conduct that can trigger liability, since the touchstone for determining whether there is Title IX liability is the effect on the child's ability to get an education. Indeed, the Court's reliance on the impact on the child's educational experience suggests that the "objective offensiveness" of a comment is to be judged by reference to a reasonable child at whom the comments were aimed. Not only is that standard likely to be quite expansive, it also gives schools—and juries—little guidance, requiring them to attempt to gauge the sensitivities of, for instance, the average seven year old.

The majority's limitations on peer sexual harassment suits cannot hope to contain the flood of liability the Court today begins. The elements of the Title IX claim created by the majority will be easy not only to allege but also to prove. A female plaintiff who pleads only that a boy called her offensive names, that she told a teacher, that the teacher's response was unreasonable, and that her school performance suffered as a result, appears to state a successful claim.

There will be no shortage of plaintiffs to bring such complaints. Our schools are charged each day with educating millions of children. Of those millions of students, a large percentage will, at some point during their school careers, experience something they consider sexual harassment. A 1993 study by the American Association of University Women Educational Foundation, for instance, found that "fully 4 out of 5 students (81%) report that they have been the target of some form of sexual harassment during their school lives." The number of potential lawsuits against our schools is staggering.

The cost of defending against peer sexual harassment suits alone could overwhelm many school districts. In addition, there are no damages caps on the judicially implied private cause of action under Title IX. As a result, school liability in one peer sexual harassment suit could approach, or even exceed, the total federal funding of many school districts. Petitioner, for example, seeks damages of $500,000 in this case. Respondent school district received approximately $679,000 in federal aid in 1992-1993. The school district sued in *Gebser* received only $120,000 in federal funds a year. Indeed, the entire 1992-1993 budget of that district was only $1.6 million.

The prospect of unlimited Title IX liability will, in all likelihood, breed a climate of fear that encourages school administrators to label even the most innocuous of childish conduct sexual harassment. It would appear to be no coincidence that, not long after the DOE issued its proposed policy guidance warning that schools could be liable for peer sexual harassment in the fall of 1996, a North Carolina school suspended a 6-year-old boy who kissed a female classmate on the cheek for sexual harassment, on the theory that "unwelcome is unwelcome at any age." A week later, a New York school suspended a second-grader who kissed a classmate and ripped a button off her skirt. The second grader said that he got the idea from his favorite book *Corduroy*, about a bear with a missing button. School administrators said only, "We were given guidelines as to why we suspend children. We follow the guidelines."

At the college level, the majority's holding is sure to add fuel to the debate over campus speech codes that, in the name of preventing a hostile educational environment, may infringe students' First Amendment rights. Indeed, under the majority's control principle, schools presumably will be responsible for remedying conduct that occurs even in student dormitory rooms. As a result, schools may well be forced to apply workplace norms in the most private of domains.

Even schools that resist overzealous enforcement may find that the most careful and reasoned response to a sexual harassment complaint nonetheless provokes litigation. Speaking with the voice of experience, the school amici remind us, "history shows that, no matter what a school official chooses to do, someone will be unhappy. Student offenders almost always view their punishment as too strict, and student complainants almost always view an offender's punishment as too lax."

A school faced with a peer sexual harassment complaint in the wake of the majority's decision may well be beset with litigation from every side. One student's demand for a quick response to her harassment complaint will conflict with the alleged harasser's demand for due process. Another student's demand for a harassment-free classroom will conflict with the alleged harasser's claim to a mainstream placement under the Individuals with Disabilities Education Act or with his state constitutional right to a continuing, free public education. On college campuses, and even in secondary schools, a student's claim that the school should remedy a sexually hostile environment will conflict with the alleged harasser's claim that his speech, even if offensive, is protected by the First Amendment. In each of these situations, the school faces the risk of suit, and maybe even multiple suits, regardless of its response.

We can be assured that like suits will follow—suits, which in cost and number, will impose serious financial burdens on local school districts, the taxpayers who support them, and the children they serve. Federalism and our struggling school systems deserve better from this Court. I dissent.

Discussion Questions

1) What is the standard that the court held need be satisfied to claim a Title IX violation?

2) How does this decision expand upon the Court's decision in *Franklin*?

3) Why does the majority feel that sexual harassment in schools must be held to a different standard than harassment in the workplace?

4) The dissent contends "the law recognizes that children— particularly young children—are not fully accountable for their actions because they lack the capacity to exercise mature judgment." Does this excuse the behavior in this case?

5) The dissent asked "whether it is either proper or useful to label this immature, childish behavior gender discrimination?" Do you agree?

6) Why should the school district be financially liable for the actions of one of its students? Is it possible for a school to eliminate all offensive behavior?

Audrey Jo DeClue v. Central Illinois Light Co.

223 F.3d 434 (2000)
United States Court of Appeals for the Seventh Circuit
Opinion by: Posner, Circuit Judge

This suit under Title VII by a female lineman for an electric company requires us to decide whether an employer's failure to alter working conditions that just happen, without any discriminatory intent, to bear more heavily on its female than on its male employees can be an actionable form of sexual harassment.

...The only significant act--omission would be more precise—of alleged sexual harassment that occurred during the limitations period was the electric company's continued failure to provide restroom facilities for the plaintiff, who was the only woman in the crew of linemen to which she was assigned--in fact the only woman lineman employed by the company. Linemen work where the lines are, and that is often far from any public restroom; nor do the linemen's trucks have bathroom facilities. Male linemen have never felt any inhibitions about urinating in the open, as it were. They do not interrupt their work to go in search of a public restroom. Women are more reticent about urinating in public than men. So while the defendant's male linemen were untroubled by the absence of bathroom facilities at the job site, the plaintiff was very troubled and repeatedly but unsuccessfully sought corrective action, for example the installation of some sort of toilet facilities in the linemen's trucks.

The question is whether the defendant's failure to respond to the plaintiff's request for civilized bathroom facilities can be thought a form of sexual harassment, and we think it cannot be. This is not because no reasonable person could think an absence of bathroom facilities an intolerable working condition; in most workplaces, such an absence would clearly be thought that. And it is not because Title VII creates remedies only against intentional discrimination. An employee may also complain about an employment practice that while not deliberately discriminatory bears harder on the members of a protected group, that is, in the jargon of discrimination law, has a "disparate impact" on that group, and the employer "fails to demonstrate that the challenged practice is job related for the position in question and consistent with business necessity." 42 U.S.C. § 2000e-2(k)(1)(A)(i); see, e.g., *Griggs v. Duke Power Co.,* 401 U.S. 424 (1971); *Wards Cove Packing Co. v. Atonio,* 490 U.S. 642 (1989); *Vitug v. Multistate Tax Comm'n,* 88 F.3d 506, 513 (7th Cir. 1996). Therefore, insofar as absence of restroom facilities deters women (normal women, not merely women who are abnormally sensitive) but not men from seeking or holding a particular type of job, and insofar as those facilities can be made available to the employees without undue burden to the employer, *Watson v. Fort Worth Bank & Trust Co.,* 487 U.S. 977 (1988); *Davey v. City of Omaha,* 107 F.3d 587 (8th Cir. 1997), the absence may violate Title VII.

We need hardly add that women are not "unreasonable" to be more sensitive about urinating in public than men; it is as neutral a fact about American women, even though it is a social or psychological rather than physical fact, as the fact that women's upper-body strength is on average less than that of men, which has been held in disparate-impact litigation to require changes in job requirements in certain traditionally male job categories. *Berkman v. City of New York,* 705 F.2d 584 (2d Cir. 1983); *Blake v. City of Los Angeles,* 595 F.2d 1367, 1375 (9th Cir. 1979); cf. *Evans v. City of Evanston,* 881 F.2d 382 (7th Cir. 1989).

But this case has not been litigated as a disparate-impact case. Neither the term nor any synonym appears anywhere in the record. The briefs are silent about it too. The plaintiff has insisted on litigating her case as a hostile-work-environment case throughout. But it is not. Sexual harassment is the form of sex discrimination in the terms or conditions of employment that consists of efforts either by coworkers or supervisors to make the workplace intolerable or at least severely and discriminatorily uncongenial to women ("hostile work environment" harassment), and also to efforts (normally by supervisors) to extract sexual favors by threats or promises ("quid pro quo" harassment). *Burlington Industries, Inc. v. Ellerth*, 524 U.S. 742 (1998). (Occasionally men can complain of sexual harassment too, but we can disregard such cases.) It is a form of, rather than a synonym for, sex discrimination. It is remote, for example, from a simple refusal to hire women, from holding them to higher standards than their male coworkers, or from refusing to make accommodations for differences in upper-body strength or other characteristics that differ systematically between the sexes. The last is the classic disparate-impact claim, and it is the claim suggested by the facts of this case but not presented by the plaintiff.

The requirements for proving, and the defenses to, charges of sexual harassment have been configured in light of the distinct nature of that form of sex discrimination. The principal defense that the law recognizes to a hostile-work-environment sexual-harassment charge, the charge made here, is that the defendant had done all he could to prevent the harassment, the principal defense to a disparate-impact claim is, as the statutory provision and cases that we cited earlier make clear, that the burden on the defendant of eliminating the disparity would be too heavy. By failing to present her case as one of disparate impact, the plaintiff prevented the defendant from trying to show that it would be infeasible or unduly burdensome to equip its linemen's trucks with toilet facilities sufficiently private to meet the plaintiff's needs. She has waived what may have been a perfectly good claim of sex discrimination, though that we need not decide.

Of course, as a purely semantic matter, it might be possible to argue that an employer who fails to correct a work condition that he knows or should know has a disparate impact on some class of his employees is perpetuating a working environment that is hostile to that class. But if this argument were accepted, it would make disparate impact synonymous with hostile work environment, erasing the important distinctions mentioned in the preceding paragraph.

The district judge was therefore right to grant summary judgment in favor of the defendant.

Affirmed.

Dissent: Rovner, Circuit Judge, Dissenting in Part

When my nomination to the Court of Appeals was announced in 1992, the late Judge Walter J. Cummings wrote me a kind note of congratulations that ended with the observation, "At long last, the ladies' room off the [judges'] conference room will have some use!"

Thank goodness there was a women's room! When women like Audrey Jo DeClue arrive in workplaces that hitherto were all-male, they often discover that the facilities for women are inadequate, distant, or missing altogether. Women know that this disparity, which strikes many men to be of secondary, if not trivial, importance, can affect their ability to do their job in concrete and material ways. As recently as the 1990s, for example, women elected to the nation's Congress--which had banned gender discrimination in the workplace some 30 years earlier-- found that without careful planning, they risked missing the vote on a bill by heeding the call of nature, because there was no restroom for women convenient to the Senate or the House chamber.

As my colleagues acknowledge, when an employer provides no restrooms at all to its employees and expects them to relieve themselves outdoors, the burden falls more heavily on women than it does on men. Not simply because women may be more reticent about relieving themselves in the open, I might add. The fact is, biology has given men less to do in the restroom and made it much easier for them to do it. If men are less reluctant to urinate outdoors, it is in significant part because they need only unzip and take aim. And although public urination is potentially a crime whether committed by a man or a woman, see, e.g., *People v. Duncan*, 259 Ill. App. 3d 308 (Ill. App. 1994) (disorderly conduct); *Elliott v. State*, 435 N.E.2d 302 (Ind. App. 1982) (public indecency), the risk of being caught in the act is arguably greater for women, for whom it is a more cumbersome, awkward, and time-consuming proposition. For all of these reasons, I agree with my brothers that an employer's failure to provide restroom facilities for its workforce can support a disparate-impact claim for female employees.

But there are respects in which the refusal to provide female employees with restrooms can be understood as creating a hostile work environment as well. See *Kline v. City of Kansas City, Mo. Fire Dep't*, 175 F.3d 660 (8th Cir. 1999) (as to hostile environment claim, error to exclude evidence of ill-fitting clothing and unequal bathroom facilities provided to female fire department employees), cert. denied, 120 S. Ct. 1160 (2000). Restroom facilities are, after all, the norm in the workplace, and the refusal to provide such facilities to workers is, most would agree, an act which alters the terms and conditions of one's employment. See generally *Meritor Sav. Bank, FSB v. Vinson*, 477 U.S. 57 (1986) (describing elements of hostile environment claim). There may be some work environments in which it is not feasible to make any type of relief facilities available to employees, but DeClue's was not one of them. For at least one two-week period, she was given the use of a "port-a-potty", and eventually, after she filed a charge with the EEOC, the company began providing "Brief Reliefs" (disposable urine bags) and privacy tents for DeClue and the other lineworkers to use at jobsites. Granted, the refusal to provide restrooms and comparable facilities is somewhat different from the affirmative acts of sexual and sex-based harassment that we typically see in hostile environment cases. 29 C.F.R. § 1604.11(a) (2000); *Baskerville v. Culligan Int'l Co.*, 50 F.3d 428, (7th Cir. 1995). Nonetheless, when, in the face of complaints, an employer fails to correct a work condition that it knows or should know has a disparate impact on its female employees—that reasonable women would find intolerable—it is arguably fostering a work environment that is hostile to women, just as surely as it does when it fails to put a stop to the more familiar types of sexual harassment. *Guess v. Bethlehem Steel Corp.*, 913 F.2d 463 (7th Cir. 1990). Indeed, the cases teach us that some employers not only maintain, but deliberately play up, the lack of restroom facilities and similarly inhospitable work conditions as a way to keep women out of the workplace. See, e.g., *Catlett v. Missouri Highway and Transp. Com'n*, 828 F.2d 1260 (8th Cir. 1987), cert. denied, 485 U.S. 1021 (1988); *Kilgo v. Bowman Transp., Inc.*, 789 F.2d 859 (11th Cir. 1986); see also *E.E.O.C. v. Monarch Machine Tool Co.*, 737 F.2d 1444 (6th Cir. 1980); see generally Vicki Schultz, "Telling Stories About Women and Work: Judicial Interpretations of Sex Segregation in the Workplace in Title VII Cases Raising the Lack of Interest Argument," 103 *Harv. L. Rev.* 1749, 1832-39 (1990).

The evidence in this case supports a hostile environment claim. First, although DeClue complained about the lack of relief facilities repeatedly, the electric company did not make them available on a consistent basis until late 1997 or early 1998, after she filed her EEOC charge.

Second, the alternatives that the company offered in response to DeClue's complaints—the use of a truck to drive to the nearest public facility, or summoning a supervisor or troubleshooter to take her to such a facility when a truck was unavailable—were both impractical (the nearest restroom might be ten or twenty miles away from the jobsite, as might be the nearest supervisor or troubleshooter, and served only to stigmatize her. Her co-workers, in fact, made harassing remarks about this very subject, and in one of DeClue's performance evaluations, her crew leader wrote that "a woman on the job of this type makes it hard with restroom facilities." Her crew leader, for example, allegedly made the following types of remarks: "You're just like my damn kids. I'm ready to leave and I have to wait for them to go to the bathroom"; "You've got the bladder of a three-year-old"; and "We'll never get to the job 'cause I'm sure we'll have to stop in Edwards for you to piss there too."

Third, on jobsites that were literally out in the open, with no trees or shrubs to hide behind, male and female workers were forced to relieve themselves with almost no privacy whatsoever: DeClue's male co-workers regularly urinated in her presence (a practice that she complained about to no avail); and on at least one occasion, she discovered to her chagrin that the bulldozer behind which she had chosen to relieve herself had given her privacy from her co-workers and passing traffic, but not from a crotchety resident who lived nearby.

Fourth, the lack of appropriate accommodations deprived DeClue of privacy among male co-workers who made a habit of keeping (and presumably viewing) pornographic magazines in company offices and in many company trucks—a practice that could only have increased the discomfort DeClue (and any reasonable woman) would have experienced relieving herself in the open. I dare say that if the tables were turned, and all but one of the employees in this environment were women, a reasonable man would be equally reticent to drop his trousers in order to relieve himself. DeClue's complaints are proof enough that she found the lack of relief facilities objectionable, and these circumstances certainly permit the inference that any reasonable woman would have felt the same. The defendant's failure to remedy the problem in turn could be viewed as a negligent response that subjects it to liability for a hostile work environment. Cf. *Guess*, 913 F.2d at 465.

Discrimination in the real world many times does not fit neatly into the legal models we have constructed. *Venters v. City of Delphi*, 123 F.3d 956 (7th Cir. 1997); *Tomsic v. State Farm Mut. Auto. Ins. Co.*, 85 F.3d 1472 (10th Cir. 1996). The hostile environment theory itself was not one that Congress anticipated or provided for in the express terms of Title VII, but instead is one that scholars, the E.E.O.C., and judges have fashioned in acknowledgment of a very real and invidious form of sex discrimination in the workplace. See *Meritor*, 477 U.S. 57. Because prejudice and ignorance have a way of defying formulaic constructs, the lines with which we attempt to divide the various categories of discrimination cannot be rigid. DeClue's complaint, insofar as it concerns the lack of restroom facilities, may fit more naturally into the disparate-impact framework that my colleagues discuss, but it also overlaps with the hostile environment framework into which she has placed it. It should be allowed to proceed within that framework.

Therefore, I respectfully dissent from the holding that the failure to provide appropriate relief facilities cannot be pursued as a hostile environment claim.

Discussion Questions

1) What is the standard that the court held need be satisfied to claim a hostile environment?

2) If the reasonable woman standard were employed in this case, would the outcome have been different?

3) Is there a difference between an environment that is "uncongenial to women" and one that is discriminatory?

Part 2
Case Studies

The Clarence Thomas Confirmation Hearings: The Awakening of America to the Issue of Sexual Harassment

Rarely does the nomination of a new Justice to the United States Supreme Court capture the public imagination. Few outside the legal community will watch the confirmation process unfold. The popular press will rarely get beyond biographical information and the views of the prospective nominee. Yet, the nomination of Clarence Thomas to the high court was not a typical nomination. For two weeks, in October of 1991, this nomination held the nation spellbound to charges of sexual harassment. The hearings that are the focus of this case study turned the country on its head and changed the way sexual harassment is viewed forever.

In 1967, President Lyndon B. Johnson nominated Thurgood Marshall to serve as an Associate Justice on the Supreme Court of the United States. As the first African American ever to be considered for such a position, this appointment caused considerable controversy. Twenty-four years later, when Justice Marshall decided to retire, a much more conservative environment existed as President George H. W. Bush was given the opportunity to replace the legendary civil rights activist on the Court.

On July 1, 1991, President Bush nominated Clarence Thomas, then a judge on the United States Court of Appeals for the D.C. Circuit, to fill the vacancy on the Supreme Court created by the retirement of Marshall. Much like the nomination of Marshall a quarter of a century before, the selection of the second African American to the Court was filled with controversy. However, unlike the ordeal that Marshall endured, the controversy surrounding Clarence Thomas had little to do with race.

There were a lot of reasons to oppose the nomination of Clarence Thomas for a slot on the nation's highest court. Thomas, at the time of his appointment, had a fairly sparse resume. He had served as a judge for little more than one year at the time of his appointment. This had followed an unspectacular term as chair of the Equal Employment Opportunity Commission. Based on his qualifications, Thomas had received the lowest recommendation ever given for any Supreme Court Justice from the American Bar Association.[1]

Qualifications aside, the nomination of Thomas also received opposition from civil rights and women's rights organizations due to his conservative philosophy. Many groups, including the NAACP, the Urban League, and the National Organization for Women, feared that Thomas's conservative stances on issues such as the rights of the accused and affirmative action would undo many of the gains that Justice Marshall had stood for during his tenure.

Others were put off by the nominee's unwillingness to discuss his legal opinions or beliefs. These groups voiced concern that, if confirmed, Thomas's vote would be the one to overturn the constitutional protection for abortion.

From September 10 through 20, 1991, the Senate Judiciary committee held hearings on Thomas' fitness to serve. In total, the nominee testified for five days followed by three additional days of other witnesses before the committee. On September 27, the Judiciary Committee vote split evenly on the nomination seven to seven, sending it to the full Senate without the committee's endorsement.

In the end, however, none of the above considerations made much of an impact. When the nomination went to the Senate floor, the real controversy had not yet begun.

Anita F. Hill, a professor of law at the University of Oklahoma, came forward with allegations that Thomas had sexually harassed her. Hill had worked for Thomas a decade earlier at both the Department of Education and later the EEOC. Hill contended that Thomas had harassed her with inappropriate discussion of sex, sexual activity, and pornography. She further alleged that Thomas has repeatedly asked to begin a personal relationship with her outside of work. Thomas strongly and categorically denied all charges.

Following the leak of Hill's name and charges, a media frenzy ensued. On October 11, 1991, the Senate Judiciary committee reconvened to hold further hearings on the nomination. The hearings, which focused specifically on the allegations leveled by Hill, lasted three full days. Both Thomas and Hill made opening statements. Judge Thomas spoke first. He began by denying all accusations made by Hill.

> Throughout the time that Anita Hill worked with me I treated her as I treated my other special assistants. I tried to treat them all cordially, professionally, and respectfully. And I tried to support them in their endeavors, and be interested in and supportive of their success.
>
> I had no reason or basis to believe my relationship with Anita Hill was anything but this way until the FBI visited me a little more than 2 weeks ago. I find it particularly troubling that she never raised any hint that she was uncomfortable with me. She did not raise or mention it when considering moving with me to EEOC from the Department of Education. And she never raised it with me when she left EEOC and was moving on in her life.
>
> During my tenure in the executive branch as a manager, as a policymaker, and as a person, I have adamantly condemned sex harassment. There is no member of this committee or this Senate who feels stronger about sex harassment than I do. As a manager, I made every effort to take swift and decisive action when sex harassment raised or reared its ugly head.
>
> The fact that I feel so very strongly about sex harassment and spoke loudly about it at EEOC has made these allegations

doubly hard on me. I cannot imagine anything that I said or did to Anita Hill that could have been mistaken for sexual harassment.[2]

Thomas then went on to describe the impact that the leak of Hill's accusations had on his life and the irony of the confirmation process.

For almost a decade my responsibilities have included enforcing the rights of victims of sexual harassment. As a boss, as a friend, and as a human being I was proud that I have never had such an allegation leveled against me, even as I sought to promote women, and minorities into non-traditional jobs. In addition, several of my friends who are women, have confided in me about the horror of harassment on the job, or elsewhere. I thought I really understood the anguish, the fears, the doubts, the seriousness of the matter. But since September 25, I have suffered immensely as these very serious charges were leveled against me....

As if the confidential allegations, themselves, were not enough, this apparently calculated public disclosure has caused me, my family, and my friends enormous pain and great harm. I have never, in all my life felt such hurt, such pain, such agony. My family and I have been done a grave and irreparable injustice. During the past two weeks, I lost the belief that if I did my best all would work out....

...in my forty-three years on this Earth, I have been able, with the help of others and with the help of God, to defy poverty, avoid prison, overcome segregation, bigotry, racism, and obtain one of the finest educations available in this country. But I have not been able to overcome this process. This is worse than any obstacle or anything that I have ever faced....

I am a victim of this process and my name has been harmed, my integrity has been harmed, my character has been harmed, my family has been harmed, my friends have been harmed. There is nothing this committee, this body or this country can do to give me my good name back, nothing.[3]

Anita Hill gave her opening statement later that morning. In her testimony, she gave a detailed, and sometimes graphic, account of the charges she had made against Thomas. Her statement began with her background, followed by her first association with Thomas, working at the Department of Education.

After approximately three months of working there, he asked me to go out socially with him. What happened next and telling the world about it are the two most difficult things, experiences of my life. It is only after a great deal of agonizing consideration and a number of sleepless nights that I am able to talk of these unpleasant matters to anyone but my close friends.

I declined the invitation to go out socially with him, and explained to him that I thought it would jeopardize what at the time I considered to be a very good working relationship. I had a normal social life with other men outside of the office. I believed then, as now, that having a social relationship with a person who was supervising my work would be ill advised. I was very uncomfortable with the idea and told him so.

I thought that by saying "no" and explaining my reasons, my employer would abandon his social suggestions. However, to my regret, in the following few weeks he continued to ask me out on several occasions. He pressed me to justify my reasons for saying "no" to him. These incidents took place in his office or mine. They were in the form of private conversations which would not have been overheard by anyone else.

My working relationship became even more strained when Judge Thomas began to use work situations to discuss sex. On these occasions, he would call me into his office for reports on education issues and projects or he might suggest that because of the time pressures of his schedule, we go to lunch to a government cafeteria. After a brief discussion of work, he would turn the conversation to a discussion of sexual matters. His conversations were very vivid.

He spoke about acts that he had seen in pornographic films involving such matters as women having sex with animals, and films showing group sex or rape scenes. He talked about pornographic materials depicting individuals with large penises, or large breasts involved in various sex acts.

On several occasions Thomas told me of his own sexual prowess. Because I was extremely uncomfortable talking about sex with him at all, and particularly in such a graphic way, I told him that I did not want to talk about these subjects. I would also try to change the subject to education matters or to nonsexual personal matters, such as his background or his beliefs. My efforts to change the subject were rarely successful....

On other occasions, he referred to the size of his own penis as being larger than normal and he also spoke on some occasions of the pleasures he had given to women with oral sex. At this point, late 1982, I began to feel severe stress on the job. I began to be concerned that Clarence Thomas might take his anger out with me by degrading me or not giving me important assignments. I also thought he might find an excuse for dismissing me....

In February 1983, I was hospitalized for five days on an emergency basis for acute stomach pain which I attributed to stress on the job. Once out of the hospital, I became more committed to find other employment and sought further to minimize my contact with Thomas....

I may have used poor judgment. Perhaps I should have taken angry or even militant steps, both when I was in the agency or after I had left it, but I must confess to the world that the course I took seemed the better, as well as the easier approach....

It would have been more comfortable to remain silent. I took no initiative to inform anyone. But when I was asked by a representative of this committee to report my experience, I felt that I had to tell the truth. I could not keep silent.[4]

The committee asked questions of each and heard from witnesses who were called to testify of behalf of both individuals. Finally, on October 15, the full Senate began the debate on the nomination. The following day, Clarence Thomas was confirmed by a vote of 52—48. This represented the closest vote in the history of the Supreme Court for confirmation of a new Justice.

It was clear, however, even during the confirmation process that the hearings had been transformed from a referendum on the fitness of Clarence Thomas to serve on the nation's highest court to a referendum on the issue of sexual harassment. Senator Edward Kennedy, in his exchange with Professor Hill during her testimony, first recognized the true importance of her statements.

> Let me just say as far as I am concerned, I think it has been enormously important to millions of Americans. I don't think that this country is ever going to look at sexual harassment the same tomorrow as it has ever at any time in its past. And if we are able to make some progress on it, I think the history books will show to a very important extent it's because of your action. The viciousness of harassment is real, it's experienced by millions of people, I hope, as a form of sex discrimination and I think all of us are hopeful that we can make progress on it.[5]

Even Senator Arlen Spector, Hill's chief inquisitor during the proceedings, recognized that despite his questions as to the veracity of her testimony, the hearings had made a substantial impact on the American workplace.

> I would join in the comment that this proceeding has been illuminating to tell America what is the law on sexual harassment. That is something which had not been known, and from what I have heard in the last few days there has been a lot of change in conduct in the workplace in this country.[6]

However, it was Senator Howard Metzenbaum who best summed up the true meaning of the hearings. He recognized that Hill's testimony, which could neither be proved nor disproved, was unlikely to sway many Senators from their party loyalties. Still, the proceedings did serve a much larger purpose.

> I don't know what impact your testimony will have on the confirmation process, but I know that your testimony will have tremendous impact on this nation from henceforth.

The women of this country, I am certain, owe you a fantastic debt of gratitude for bringing this issue of sexual harassment to the fore. But as one of those 98 men in the United States Senate, I think I speak for all of us, and I say we owe you a debt of gratitude as well, for bringing this issue up to the fore in a more striking, more sympathetic, more concerned manner than ever before. I think you've made this nation, men and women alike, more enlightened, more aware, more sensitive. And the nation will never be the same.[7]

The Aftermath

Despite the seriousness of the charges made by Anita Hill, Clarence Thomas did gain a seat on the nation's highest court. For those who believed Hill and those who opposed Thomas on ideological grounds, Thomas's confirmation was a defeat. However, The Clarence Thomas-Anita Hill hearings had other long-term consequences for the American public beyond Justice Thomas's place on the Court. Most importantly, the national consciousness about sexual harassment was raised significantly. This is obvious from just about any objective measure.

The clearest indication of the impact of the hearings is found in the increased number of sexual harassment claims. According to the Equal Employment Opportunity Commission, statistics in all areas of sexual harassment have risen substantially since Anita Hill first became a public figure. For example, in 1990, the year before the hearings, there were 6,127 sexual harassment charges filed.[8] In 1992, the year after the hearings, there were 10,532. This represented an increase of 72% in the first year alone. Further, these numbers have risen consistently over time. In 1995, for example, the total of sexual harassment claims for that year alone reached 15,549. In just four years, after the hearings took place, this denotes an increase of 154%. Even more telling is the fact that after 1995, the number of claims has remained remarkably consistent, never deviating by more than three hundred claims in either direction from the 1995 baseline. This clearly demonstrates the lasting impact of the hearings. Once sexual harassment was brought to the fore, it is destined to remain one of the most discussed and most litigated aspects of American life and law.

Also worth noting is the rise in monetary benefits brought about as a result of these charges. Once again, using the same baselines, the results are quite telling. In 1990, the total monetary settlements amounted to $7.7 million. By 1992, the settlement benefits had risen to $12.7 million. While claims had risen 72% in this time period, benefits had risen a nearly corresponding 65%. By 1995, monetary benefits had reached $24.3 million. Again, during this time period, claims had risen 154%, but settlement costs had now grown 216%.

Even more striking is the fact that while claims had leveled off after 1995 monetary benefits continue to rise, at an astronomical rate, to this day. In 2000, settlement benefits had reached an all-time high of $54.6 million. Over the ten-year period in question, monetary benefits have risen more than 600%. Further, there are no indications that this trend will change anytime in the foreseeable future. Further, these figures represent only those claims settled by the EEOC. Keeping in mind that these figures do not include awards reached through litigation, the total cost, in damages, of sexual harassment claims in the United States must exceed $100 million annually. These figures are broken out below.

Statistics	*1990*	*1991*	*1992*
Total Claims	6,127	6,883	10,532
Resolutions	5,671	6,718	7,484
Monetary Benefits (In Millions)	7.7	7.1	12.7
Statistics	*1993*	*1994*	*1995*
Total Claims	11,908	14,420	15,549
Resolutions	9,971	11,478	13,802
Monetary Benefits (In Millions)	25.1	22.5	24.3

Statistics	1996	1997	1998	1999	2000
Total Claims	15,532	15,889	15,618	15,222	15,836
Resolutions	15,861	17,333	17,115	16,524	16,726
Monetary Benefits (In Millions)	27.8	49.5	34.3	50.3	54.6

Continuing Interest

The Thomas-Hill hearings roused the nation to the concept of sexual harassment. Yet, long after the debate over the confirmation, the debate about Thomas and sexual harassment rages on. There have been at least 15 books written about the Thomas-Hill hearings. Several of these are blatantly one sided in favor of either Thomas or Hill. Others are compilations of essays on virtually every aspect of the subject. Some collections of essays attack the subject from a racial perspective, others from a gender perspective. Most are highly critical of Thomas. One book, *Strange Justice: The Selling of Clarence Thomas* by Jane Mayer and Jill Abramson[9] was even adapted into a movie for the *Showtime* network in 2000.

In addition to the popular press, the academic crowd has also weighed in quite heavily on the subject. A search of the *Lexis-Nexis* database using the keywords Clarence Thomas and sexual harassment, revealed no fewer than 594 law review articles published since 1992. In addition, the same *Lexis* search turned up at least 2,226 articles in major newspapers using the aforementioned search parameters.

While it is not surprising to find a large quantity of articles in the immediate aftermath of the hearings, what is intriguing is the consistency of articles from year to year. In the nine years following the hearings, law reviews published an average of 66 feature articles per year that include reference to Thomas and sexual harassment. This total ranged from a high of 81 in 1993 to a low of 54 in 2000.

Newspapers ran an average of 247 articles per year. This ranged from a high of 810 articles in the immediate aftermath of the hearings in 1992 to a low of 82 articles in 1999. What is most interesting about the pattern of newspaper articles is how often Thomas was mentioned in articles dealing with other famous sexual harassment charges. For example, in 1998, when President Clinton was facing impeachment over an improper sexual relationship, Clarence Thomas and sexual harassment were mentioned in 236 newspaper articles that year alone. It seems that the Thomas-Hill charges are the standard that the American public continues to use to measure the seriousness of sexual harassment accusations.

Thomas' Impact on the Supreme Court

Interestingly enough, Clarence Thomas played a major role in shaping the standard for sexual harassment long before Anita Hill went public with her accusations. As chairman of the Equal Employment Opportunity Commission, Thomas was instrumental in legitimizing the hostile environment standard by which he was judged.

In the early 1980s, when Thomas was at the EEOC (and Hill worked for him), Hill would have had a hard time taking legal action even if all her allegations were true. The courts, at that time, simply did not recognize verbal sexual conduct as harassment. At that time, the sexual harassment standards were still new and the law was still evolving. It was not until 1986 that the United States Supreme Court would legitimize the hostile environment standards first given legal voice by the EEOC earlier in the decade.

In *Meritor Savings Bank v. Vinson*[10] the Supreme Court first considered the scope of sexual harassment workplace regulations. This decision cemented that all forms of sexual harassment, even those without direct threats attached, were in violation of Title VII. This greatly expanded the range of complaints that would now receive legal standing.

Following the hearings, the Supreme Court revisited the issue in the 1993 case of *Harris v. Forklift Systems Inc.*[11] In this decision, the Court again expanded the reach of sexual harassment protection. However, in his first sexual harassment case while a sitting Justice, Thomas remained silent on the subject, simply signing on with the majority in this unanimous opinion.

It would not be until 1998 that Thomas would speak for himself in a sexual harassment decision. In companion cases addressing the scope of employer liability, Thomas took a very strong stand.[12] As EEOC director and later as a Justice, Thomas had been an active participant in expanding the scope of sexual harassment regulations. However, dating back to his days at the EEOC, Thomas had been a strong opponent of strict liability for employers. In *Burlington Industries v. Ellerth* (as well as *Faragher v. City of Boca Raton*), the Court held that an employer may be liable for sexual harassment in their workplace, even if they had no knowledge nor any reasonable way of knowing of the harassment, subject to an affirmative defense. Perhaps drawing on his own personal experience, Thomas wrote a scathing dissent attacking the Court for going too far in this area.

> The Court today manufactures a rule that employers are vicariously liable if supervisors create a sexually hostile work environment, subject to an affirmative defense that the Court barely attempts to define. This rule applies even if the employer has a policy against sexual harassment, the employee knows about that policy, and the employee never informs anyone in a position of authority about the supervisor's conduct. As a result, employer liability under Title VII is judged by different standards depending upon whether a sexually or racially hostile work environment is alleged. The standard of employer liability should be the same in both instances: An employer should be liable if, and only if, the plaintiff proves that the employer was negligent in permitting the supervisor's conduct to occur….
>
> If a supervisor creates a hostile work environment, however, he does not act for the employer. As the Court concedes, a supervisor's creation of a hostile work environment is neither within the scope of his employment, nor part of his apparent

authority. Indeed, a hostile work environment is antithetical to the interest of the employer. In such circumstances, an employer should be liable only if it has been negligent. That is, liability should attach only if the employer either knew, or in the exercise of reasonable care should have known, about the hostile work environment and failed to take remedial action.

Sexual harassment is simply not something that employers can wholly prevent without taking extraordinary measures—constant video and audio surveillance, for example--that would revolutionize the workplace in a manner incompatible with a free society.[13]

Thomas stuck a similar note in the *Faragher* decision, which applied vicarious liability to public as well as private employers for sexual harassment in the workplace. In both instances, he places great emphasis in finding liability only where intentional negligence is present. He further takes great exception to the intrusion into private lives that these inquiries tend to take. Based on his personal experience, it is hard to fault him on either score.

In the end, we will never know, with any degree of certainty, whether Anita Hill's charges were true. We will never know for sure if Clarence Thomas was a crude and boorish employer or a victim himself in the entire fiasco. There are only two people who know for sure what happened nearly twenty years ago, Hill and Thomas. Nonetheless, Thomas will always carry the burden of the hearings. Sexual harassment, as Thomas has surely come to realize, is one area of law where a person is guilty until proven innocent. No charges were ever filed against Clarence Thomas. No indisputable evidence was ever brought forth against Clarence Thomas. Yet, polls indicate that a full year after the hearings, most people believed Thomas to be guilty.[14] Accordingly, it is not surprising that Thomas, particularly if his testimony was the truth, would remain particularly sensitive about this subject. In the end, rightly or not, the name Clarence Thomas will always trigger a reference to sexual harassment.

Conclusions

Polls showed from the very outset of the hearings that this nomination would have far reaching implications well beyond a seat on the Court. There were consequences to these hearings, both for the Supreme Court as well as for society at large.

After watching the hearings, a majority of Americans agreed that our leaders in Washington "just don't get it when it comes to women's concerns."[15] The spectacle of watching the all-white, all-male Judiciary committee in its questioning of Anita Hill made that abundantly clear. The result was that one year later, in 1992, the "Year of the Woman" in politics saw record numbers of women elected to Congress. In 1992 alone, 106 women won primary elections for House seats. Eleven women won major party nominations for the Senate.[16] In the end, nineteen new women House members were elected in 1992, raising the total membership in the House of Representatives to forty-seven.[17]

Four new women won Senate seats raising the number of women in that body to a then all-time high of six. Included in that freshman group was Carol Mosley Braun, who became the first black woman in history to serve in the Senate. Braun had shocked incumbent Senator Alan Dixon in the Democratic primary. Dixon was one of only five democrats to vote in favor of the Thomas confirmation.

Polls also indicated that most Americans felt that as a result of the hearings that women would be more likely to report cases of sexual harassment.[18] Further, 68% of those surveyed indicated that, in the week following the hearings, they had discussed the issue of sexual harassment with other people.[19] Further, an overwhelming 76% felt that the attention on the issue of sexual harassment as a result of the charges against Thomas would make men more careful in the way they relate to women.[20]

The following year, polls showed that 66% of those surveyed felt that bosses had become more sensitive to the problem of sexual harassment[21] and that 58% felt that men in general had become more sensitive to the subject.[22] The number of claims filed and the awards received through sexual harassment claims in the decade since the hearings clearly bear out these initial reactions.

In the end, considerably more than the membership of the Supreme Court changed in October 1991. The landscape of how men and women relate to each other has changed as well. Sexual harassment has always been a problem in the United States, but following the Clarence Thomas/Anita Hill hearings, it was no longer a problem that was not discussed. These discussions have proven healthy for the nation, and the cause of women has been greatly advanced as a result.

1. Rucinski, Diane, "Rush to Judgement? Fast Reaction Polls in the Anita Hill-Clarence Thomas Controversy." *Public Opinion Quarterly* 14 (1993): 575.
2. Miller, Anita, *The Complete Transcripts of the Clarence Thomas-Anita Hill Hearings* (Chicago: Academy Chicago Publishers, 1994): 14–18.
3. Miller, 14–18.
4. Miller, 22–26.
5. Miller, 98.
6. Miller, 98.
7. Miller, 99.
8. All statistics were provided to the author by the Equal Employment Opportunity Commission and are on file with the author. Statistics from 1992–2000 are available at www.eeoc.gov on the world wide web.
9. Mayer, Jane, and Jill Abramson, *Strange Justice: The Selling of Clarence Thomas* (Boston: Houghton Mifflin Company, 1994).
10. *Meritor Savings Bank v. Vinson*, 477 U.S. 57 (1986).
11. *Harris v. Forklift Systems Inc.*, 510 U.S. 17 (1993).
12. *Burlington Industries v. Ellerth*, 524 U.S. 742 (1998) and *Faragher v. City of Boca Raton*, 524 U.S. 775 (1998).
13. *Burlington Industries v. Ellerth*, 524 U.S. 742 (1998)
14. Three separate polls, coinciding with the one-year anniversary of the hearings found more people believed Hill than Thomas. A Gallup poll (December 17–18, 1992) showed 51% believed Thomas was guilty, a CNN/*U.S.A. Today* poll (October 1–3, 1992) showed 43% believed Hill as opposed to 39% who believed Thomas, and

an ABC News/*Washington Post* poll (December 11–14, 1992) found 43% believed Hill with only 27% who believed Thomas.

15. *U.S.A. Today* Poll, December 9–10. 1991.
16. Hershey, Marjorie Randon, "The Congressional Elections." *The Election of 1992* (Chatham, New Jersey: Chatham House Publishers, 1993): 177.
17. Hershey, 178.
18. In a Gallup Poll conducted October 17–20, 1991, 60% felt that women would be more likely to report cases of sexual harassment.
19. ABC News Poll, conducted October 13, 1991.
20. ABC News Poll, conducted October 13, 1991.
21. Gallup/*Newsweek* Poll, conducted December 17–18, 1992.
22. Ibid.

Taking the Science Out of Decision Making: Sexual Harassment Policy and Human Resource Management

Introduction

In the Twentieth century, political scientists have spent a considerable amount of time and effort attempting to explain how decisions come to be made. Much credence has been given to the various theories as one has built upon another in order to reach ever-more realistic depictions of the decision making process. These efforts have enabled students of political science, public administration, personnel management, and others to gain valuable insights and, in the case of practitioners, to apply this knowledge within their given spheres. In the area of sexual harassment, however, much of this learning does not apply. This case study examines one real-world example of how decision makers are restrained in their ability to effectively exercise control over the policy decisions they make.

The Dilemma of Vicarious Liability

On March 19, 1996, Ron Baldasaro was suspended and ultimately demoted from his job in the Public Works department in the City of Cambridge, Massachusetts. City Manager Robert W. Healy made this decision based upon his finding that Baldasaro was guilty of sexual harassment towards a fellow city employee. This would have been an unexceptional occurrence had it not been for the fact that Baldasaro's actions had not occurred in the workplace and involved no action on behalf on his department or the city.

On this fateful day, Baldasaro, while off duty, illegally parked his jeep in a loading zone on a city street. A city meter maid, while checking the street for illegally parked cars, asked Baldasaro to move. Baldasaro asked for five minutes so he could complete his business. When the meter maid refused, Baldasaro screamed vulgar and abusive remarks at the woman. Included in this tirade were derogatory names based on the meter maid's gender and a sexual comment about the woman and her boss.

Shaken by this episode, and fearing for her safety, the meter maid reported the incident to her supervisor, who, in turn, reported it to the city manager. Healy, the City Manager, suspended Baldasaro for five days. However, after an evidentiary hearing, he increased the suspension to sixty days and included a demotion in rank. Healy felt, according to court records, that Baldasaro's conduct had contributed to the creation of a hostile work environment which "interfered with the work of employees in the traffic department and reflected poorly on the city by undermining confidence in city operations by members of the public and fellow employees."[1]

Baldasaro appealed his punishment. Holding that Baldasaro's actions had not prevented the meter maid from doing her job, the Civil Service Commission overturned the City's decision. An Appeals Court in Massachusetts upheld the ruling, striking the suspension and demotion.

In many ways, Cambridge, Massachusetts, is considered one of the most elite, most politically liberal, and most socially progressive cities in America. On the other hand, it also has a long history as a blue-collar town with factories set alongside of some of America's best institutions of higher education.

The question of whether a person can be suspended from work for actions (or words) that occur outside of the workplace is still an open one. Yet this is a question that the City of Cambridge is determined to answer. They have appealed the Baldasaro decision to the Supreme Judicial Court, the highest state court in Massachusetts.

Regardless of the ultimate disposition of this case, individuals in management positions everywhere will undoubtedly face similar dilemmas. Proper handling of the issue of sexual harassment has become a major issue for all managers. The difficulty lies in the fact that it is not always easy to determine what actually constitutes sexual harassment. Sometimes what is called sexual harassment by one person might be considered by another to be immaturity, ignorance, or simply bad manners. Today, sexual harassment is a major issue in the workplace, but there is no consensus among managers (or courts) regarding how it is defined or what the boundaries of this offense may be.

Sexual Harassment Law and the Courts

In the United States, the laws regarding discrimination in employment have been developed, it might seem, in a constitutional vacuum. Most sexual harassment cases arise under Title VII of the Civil Rights Act of 1964. Its original purpose as a civil rights measure was to outlaw racial segregation. Sex, as a category, was added at the last minute as an amendment in a cynical attempt to defeat the bill altogether.[2] Though an afterthought, sex-based criteria have developed into one of the most litigated parts of the civil rights agenda. Title VII does not specifically outlaw sexual harassment or sexually offensive speech. Instead, its broad proclamation makes it illegal for an employer to discriminate "against any individual with respect to his compensation, terms, conditions, or privileges of employment, because of such individual's race, color, religion, sex, or national origin."[3]

Sexual harassment can take two separate and distinct forms. The first of these is called quid pro quo harassment. This entails something for something, such as an employer demanding sex in exchange for a job or promotion. This is fairly straightforward and does not pose great problem for managers.

The second and more problematic form of sexual harassment is what is called hostile environment harassment. This occurs when the workplace is so polluted with discrimination that it makes the environment of the employment setting hostile or intimidating.

The first case to test the hostile environment theory in the United States Supreme Court was *Meritor Savings Bank v. Vinson* (1986).[4] In this decision, the Supreme Court, relying upon Equal Employment Opportunity Commission guidelines, upheld the hostile environment concept. Though the Court was careful to point out that there are limits as to how far the scope of this hostile environment theory could go, they were not specific in identifying the dividing line. Chief Justice Rehnquist delivered the opinion of the Court, saying that Title VII hostile environment claims would receive wide consideration.

> Not all workplace conduct that may be described as "harassment" affects a "term, condition, or privilege" of employment within the meaning of Title VII. Mere utterance of an ethnic or racial epithet which engenders offensive feelings in an employee would not affect the conditions of employment to sufficiently significant degree to violate Title VII. For sexual harassment to be actionable, it must be sufficiently severe or pervasive "to alter the conditions of employment and create and abusive environment."[5]

The *Meritor* case was a relatively easy one to decide on the facts. It involved a sexual relationship between an employer and employee that included assault and forcible rape, among the other things, that added up, in the Court's view, to a hostile work environment. This behavior was sufficiently severe and pervasive to qualify as sexual harassment.

However, it was not surprising that the lower federal courts struggled to give a consistent meaning to this standard in less clear circumstances. Determining the level and severity of hostility needed to create a hostile environment is an inherently subjective question and has been interpreted in many different ways.

Sexual Harassment After *Meritor*

Following the *Meritor Savings Bank* decision, the Sixth Circuit Court of Appeals was the first court to apply the new standard of "hostile environment sexual harassment." In *Rabidue v. Osceola Refining Co.* (1986), the Court of Appeals found that offensive behavior, by itself, was not sufficient to constitute sexual harassment. [6] In this case, the court found that offensive conduct that originates mostly from one coworker with little direct power over the plaintiff would not be threatening, even if such conduct were gravely offensive. In this case, the co-worker consistently made obscene comments about women in general and hung a sign on his desk stating, "Even male chauvinist pigs need love," as well as posting pornographic pictures around his office.[7] In finding that this situation was not a hostile environment within the meaning of Title VII, the court argued the "sufficiently severe" standard must include some type of tangible injury or reasonable fear of injury.

> The test for whether or not sexual harassment rises to the level of a hostile work environment is whether the harassment is conduct which would interfere with the hypothetical reasonable individual's work performance and affect seriously the psychological well-being of that reasonable person under like circumstances. Once the objective reasonable person test is met, the court must next determine if the victim was subjectively offended and suffered an injury from the hostile work environment.[8]

The Sixth Circuit Court of Appeals goes on to make the point that Title VII is aimed at harassing conduct, not mere offensive language:

> It cannot be seriously disputed that in some work environments, humor and language are rough hewn and vulgar. Sexual jokes, sexual conversation, and girlie magazines may abound. Title VII was not meant to—or can—change this. It must never be forgotten that Title VII is the federal court mainstay in the

struggle for equal employment opportunity for the female workers of America. But it is quite different to claim that Title VII was designed to bring about a magical transformation in the social mores of American workers.[9]

In essence, the Sixth Circuit decided that unless there is a real and substantial injury suffered by the plaintiff, offensive or crude behavior is not sufficiently severe to trigger a violation of Title VII. In order for Title VII to apply, this harassment must affect a term, condition, or privilege of employment. Failure to show actual harm in one of these areas will result in failure with a hostile environment suit.

A few years later, a District Court in Florida interpreted the law quite differently. In *Robinson v. Jacksonville Shipyards* (1991), offensive conduct was deemed to create a hostile environment since it was so pervasive throughout the workplace as to make it unavoidable, thus becoming a condition of employment.[10] This case concerned offensive behaviors similar to those in *Rabidue*. Male coworkers at the Jacksonville Shipyards had placed nude and partially nude pictures of women around the workplace and refused to stop doing so although the plaintiff was gravely offended by these photographs. Some pictures were within Robinson's view and several lewd comments were made specifically toward the plaintiff. Other pictures and photographs were kept in lockers and private areas. Comments made included statements that the shipyard was a "boys club" and "more or less a man's world."[11] The pictures in question came from a broad spectrum of sources and represented a large number of groups. They included "magazines, plaques on the wall, and calendars supplied by advertising tool supply companies" featuring women "in various stages of undress and sexually suggestive or submissive poses."[12]

The court in this case chose to concentrate on the second half of the standard laid out in *Meritor*. Rather than focus on whether the conduct in question was "sufficiently severe," the court instead zeroed in on whether it was overly pervasive. It held that even if the conduct was not directed at any one individual, and even if no specific tangible harm could be shown by that individual, a sexual harassment claim was still possible. A hostile environment could still exist if a reasonable person in similar circumstances would view the workplace as pervaded with harassing materials. In this case, since these materials were constantly in view of Robinson and she was subjected to them on a routine basis, the conduct was actionable. Regardless of whether her job, future promotions, or pay were affected by the offensive behavior, these actions could still be a violation of Title VII by creating a disparate impact on women in the workplace.

> Actionable conduct under Title VII is behavior that is not directed at a particular individual or group of individuals, but is disproportionately more offensive or demeaning to one sex....Harassing behavior lacking sexually explicit content but motivated by animus against women satisfies requirements for hostile work environment.[13]

The court held that whether allegedly discriminatory conduct can rise to the standard of being "sufficiently severe as to affect a term, condition, or privilege of employment" must be viewed under both "objective and subjective standards."[14] In contrast to the *Rabidue* court, the court in *Robinson* ruled that Title VII could lead to the removal of sexually explicit materials from the workplace. The court held that "this type of behavior would be insulting and intimidating to a reasonable woman. While men may not find such conduct offensive, it could be construed as creating a hostile environment for women."[15]

Harris and the Danger of Unguided Juries

These two lower courts clearly had profound disagreement about the meaning of the standard put forth by the United States Supreme Court in *Meritor Savings Bank v. Vinson*. For two separate courts to have such divergent views about what was "severe" and "pervasive" left a wide gulf that the United States Supreme Court needed to bridge. In 1993, the Court faced such an opportunity in *Theresa Harris v. Forklift Systems Inc.*

Teresa Harris worked as a manager at Forklift Systems Inc. for more than two years.[16] During that time, her boss, Charles Hardy, had, among other things, made insulting and demeaning comments to Ms. Harris about herself as well as women in general. More than once, Hardy had told her, "You are a woman, what do you know," and "We need a man as rental manager," among other remarks of this nature. Harris sued Forklift Systems, claiming that Hardy's actions, including comments such as these, had created a hostile working environment based upon her sex.[17]

In rejecting her claim, the District Court for the Middle District of Tennessee found that Hardy's behavior did not rise to the level necessary for hostile environment sexual harassment to exist. It found that his comments were indeed offensive and likely to be found offensive by a reasonable person.[18] However, despite their offensive nature, Hardy's words did not affect her terms or conditions of employment.

The District Court held that the conduct in question was not

> so severe as to be expected to seriously affect Harris' psychological well-being. A reasonable woman manager under like circumstances would have been offended by Hardy, but his conduct would not have risen to the level of interfering with that person's work performance. Neither do I believe that Harris was subjectively so offended that she suffered injury. Although Hardy may at times have genuinely offended Harris, I do not believe that he created a working environment so poisoned as to be intimidating or abusive to Harris.[19]

The District Court reasoned that in order for the governmental interest in suppressing speech to be compelling, there must be some tangible harm done. After the District Court's decision was upheld by the Sixth Circuit Court of Appeals, the Supreme Court granted certiorari.

Justice Sandra Day O'Connor, writing for a unanimous Court, overturned the decision and found in favor of Harris. In explaining the Court's reasoning, Justice O'Connor tries to walk the middle ground between what the two Circuits had decided.

> This standard...takes a middle path between making actionable any conduct that is merely offensive and requiring the conduct to cause a tangible psychological injury. . . . Conduct that is not severe or pervasive enough to create an objectionably hostile or abusive work environment—an environment that a reasonable person would find abusive or hostile—is beyond Title VII's purview. Likewise, if the victim does not subjectively perceive the environment to be abusive, the conduct has not actually altered conditions of the victim's employment, and there is no Title VII violation.
>
> But Title VII comes into play before the harassing conduct leads to a nervous breakdown. A discriminatorily abusive work environment, even one that does not seriously affect employees' psychological well-being, can and often will detract from employee's job performance, discourage employees from remaining on the job, or keep them from advancing in their careers.
>
> Moreover, even without regard to these tangible effects, the very fact that the discriminatory conduct was so severe or pervasive that it created a work environment abusive to employees because of their race, gender, religion, or national origin offends Title VII's broad rule of workplace equality.[20]

O'Connor goes on to specify that while no single factor will be a clear indication of a hostile environment, a lack of any tangible harm will not by itself sink a sexual harassment claim.

> We therefore believe that the District Court erred in relying on whether the conduct "seriously affected plaintiff's psychological well-being" or led her to "suffer injury." Such an inquiry may needlessly focus the fact-finder's attention on concrete psychological harm, an element Title VII does not require. So long as the environment would reasonably be perceived, and is perceived, as abusive or hostile, there is no need for it also to be psychologically injurious.[21]

O'Connor concludes the Court's opinion with a statement portending obvious problems that lay ahead following this ruling.

> This is not, and by its nature, cannot be, a mathematically precise test. We need not answer today all the potential questions it raises, nor specifically address the EEOC's new regulations on the subject. But we can say that whether an environment is "hostile" or "abusive" can be determined only by looking at all the circumstances....But, while psychological harm, like any other relevant factor, may be taken into account, no single factor is required.[22]

While agreeing with the outcome of the case, Justice Scalia, in a harsh concurrence, points to the potential for problems in applying this new and imprecise standard.

> "Abusive" or "hostile" (which in this context I take to mean the same thing) does not seem to me a very clear standard—and I do not think clarity is at all increased by adding the adverb "objectively" or by appealing to a "reasonable person's" notion of what the vague word means. Today's opinion does list a number of factors that contribute to abusiveness, but since it neither says how much of each is necessary (an impossible task) nor identifies any single factor as determinative, it thereby adds little certitude. As a practical matter, today's holding lets virtually unguided juries decide whether sex-related conduct engaged in (or permitted by) an employer is egregious enough to warrant an award of damages. One might say that what constitutes "negligence" (a traditional jury question) is not much more clear and certain than what constitutes "abusiveness". Perhaps so. But the class of plaintiffs seeking to recover for negligence is limited to those who have suffered harm, whereas under this statute, "abusiveness" is to be the test of whether legal harm has been suffered, opening more expansive vistas of litigation.[23]

Title VII After *Harris*

With the standard put forth by the Supreme Court in *Harris v. Forklift Systems Inc.*, the Court has chosen a very broad rule. However, the real issue for managers comes not from recognizing sexual harassment in the workplace, but rather from their liability when they do not recognize sexual harassment in the workplace.

The Supreme Court addressed the liability of employers with two decisions in the 1998 term. In *Burlington Industries v. Ellerth* and *Faragher v. City of Boca Raton* the Supreme Court held that an employer may be liable for the actions of its employees, even if it had no knowledge or any reasonable way of knowing that the harassment took place.[24] Justice Kennedy, writing for the Court, held that "an employee who refuses the unwelcome sexual advances of a supervisor, yet suffers no adverse, tangible job consequences, may recover against the employer without showing the employer is negligent or otherwise at fault for the supervisor's actions."[25]

In other words, if a jury or arbiter were to rule against an employee, the employer could be vicariously, and thus financially, liable for damages. These rulings certainly must have an effect on all managers when confronted with a charge of sexual harassment in the workplace. Vicarious liability forces managers such as Robert Healy, the Cambridge City Manager to pursue all claims of harassment to the fullest. To do anything less would leave the city open to tremendous financial exposure.

Turning Decision Making Theory on its Head

Ideally, public administration is based on the fundamental idea that government decisions should follow the established rule of law. In order to govern according to the law, public managers must understand that law applies to their conduct and that all of their decisions may, at some point, have legal ramifications. Important public values (such as providing a workplace free from discrimination) may conflict with basic legal values (such as due process of law). When such a situation occurs, the task of the responsible manager is to make decisions that will reconcile this conflict. In the world of the real, however, decision making is never so clear cut. Managers must make their decisions not based on a set of ideal circumstances, but within the context of a range of pressures—some known and some only vaguely understood. The public policy literature on the "science" of decision making is filled with attempts, by both theorists and practitioners, to develop a framework upon which to begin modeling the method through which decisions are made within the context of real-world public administration.

Historically, there have been several schools of thought surrounding the process of decision making used by administrators. The rational comprehensive model (what Lindblom termed the root method), the incremental model of successive limited comparisons (what Lindblom termed the branch method), and Cohen, March, and Olsen's Garbage Can model (which led to Kingdon's model of the "policy primeval soup" and the three streams of problems, politics and policies) represent serious attempts to develop an explanation for how public policy decisions are made by real-world administrators. However, where decisions must be made regarding sexual harassment, within the context of vicarious liability, these traditional approaches are lacking in explanatory power.

The Traditional Models of Decision Making

Perhaps the oldest explanation of how public managers make decisions is the rational comprehensive model.[26] If managers were operating according to this theory, they would first define their goals and set clear standards to achieve them. Then, they would consider all possible alternatives which would achieve these goals. Finally, after weighing the costs and benefits of these options, they would select the alternative that would achieve their goal at the least cost. The rational comprehensive model emphasizes finding and applying methods unique to each individual set of circumstances, assuming the time, resources and, perhaps most importantly, complete information necessary to analyze each decision are available.

In making personnel decisions within the context of vicarious liability, such as the one faced by Mr. Healy in the case above, the rational comprehensive model does not carry significant explanatory weight. The manager's foremost concern here is to avoid excessive financial liability. This is especially true where, as Justice Scalia has pointed out, "unguided juries decided whether sex related conduct is egregious enough to warrant an award of damages."[27] Given that there is a real possibility that the employer may be held responsible for the actions of its employees and that, in the American system of jurisprudence, there is no way to assure the availability of complete information, the administrator is unable to select among a set of best possible choices. The only practical decision, therefore, was to discipline Mr. Baldasaro to the fullest extent of Mr. Healy's powers. If the city were to lose in court, Mr. Baldasaro would be returned to his former position and perhaps receive back pay. However, if the city did not take action against Mr. Baldasaro, believing that his conduct did not cause a hostile environment and thus did not constitute sexual harassment, it would be left open to potentially tremendous liability. If the city were sued by the meter maid for sexual harassment, and lost, it may have faced exposure to damages in the range of hundreds of thousands of dollars if not more. Thus, without ever considering alternatives or weighing the costs and benefits of each given the circumstances of each individual situation, managers such as Mr. Healy will be constrained in their range of possible choices of action.

Another major school of thought regarding decision making, and one that more closely mirrors actual practice in most instances (where, for example, only limited information is available), is that of incrementalism.[28] According to this approach, decision makers take what they presently do as a given and then tweak that through small, incremental adjustments in their current practices to meet new situations. As in many real-world decision making situations, managers need not even agree on specific sets of objectives, but only on broadly defined goals. By doing this, managers need not explore a full range of options and alternatives nor apply a cost benefit analysis, thus saving considerable time. The inevitable result of this is that changes to existing practices are made in small, gradual steps, and the resultant policies tend to take on the aspect of a "branch" that juts off from the original policy.

In response to sexual harassment allegations, the incremental approach also appears lacking as an explanation for how decisions come to be made. In most personnel decisions, a manager will weigh any number of factors in reaching a final determination. However, when the need arises to make a decision regarding employee behavior in a case of alleged sexual harassment within the context of vicarious liability, the range of potential choices is severely restricted. Since, as we noted above, a manager wishes to reduce the potential exposure to financial liability to a minimum, he or she does not have the luxury of making incremental adjustments. Their course of action requires a significant departure from policies they might otherwise consider in different kinds of situations involving workplace behavior. Liability for sexual harassment, unlike forms of potential liability, such as negligence, does not require proof of harm and thus poses a much greater danger to the financial well-being of the employer. In summary, incrementalism requires that policy remain malleable and ultimately changeable from its present form. Under the standard of vicarious liability as expounded by the Court, however, policy is unchangeable, and rational decision makers are bound to treat all sexual harassment allegations, regardless of the specifics involved, in a similar fashion.[29]

A third major model of decision making is the garbage can model of organizational choice.[30] Running through the so-called "garbage can" are four separate policy "streams": problems, solutions, participants, and choice opportunities. Each stream is a sphere unto itself and is separate from the others. Rather than identify the problems and look for the proper solutions, this model contends that an organization is "a collection of choices looking for problems, issues and feelings looking for decision situations in which they might be aired, solutions looking for issues to which they might be the answer, and decision makers looking for work."[31] Each circumstance that arises then depends upon "a garbage can into which various kinds of problems and solutions are dumped by participants as they are generated."[32] As a result, when a new problem needs to be addressed, the manager would look into the garbage can and pull out the best solution. The outcome is based upon the mix of garbage. Often, managers will go through this process in reverse. They will devise a solution and cast about in the garbage can for a problem to solve.

Many consider the garbage can model to be a very realistic portrayal of how policy decisions are made. However, in addressing a sexual harassment issue, there is no need for a garbage can. The course of action is predetermined by the law. In order to avoid liability, decision makers must act swiftly and decisively. In fact, however, part of the garbage can may be applicable since managers have been given the solution for all of their sexual harassment policy problems. They do not, however, need to search the garbage can for the best possible fit of a solution to the problem. Rather, the power to actually make the decision has effectively been taken from them, and they must apply a uniform decision regardless of what the garbage may throw at them.

Concluding Thoughts

In essence, addressing a sexual harassment accusation is unlike any other decision that a manager must make. In most instances, policy decisions can be explained using one of the models described above. Each model allows a significant degree of discretion to accrue to those whose task it is to make the decision at hand. However, when it comes to decisions involving sexual harassment, this power of choice has been removed from the manager. The law, as presently applied by the courts, leaves no room for a manager to consider his or her options and make reasoned judgments based on the merits of individual cases. Rather, by casting the term sexual harassment so broadly, and leaving an unguided jury to determine the meaning of the term on a case-by-case basis, managers are faced with a degree of uncertainty so profound as to drastically reduce their ability to apply a proportional response. As a result, managers are faced with the prospect of always reacting in the harshest possible manner when faced with a complaint of sexual harassment so as to mitigate the greater danger of being left open to potentially devastating liability down the road. The abrogation of one individual's due process is the lesser of two evils for the manager who must decide what is better for his department, company, university, or other organization.

Making it even more dangerous for the manager is the further threat of vicarious liability. As a result of recent rulings, an employer may be liable for the actions of its employees, even if it had no knowledge nor any reasonable way of knowing about the harassment. However, this is subject to an affirmative defense. The only safe course of action is to provide the affirmative defense that the employer took every possible step to punish the accused harasser. Anything short of this may leave the employer exposed to significant damages.

In Mr. Baldasaro's case, this is the decision facing the City Manager, Mr. Healy. We certainly do not contend to suggest a proper solution to this dilemma. However, this is exactly the point. As long as the courts define the law so broadly, it will not matter what the proper course of action should be. For in the present environment, there can be only one course of action.

1. *City of Cambridge v. Edward Ronald Baldsasaro*, 2000 Mass. App. LEXIS 735 (2000).

2. *Barnes v. Costle*, 183 U.S. App. D.C. 90, 561 F. 2D 983 (1977).

3. Title VII, Civil Rights Act of 1964, 42 U.S.C., section 2000e-2.

4. *Meritor Savings Bank v. Vinson*, 477 U.S. 57 (1986).

5. *Meritor Savings Bank v. Vinson*, 477 U.S. 57 (1986).

6. *Rabidue v. Osceola Refining Co.*, 805 F. 2D 624 (1986).

7. *Rabidue v. Osceola Refining Co.*, 805 F. 2D 624 (1986).

8. *Rabidue v. Osceola Refining Co.*, 805 F. 2D 624 (1986).

9. *Rabidue v. Osceola Refining Co.*, 805 F. 2D 624 (1986).

10. *Robinson v. Jacksonville Shipyards*, 760 F. Supp. 1486 (M.D. Fla. 1991).

11. *Robinson v. Jacksonville Shipyards*, 760 F. Supp. 1493 (M.D. Fla. 1991).

12. *Robinson v. Jacksonville Shipyards*, 760 F. Supp. 1490 (M.D. Fla. 1991).

13. *Robinson v. Jacksonville Shipyards*, 760 F. Supp. 1487 (M.D. Fla. 1991).
14. *Robinson v. Jacksonville Shipyards*, 760 F. Supp. 1542 (M.D. Fla. 1991).
15. *Robinson v. Jacksonville Shipyards*, 760 F. Supp. 1542 (M.D. Fla. 1991).
16. *Harris v. Forklift Systems Inc.*, 62 USLW 4004 (1993).
17. *Harris v. Forklift Systems Inc.*, 62 USLW 4004 (1993).
18. *Harris v. Forklift Systems Inc.*, 62 USLW 4005 (1993).
19. *Harris v. Forklift Systems Inc.*, 62 USLW 4005 (1993).
20. *Harris v. Forklift Systems Inc.*, 62 USLW 4006 (1993).
21. *Harris v. Forklift Systems Inc.*, 62 USLW 4006 (1993).
22. *Harris v. Forklift Systems Inc.*, 62 USLW 4006 (1993).
23. *Harris v. Forklift Systems Inc.*, 62 USLW 4007 (1993).
24. *Burlington Industries v. Ellerth*, 118 U.S. 2257 (1998), *Faragher v. City of Boca Raton*, 118 U.S. 2275 (1998).
25. *Burlington Industries v. Ellerth*, 118 U.S. 2257 (1998).
26. For examples of the rational comprehensive model, see James March and Herbert Simon, *Organizations* (New York: Wiley, 1958); Aaron Wildavsky, *The Politics of the Budgetary Process*, (Boston: Little, Brown and Company, 1979); and John Kingdon, *Agendas, Alternatives, and Public Policies* (Boston: Little, Brown, and Company, 1984).
27. *Harris v. Forklift Systems Inc.*, 62 USLW 4007 (1993).
28. For examples of incrementalism, see Charles Lindblom, "The Science of Muddling Through," *Public Administration Review* 14 (Spring 1959): 79-88; and John Kingdom, *Agendas, Alternatives, and Public Policies* (Boston: Little, Brown, and Company, 1984).
29. See *Burlington Industries v. Ellerth*, 118 U.S. 2257 (1998), *Faragher v. City of Boca Raton*, 118 U.S. 2275 (1998) as an example of the Court's present application of vicarious liability.
30. For the origin of the garbage can model, see Michael Cohen, James March and Johan Olsen, "A Garbage Can Model of Organizational Choice," *Administrative Studies Quarterly* 17 (March 1972); 1-25.
31. Ibid., p. 2.
32. Ibid.

Sexual Harassment and Free Speech: The Lessons of the Campus Speech Code Controversies

A focal point for the debate about sexual harassment can be found in the battle for free expression being waged across the country over speech codes on college campuses. In both instances, advocates of speech restrictions propose limitations upon speech that is unpopular or offensive. They claim a compelling interest in providing equal opportunity in school and at work.[1]

Critics point to similar constitutional problems in the workplace as well as the classroom.[2] Restrictions are overly broad and vague. They tend to sweep up much protected speech and in some instances, have a chilling effect on speech altogether. Yet, in court, these seemingly similar restrictions produced cases that were decided very differently. The sexual harassment regulations, such as those in *Harris v. Forklift Systems* (1993), found offensive speech about women in the workplace to be outside the boundary of First Amendment protection.[3] Yet in two major cases involving campus speech codes, a different outcome was reached as to the constitutionality of offensive speech. [4] Campus speech policies at both the University of Michigan and the University of Wisconsin at Madison were struck down as unconstitutional violations of the First Amendment. This case study will look at these cases, the logic applied in the decisions, and show the relationship between speech codes at school with those at work.

The United States Supreme Court has laid out certain areas over the years that are outside the scope of First Amendment protection. Any content-based restriction would be facially unconstitutional, thus the speech codes at both the University of Michigan and the University of Wisconsin were crafted with these areas in mind. Limitations on speech passed by the two universities were patterned closely after the fighting words doctrine outlined in the case of *Chaplinsky v. New Hampshire* (1942). In *Chaplinsky*, the United States Supreme Court ruled that face-to-face confrontations that are likely to provoke violence or incite a breach of the peace are not protected by the First Amendment. Justice Murphy spoke for the Court in a very broad proclamation of what constitutes fighting words.

> It is well understood that the right of free speech is not absolute at all times and under all circumstances. There are certain well-defined and narrowly limited classes of speech, the prevention and punishment of which have never been thought to raise any Constitutional problem. These include the lewd and obscene, the profane, the libelous, and the insulting or fighting words—those which by their very utterance inflict injury or tend to incite an immediate breach of the peace. It has been well observed that such utterances are no essential part of any exposition of ideas, and are of such slight social value as a step to truth that any benefit that may be derived from them is clearly outweighed by the social interest in order and morality. Resort to epithets or personal abuse is not in any proper sense communication of information or opinion safeguarded by the Constitution.[5]

The universities felt that by tailoring their speech codes to this fighting words standard, they would be within established guidelines. However, it is questionable whether *Chaplinsky* is still good law.[6] This is evidenced by the fact that the Supreme Court has not sustained a single conviction based on the fighting words doctrine since *Chaplinsky* was handed down nearly sixty years ago. Since then, however, the Supreme Court has taken steps to significantly narrow this exception. While it has not explicitly overturned the fighting words standard, the Supreme Court has rendered it unrecognizable, stripping away parts of it until all that is left is the restriction against causing imminent and immediate lawless action. Justice Murphy's ruling not only dealt with words or action that would result in disorder, but also included limits on offensive speech to protect the sensibilities of the audience. The Supreme Court has upheld the first part of this test many times. Limits on provocation and violence are not much different than the clear and present danger standard long recognized by the Court.[7] However, the part about limiting offensive speech has never again been used and has been rejected in several cases.

A few years later, in *Terminiello v. Chicago* (1949), the Supreme Court rejected the *Chaplinsky* standard in reversing the breach of the peace conviction of a speaker who had purposely agitated a crowd, calling them "snakes" and "scum" among other things. Speaking for the Court, Justice Douglas seemed to abandon the offensive speech portion of *Chaplinsky* altogether in noting that: "Free speech may best serve its high purpose when it induces a condition of unrest, creates dissatisfaction with conditions as they are, or even stirs people to anger."[8]

Then in 1969, in the case of *Brandenburg v. Ohio*, a unanimous Supreme Court curbed the *Chaplinsky* restrictions even further.[9] This time it dealt with the first part of the fighting words standard dealing with provocation. The Supreme Court scaled these limits back to include only an immediate and certain breach. The *Brandenburg* decision draws a distinction between speech and actual violence or action. Clarence Brandenburg, at a rally of the Ku Klux Klan, called for violence and revenge in stirring up an angry mob. He was convicted under an Ohio criminal syndicalism statute. In reversing, the Court stated:

> The mere abstract teaching of the moral propriety or even moral necessity for a resort to force and violence, is not the same as preparing a group for violent action and steeling it to such action. A statute which fails to draw this distinction impermissibly intrudes upon the freedoms guaranteed by the First and Fourteenth Amendments. It sweeps within its condemnation speech which our Constitution has immunized from government control.[10]

Two years later, in *Cohen v. California* the Court continued in this direction. In *Cohen,* the United States Supreme Court reversed the conviction of a man for wearing a jacket with an obscene message about the draft. Although the word in question was lewd and offensive, the Court ruled that he had a right to express his views on important issues regardless of how they were perceived by the public. Though he could have expressed the same message in a less offensive manner, his speech was still protected. Justice Harlan spoke for the Court:

> The conviction quite clearly rests upon the asserted offensiveness of the words Cohen used to convey his message to the public. The only conduct which the state sought to punish is the fact of communication...Further, the state certainly lacks the power to punish Cohen for the underlying content of the message the inscription conveyed.[11]

The Court next addressed the fighting words rule and its applicability to these circumstances.

> This Court has also held that the states are free to ban the simple use of so called fighting words, those personally abusive epithets which, when addressed to the ordinary citizen, are, as a matter of common knowledge, inherently likely to provoke violent reaction. While the four-letter word displayed by Cohen in relation to the draft is not uncommonly employed in a personally provocative fashion, in this instance it was clearly not directed to the person of the hearer. No individual actually or likely to be present could reasonably have regarded the words on appellant's jacket as a direct personal insult.[12]

In the 1972 decision of *Gooding v. Wilson,* the Supreme Court reversed the conviction of a man punished under a Georgia statute which provided that "any person, without provocation, use to or of another, opprobrious words or abusive language, tending to cause a breach of the peace"[13] was guilty of a criminal act. The Supreme Court felt that this categorization was too broad and might limit protected expression. Justice Brennan delivered the opinion of the Court.

> The statute must be carefully drawn or be authoritatively construed to punish only unprotected speech and not be susceptible of application to protected expression. Because First Amendment freedoms need breathing space to survive, government may regulate in the area only with narrow specificity.[14]

The Court draws a clear distinction in *Wilson*. Here, as in *Brandenburg*, there is a difference between provocation and action. In this instance, no one responded to Cohen's speech with a violent reaction. Therefore, no matter how offensive, his speech cannot be considered fighting words. Mere offensiveness, without more, was no longer a viable standard of *Chaplinsky*. All that remains of the fighting words doctrine is the idea that speech, to be regulable, must cause immediate lawless action. In these cases, the speech did not rise to such a level. Although speech codes on college campuses were drawn according to *Chaplinsky* standards, they have failed in the courts whenever they have been challenged. Codes that go beyond the stripped-down version of fighting words or those presenting a clear and present danger will face great difficulties. Speech codes going further than these standards would allow will likely be considered overbroad and be found unconstitutional. Likewise, codes that are not clear and specific about what speech is prohibited are subject to fall victim to the void for vagueness doctrine. Finally, if the university punished individuals using these speech codes based upon the content of the speech in question, they will most likely fail to pass constitutional barriers. Two universities that have tried the courts on the constitutionality of their speech codes have both failed for each of these reasons. The codes chill expression (which was their intention), are not narrowly tailored to prevent only fighting words, and are impermissibly vague.

Speech Codes at the University of Michigan

In *John Doe v. University of Michigan* (1989), a United States District Court struck down the Michigan speech policy on the grounds that it was overbroad, content based, and so vague as to make enforcement selective at best and impossible at worst.[15]

This was the first case in which a student challenged a campus speech code in federal court. The Michigan code is particularly useful for the purposes of comparison to sexual harassment because its language so closely mirrors that of Title VII itself and the rules for workplace regulations. Part of the code prohibits "behavior that creates an intimidating, hostile, or demeaning environment for educational pursuits, employment, or participation in University sponsored activities."[16] Since this language was ultimately held to be overly broad, it is not a stretch to suggest that the language of Title VII, if viewed under a First Amendment light, might also face serious problems with the same issues.

Doe was a graduate student in biopsychology, which is an interdisciplinary study of the biological basis of differences in people's behaviors. Because the university speech policy applied to classrooms and other academic centers, he was concerned that certain controversial biological theories could be taken by some students to be racist or sexist. Since he feared that discussion of such theories might be sanctionable under the new speech policy, he felt his rights to a free academic discussion might be forever limited. In other words, the threat of application of this policy in a classroom setting was enough to chill controversial thoughts altogether, even if it was never actually enforced.

The District Court for the Eastern District of Michigan struck down the campus speech policy as a violation of the First Amendment. It was found to fail on the grounds of overbreadth as well as vagueness. The District Court worried that the code was so broad that it included constitutionally protected speech. Further, its vagueness was embedded in key words such as "stigmatize" and "victimize" which are difficult to define with precision. The final blow dealt with the content regulations inherent in the speech code. After outlining forms of unprotected speech such as fighting words that the university was free to regulate, the court turned to the fatal flaw in this policy.

> What the University could not do, however, was establish an anti-discrimination policy which had the effect of prohibiting certain speech because it disagreed with ideas or messages sought to be conveyed. Nor could the University proscribe speech simply because it was found to be offensive, even gravely so, by large numbers of people. It is firmly settled that under our Constitution the public expression of ideas may not be prohibited merely because the ideas are themselves offensive to some of their hearers.[17]

In turning to the overbreadth claim, the court gave a litany of United States Supreme Court precedent in this area, which they deemed to be applicable to this attempt at speech restriction.

> The Supreme Court has consistently held that statutes punishing speech or conduct solely on the grounds that they are unseemly or offensive are unconstitutionally over broad. In *Houston v. Hill*, the Supreme Court struck down a city of Houston ordinance which provided that it shall be unlawful for any person to assault or strike or in any manner oppose, molest, and abuse or interrupt any policeman in the execution of his duty. The Supreme Court also found that the ordinance was over broad because it forbade citizens from criticizing and insulting police officers, although such conduct was constitution-ally protected. The fact that the statute also had a legitimate scope of application in prohibiting conduct which was clearly unprotected by the First Amendment was not enough to save it. In *Gooding v. Wilson*, the Supreme Court struck down a Georgia statute which made it a misdemeanor for any person to without provocation, use to or of another, and in his presence... opprobrious words or abusive language, tending to cause a breach of the peace. The Supreme Court found that the statute was over broad as well, because it punished speech which did not rise to the level of fighting words as defined in *Chaplinsky v.*

New Hampshire. The Supreme Court struck down a similar ordinance in *Lewis v. New Orleans* on the same grounds. In *Papish v. University*, the Supreme Court ordered the reinstatement of a university student expelled for distributing an underground newspaper sporting the headline "Motherfucker Acquitted" on the grounds that mere offensive dissemination of ideas—no matter how offensive to good taste—on a state university campus may not be shut off in the name alone of conventions of decency. Most recently, in *Texas v. Johnson*, the Supreme Court invalidated a Texas statute prohibiting burning of the American flag on the grounds that there was no showing that the prohibited conduct was likely to incite a breach of the peace. These cases stand generally for the proposition that the state may not prohibit broad classes of speech, some of which may indeed be legitimately regulable, if in doing so a substantial amount of constitutionally protected conduct is also prohibited. This was the fundamental infirmity of this Policy.[18]

The court summed up its opinion by recognizing the well-intentioned reasoning of the University of Michigan in wanting to provide equal access for education to all, but noted that good intentions alone cannot save this speech code.

While the Court is sympathetic to the University's obligation to ensure equal educational opportunities for all of its students, such efforts must not be at the expense of free speech. Unfortunately, this was precisely what the University did....There is no evidence in the record that any officials at the University ever seriously attempted to reconcile their efforts to combat discrimination with the requirements of the First Amendment.[19]

The court, in this decision, recognized that this speech code covered much more than just speech. It tried to regulate behaviors and thoughts, and in doing so, was out of bounds. Its purpose was not only to limit fighting words but also offensive speech. Although the university had a legitimate interest in providing for equal education for its students, it went too far in deciding how to accomplish this goal.

In reviewing how the code had worked in practice, the court found that although well intentioned, it had been used to restrict more than just fighting words, resulting in a chilling effect on all speech. The court cited three examples in which students had been disciplined or threatened with discipline under this speech policy. One involved a graduate student in the School of Social Work who openly stated in a research class that he believed that homosexuality was a disease. A formal hearing was held but ruled that the policy was not violated. Still, according to the court, this had an effect on all future classroom discussions.

The second example cited by the court involved a complaint filed against a student in the School of Business Administration for reading an "allegedly homophobic" limerick during a scheduled class public speaking exercise. This case was settled informally but involved a letter of apology to the school newspaper from the student and an agreement to attend an educational "gay rap" session.

The third incident occurred during an orientation session of a pre-clinical dentistry class. During a breakout session into small groups, a student commented that he had heard that minorities had great difficulties in the course and were not treated fairly. A minority professor claimed that such comments were unfair and could potentially hurt her chances at tenure. Again, this was resolved informally with the student writing a formal letter of apology to the professor who had filed the complaint.

A further example included a charge of sexual harassment against a sophomore at the University of Michigan for submitting an essay in a political science research methods class which contained the fictionalized characters "Dave Stud" and "Joe Sixpack."[20]

The court concluded from these examples that "the Administrator's manner of enforcing the policy was constitutionally indistinguishable from a full blown prosecution."[21] The intention of the policy may not have been to silence criticism or differing points of view, yet in practice, this was the ultimate result of the speech restrictions. The remedy was worse than the cure. The court also noted that although this policy was designed to protect powerless groups, the policy was applied more often against minorities than any other group.[22]

Speech Codes at the University of Wisconsin

Two years after the Michigan policy was overturned, a Federal District Court in Wisconsin ruled that the speech code at the University of Wisconsin also violated the First Amendment to the Constitution. The Wisconsin policy was more narrowly written than the one struck down at the University of Michigan in an attempt to survive First Amendment scrutiny, yet still it suffered many of the same problems. The University of Wisconsin claimed that, as worded, its speech code applied only to fighting words as approved by the Supreme Court in *Chaplinsky* as well as those which were accepted in Title VII for workplace speech as words that create a hostile environment. The Wisconsin policy covered "racist or discriminatory comments, epithets, or other expressive behavior directed at an individual or creating an intimidating, hostile, or demeaning environment for education." Therefore, under this policy, the students at Michigan who were punished for expressing controversial thoughts in a classroom setting would not have fit the definition of proscribed behavior at Wisconsin.

A group of students brought suit challenging the policy on basically the same grounds that the court in Michigan had applied to the speech policy in that state. They contended that this policy was still overly broad and vague as well as representing a content-based restriction. The United States District Court for the Eastern District of Wisconsin agreed and found the rule to be unconstitutional.

In addressing the University of Wisconsin's claim that the policy covered nothing more than fighting words, the court felt that their application was incorrect. The University had argued that fighting words covered words of " such slight social value" as well as words that could provoke a reasonable person to violence. The District Court pointed out that the United States Supreme Court had narrowed that distinction in cases subsequent to *Chaplinsky*. They felt that since the speech code did not require as a necessary condition that the regulated speech actually incite violent reaction, it went beyond the scope of the accepted definition of fighting words. Racist, discriminatory, or demeaning words by themselves were not enough to allow for limitations.

The Court also rejected the parallel to Title VII workplace regulations. While the Court did not claim that Title VII or rules of that ilk were unconstitutional, they said that though not applicable here, these rules may go against the principles of the Constitution. The court noted that "Title VII is only statute, it cannot supersede requirements of the First Amendment."[23] The court recognizes that content-based restrictions on speech are unconstitutional. The court also found the policy to be both too vague and too broad.

The speech policy was originally adopted in May 1988, a full year before the policy at the University of Michigan was rejected in court. However, Wisconsin may have felt that the Michigan policy was doomed to failure and was careful in the writing of their policy as to avoid some potential problems that Michigan was sure to face. The policy was developed by some of the most distinguished law professors in the country who were faculty members at the University of Wisconsin at the time, including Richard Delgado and Gordon Baldwin. These professors felt that their policy was different than the one at the University of Michigan because it was framed in a way so as to mirror an existing limitation, Title VII of the Civil Rights Act of 1964. In its review, the court acknowledged both the reasons for the policy as well as its construction. They pointed to the fact that the policy was not designed by the University as a limit on speech but as "a plan to increase minority representation, multicultural understanding, and greater diversity throughout the University of Wisconsin system."[24] It was further noted that the professors who wrote the policy all agreed that "the proposed rule would likely withstand attack on First Amendment grounds if it included a requirement that the speaker intended to make the educational environment hostile for the individual being addressed."[25] It was as if the authors of the plan were trying to head off attack on First Amendment grounds by carefully patterning it after existing law and accepted doctrine such as fighting words, as well as the *O'Brien* hurdle that the law must not be aimed at the suppression of free speech.[26]

The similarities between the speech policy and Title VII ultimately raise some interesting comparisons. Since it was held to be too broad and vague in the classroom, it can be no less broad or vague in the workplace. The test for overbreadth and vagueness knows no boundaries. If a restriction sweeps up protected speech in its limitations, it is too broad, regardless of where the limitation takes place. If a restriction is unclear as to its meaning, it will still be unclear, regardless of where the limitation takes place.

Examples laid out in the decision of how the rule was enforced at the University of Wisconsin included: discipline against a student who called another student "shakazulu," a student telling an Asian-American student that "It's people like you, that's the reason this country is screwed up" and "You don't belong here," a student who hung a sign from his dorm room proclaiming "Death to all Arabs," and a student who harassed a Turkish-American student by pretending to be an immigration official and asking to see immigration documents.[27]

The District Court struck down the University of Wisconsin policy in October 1991. The first and perhaps largest problem the court addressed in its opinion was the overbreadth of the policy and the implications that had for free expression on the campus of the University of Wisconsin.

> The University of Wisconsin rule has overbreadth difficulties because it is a content based rule which regulates a substantial amount of protected speech. In *Police Department v. Mosely*, the Supreme Court explained the great import of protecting speech from content based regulation. Above all else, the First Amendment means that the government has no power to restrict

expression because of its message, ideas, its subject matter, or its content. To permit the continued building of our politics and culture, and to assure self fulfillment for each individual, our people are guaranteed the right to express any thought, free from government censorship. The essence of this forbidden censorship is content control. Any restriction on expressive activity because of its content would completely undercut the profound national commitment to the principle that debate on public issues should be uninhibited, robust, and wide open. Although the First Amendment generally protects speech from content-based regulation, it does not protect all speech. The Supreme Court has removed certain narrowly limited categories of speech from First Amendment protection....The categories include fighting words, obscenity, and to a limited extent, libel.[28]

After reviewing the standard for content-based restrictions, the court applies that standard to invalidate this speech policy. It reviewed United States Supreme Court cases explaining the transition of the fighting words doctrine. It cites several cases to point to the fact that the sensibilities portion of *Chaplinsky* is dead, and that fighting words now only constitute words that incite an immediate breach of the peace. Since none of the examples listed by the court of the university's enforcement of this policy involved breaches of the peace, immediate or otherwise, the fighting words doctrine could not apply here.

The court further found that the intention of the policy was not to limit fighting words, but from the way the policy was written, its purpose was to limit racial and discriminatory words, thus getting into the content of the speech in question. Paying special attention to the section of the Wisconsin code mirroring Title VII, the court ruled that there is no separate, specific exception for "hostile environments," and the type of speech likely to cause a hostile environment does not fit the exception for fighting words.

The University of Wisconsin rule requires that the prohibited speech create an intimidating, hostile, or demeaning environment. An intimidating, hostile or demeaning environment certainly disturbs the public peace or tranquility enjoyed by the citizens of a University community. However, it does not necessarily incite violent reaction. The creation of a hostile environment may tend to incite an immediate breach of the peace under some circumstances. Nevertheless, the term hostile covers non-violent as well as violent situations. Moreover, an intimidating or demeaning environment is unlikely to incite violent reaction. To intimidate means to make timid or to inhibit by or as if by threats. To demean is to debase in dignity or stature. Given these definitions, this Court cannot properly find that an intimidating or demeaning environment tends to incite an immediate breach of the peace....It is unlikely that all or nearly all demeaning discriminatory comments, epithets, or other expressive behavior which creates an intimidating, hostile, or demeaning environment tend to provoke a violent response. Since the University of Wisconsin rule covers a substantial number of situations where no breach of the peace is likely to result, the rule fails to meet the requirements of the fighting words doctrine.[29]

The court further addressed the ultimate failure of the policy—that it is based on the content of the speech. It referred to the Seventh Circuit's decision in *American Book Sellers Association v. Hudnut* as the proper standard to apply here. In striking down an Indianapolis anti-pornography ordinance, the Seventh Circuit spoke of content being the one hurdle that a law cannot clear.

The *American Book Sellers* court's reluctance to apply a balancing approach to content based restrictions is well founded. The First Amendment's protection of speech constitutes a pre-commitment by the government to refrain from restricting the expression of ideas. This pre-commitment ensures the continued building of our politics and culture as well as self-fulfillment for each individual. This commitment to free expression must be unwavering, because there exist many situations where, in the short run, it appears advantageous to limit speech to solve pressing social problems, such as discriminatory harassment. If a balancing approach is applied, these pressing and tangible short run concerns are likely to outweigh the more amorphous and long run benefits of free speech. However, the suppression of free speech, even where the speech's content appears to have little value and great costs, amounts to governmental thought control. An individual instance of thought control may not appear to impose great costs on society. However, if a balancing test is used there are likely to be many such instances. Taken as a whole, these instances will work to dissolve the great benefits which free speech affords.[30]

The court summed up its opinion by placing the issue in the larger perspective of our national history and tradition of free speech.

The Founding Fathers of this nation produced a remarkable document in the Constitution but it was ratified only with the promise of a Bill of Rights. The First Amendment is central to our concept of freedom. The "God-given" unalienable rights that the infant nation rallied to in the Declaration of Independence can be preserved only if rigorously analyzed. The problems of bigotry and discrimination sought to be addressed here are real and truly corrosive of the educational environment. But freedom of speech is almost absolute in our land, and the only restriction the fighting words doctrine can abide is that based on the fear of violent reaction. Content based prohibitions such as that in the University of Wisconsin rule, however well intentioned, simply cannot survive the screening which our Constitution demands.[31]

Conclusions

Taken together, the University of Michigan and University of Wisconsin decisions show that speech codes of this form violate the First Amendment. For many of the same reasons, speech limitations that are content based, overly broad, and vague may face legal challenges in the workplace as well. Until now, the Supreme Court has not addressed the First Amendment implications of its Title VII rulings. Nonetheless, the impact of those rulings on workplace speech has been profound.

These implications were alluded to in Justice White's opinion in another important speech case, *R.A.V. v. St. Paul.*[32] This decision, which struck down St. Paul's bias-motivated crimes ordinance as overly broad and vague, caused Justice White to ponder the reach of the Court's doctrine.

> ...Under the general rule the Court applies in this case, Title VII hostile work environment claims would suddenly be unconstitutional. Title VII regulations covering hostile workplace claims forbid "sexual harassment," which includes "unwelcome sexual advances, requests for sexual favors, and other verbal or physical conduct of a sexual nature" which creates "an intimidating, hostile, or offensive working environment." The regulation does not prohibit workplace harassment generally; it focuses on what the majority would characterize as the "disfavored topic" of sexual harassment. In this way, Title VII is similar to the St. Paul ordinance that the majority condemns because it "imposes special prohibitions on those speakers who express views on disfavored subjects."[33]

In practice, the experiences of Teresa Harris in dealing with the offensiveness of her employer are not that much different from those related by the courts in the cases involving the students at the University of Michigan as well as the University of Wisconsin.[34] Harris was successful in her court battle against her employer for his offensive statements. His statements were not fighting words. Nonetheless, they were found in violation of the law as a hostile environment and not protected by the First Amendment.

Further, the Court's attempts to differentiate between protected workplace speech and sexual harassment have been equally broad. In *Oncale v. Sundowner Offshore Services, Inc.,* a case addressing the issue of same-sex harassment, the Court addressed concerns about the breadth of sexual harassment regulations by stating:

Respondents and their amici contend that recognizing liability for same-sex harassment will transform Title VII into a general civility code for the American workplace.... The real social impact of workplace behavior often depends on a constellation of surrounding circumstances, expectations, and relationships which are not fully captured by a simple recitation of the words used or the physical acts performed. Common sense, and an appropriate sensitivity to social context, will enable courts and juries to distinguish between simple teasing or roughhousing among members of the same sex, and conduct which a reasonable person in the plaintiff's position would find severely hostile or abusive. [35]

The same problems that the Court struck down in the college speech code cases are apparent in its own problematic definition of sexual harassment workplace limits. Quoting *Oncale*, the court says that "the statute does not reach genuine but innocuous differences in the ways men and women routinely interact" and "the prohibition of harassment on the basis of sex requires neither asexuality nor androgyny in the workplace."[36] Yet, exactly how the workplace differs from the other forums such as the college campus has yet to be addressed.

The importance of employment and the workplace is not to be underestimated. Yet despite language that paralleled Title VII, speech restrictions for universities were struck down. It was an unconstitutional restriction based upon content in the university setting; it is no less content based in the workplace. It was overly broad in the university setting, sweeping up much protected as well as unprotected speech; it will have the same effect in the workplace. It was overly vague, its meaning being very hazy and unclear. The workplace does not transform the words "hostile" or "discriminatory" into ones that are clearly understood.

1.   See "Regulating Racist Speech on Campus: A Modest Proposal?" *Duke Law Journal* 484 (1992), Charles Lawrence, "If He Hollers Let Him Go: Regulating Racist Speech on Campus," *Duke Law Journal* 431 (1990), Mari Matsuda, "Public Response to Racist Speech:

Considering the Victim's Story," *Michigan Law Review* 87 (1989), Kent Greenawalt, *Fighting Words* (Princeton, N.J.: Princeton University Press, 1995), as examples of this line of thought.

2. See Nat Hentoff, *Free Speech for Me- But Not for Thee* (New York: Harper Collins Press, 1993), Melanie Moore, "Free Speech on College Campuses," *West Virginia Law Review*, 96 (1994), Edward Cleary, *Beyond the Burning Cross* (New York: Random House Publishers, 1994), Nadine Strossen, *Defending Pornography* (New York: Scribner Press, 1995), Nadine Strossen, B.C. Adams, "Shouting Epithets on a Crowded Campus—A Lesson in Tolerating Intolerance," *Alabama Law Review*, 44, 1, (1992), Kent Greenawalt, *Fighting Words* (Princeton, NJ: Princeton University Press, 1995) as examples of this debate.

3. *Harris v. Forklift Systems Inc.*, 62 USLW 4004 (1993). In this case, Ms. Harris was subjected to repeated chauvinistic statements by her employer. Among other things, the statements included "You are a woman, what do you know?" and "We need a man for this job." The Supreme Court found that a hostile environment can exist even without a showing of tangible harm.

4. See *John Doe v. University of Michigan*, 721 F. Supp. 852, 1989 as well as *The UWM Post Inc. v. Board of Regents of the University of Wisconsin System*, 774 F. Supp. 1163 (1991).

5. *Chaplinsky v. New Hampshire*, 315 U.S. 568 (1942).

6. See Shepard's Citation Service indicating negative treatment in 189 cited decisions.

7. The clear and present danger test was first enunciated in *Schenck v. United States*, 249 U. S. 47 (1919).

8. *Terminiello v. Chicago*, 337 U.S. 1131 (1949).

9. *Brandenburg v. Ohio*, 395 U.S. 444 (1969).

10. *Brandenburg v. Ohio*, 395 U.S. 444 (1969).

11. *Cohen v. California*, 403 U.S. 15 (1971).

12. *Cohen v. California*, 403 U.S. 15 (1971).

13. *Gooding v. Wilson*, 405 U.S. 518 (1972).

14. *Gooding v. Wilson*, 405 U.S. 518 (1972).

15. *John Doe v. University of Michigan*, 721 F.Supp. 852 (1989).

16. *John Doe v. University of Michigan*, 721 F.Supp. 852 (1989).

17. *John Doe v. University of Michigan*, 721 F.Supp. 852 (1989).

18. *John Doe v. University of Michigan*, 721 F.Supp. 852 (1989).

19. *John Doe v. University of Michigan*, 721 F.Supp. 852 (1989).

20. Melanie Moore, "Free Speech on College Campuses," *West Virginia Law Review*, 96 (1994):518.

21. Moore, 518.

22. Moore, 518.

23. *The UWM Post, Inc. v. Board of Regents of the University of Wisconsin System*, 774 F. Supp. 1163, (1991).

24. *The UWM Post, Inc. v. Board of Regents of the University of Wisconsin System*, 774 F. Supp. 1163, (1991).

25. *The UWM Post, Inc. v. Board of Regents of the University of Wisconsin System*, 774 F. Supp. 1163, (1991).

26. See *United States v. O'Brien* 391 U.S. 367, 88 S.Ct. 1673, (1968), which sets out the standard for separating speech from conduct. In order to withstand challenge, a law must be within the constitutional power of the government it must further an important governmental interest; the governmental interest must be unrelated to the suppression of free expression; and the incidental restriction on alleged First Amendment freedoms must be no greater than is essential to the furtherance of that interest.

27. *The UWM Post, Inc. v. Board of Regents of the University of Wisconsin System*, 774 F. Supp. 1163, (1991).

28. *The UWM Post, Inc. v. Board of Regents of the University of Wisconsin System*, 774 F. Supp. 1163, (1991).

29. *The UWM Post, Inc. v. Board of Regents of the University of Wisconsin System*, 774 F. Supp. 1163, (1991).

30. *The UWM Post, Inc. v. Board of Regents of the University of Wisconsin System*, 774 F. Supp. 1163, (1991).

31. *The UWM Post, Inc. v. Board of Regents of the University of Wisconsin System*, 774 F. Supp. 1163, (1991).

32. *R.A.V. v. St. Paul*, 505 U.S. 377 (1992).

33. *R.A.V. v. St. Paul*, 505 U.S. 377 (1992).

34. *Harris v. Forklift Systems Inc.*, 62 USLW 4004.

35. *Oncale v. Sundowner Offshore Services Inc.*, 523 U.S. 75 (1998).

36. *Oncale v. Sundowner Offshore Services Inc.*, 523 U.S. 75 (1998).

Part 3
Commentary

What Speech Does "Hostile Work Environment" Harassment Law Restrict?

Eugene Volokh, UCLA Law School

Introduction

Workplace harassment law is a speech restriction of remarkable breadth. It goes far beyond slurs, hardcore pornography, repeated vulgar sexual propositions, and the like, and can suppress, among other things,

- political statements,
- religious proselytizing,
- legitimate art (such as prints of Francisco de Goya paintings),
- sexually themed (perhaps not even misogynistic) jokes,
- and other kinds of speech that are generally seen as being entirely constitutionally protected.

I aim to prove this claim below.

Political, Artistic, Religious, and Socially Themed Speech May Constitute "Harassment"

The Formal Definition of "Harassment"

The first place to look in determining the scope of harassment law, of course, is the definition of "harassment." Speech can be punished as workplace harassment if it's:

- "severe or pervasive" enough to
- create a "hostile or abusive work environment"
- based on race, religion, sex, national origin, age, disability (including obesity), military membership or veteran status, or, in some jurisdictions, sexual orientation, marital status, transsexualism or cross-dressing, political affiliation, criminal record, occupation, citizenship status, personal appearance, "matriculation," tobacco use outside work, Appalachian origin, receipt of public assistance, or dishonorable discharge from the military
- for the plaintiff and for a reasonable person.[1]

Note what the definition does not require. It does not require that the speech consist of obscenity or fighting words or threats or other constitutionally unprotected statements. It does not require that the speech be profanity or pornography, which some have considered "low value." Under the definition, it is eminently possible for political, religious, or social commentary, or "legitimate" art, to be punished.

"David Duke for President" posters, after all, might well be quite offensive to many reasonable people based on their race, religion, or national origin, and may create a hostile environment; likewise for confederate insignia. This would be even more true of bigoted or insensitive remarks about minority or female political candidates. Many reasonable people might view strident denunciations of Catholicism, whether political or religious, as creating a hostile environment for devout Catholics, or criticisms of feminism as creating a hostile environment for women.

The Cases

Religious Speech. If some complainants make these claims, some fact-finders may well agree. A state court has in fact found that it was religious harassment for an employer to put religious articles in its employee newsletter and Christian-themed verses on its paychecks.[2] The EEOC likewise found that a claim that an employer "permitted the daily broadcast of prayers over the public address system" over the span of a year was "sufficient to allege the existence of a hostile working environment predicated on religious discrimination."[3] A recent article by two employment lawyers gives "repeated, unwanted 'preaching' episodes [by a fundamentalist Christian employee] that offend coworkers and adversely affect their working conditions" as a "bright-line example" of actionable harassment; an employer in such a situation would be "well advised to take swift remedial action."[4]

If polite religious proselytizing can be harassment, then of course harsher criticism of religion would be, too. In the EEOC's words, "disparag[ing] the religion or beliefs of others" in the workplace may be illegal; "a Christian employee would have recourse under Title VII if a 'secular humanist' employer"—or presumably secular humanist coworkers—engaged in a pattern of ridiculing the employee's religious beliefs."[5] Likewise, a federal district court has held that a pattern of religiously themed comments, which mostly consisted of statements that the target was a sinner and had to reprent, and didn't include any religious slurs, could be religious harassment.[6]

Social and Political Commentary. Likewise, one court has said that coworkers' use of job titles such as "foreman" and "draftsman" may constitute sexual harassment,[7] and a Kentucky human rights agency has gotten a company to change its "Men Working" signs (at a cost of over $35,000) on the theory that the signs "perpetuat[e] a discriminatory work environment and could be deemed unlawful under the Kentucky Civil Rights Act."[8] Another court has characterized an employee's hanging "pictures of the Ayatollah Khome[i]ni and a burning American flag in Iran in her own cubicle" as "national-origin harassment" of an Iranian employee who saw the pictures.[9]

In another case, the EEOC concluded that an employer had racially harassed a Japanese-American employee by (1) creating an ad campaign that used images of samurai, kabuki, and sumo wrestling to refer to its Japanese competition, and (2) referring to the competition in internal memos and meetings using terms such as "Jap" and "slant-eyed." There were no allegations that the slurs were used to refer to the complaining employee (though it's of course understandable that he found them offensive). Curiously, the EEOC did not focus exclusively or even primarily on the slurs; it seems to have viewed the ads themselves as being as offensive—and as illegal—as the slurs. The case was finally settled "for undisclosed monetary terms and other commitments."[10]

Offensive union-related speech can also lead to harassment liability. Thus, in *Bowman v. Heller*, an employee who disliked a certain female candidate for union office gave some of his coworkers a *Hustler* centerfold with the candidate's picture superimposed over the model's head. The trial court concluded that this constituted sexual harassment of the candidate. (An appellate court agreed that the speech was constitutionally unprotected, but reversed the harassment portion of the judgment on unusual state-law grounds.)[11] The NLRB has likewise suggested that it would be racial harassment for employees to use the words "Spics, Kikes, and Broads" to criticize the president of the employee union.[12]

And courts are not bashful about this. The Sixth Circuit put it quite plainly:

> In essence, while [harassment law] does not require an employer to fire all "Archie Bunkers" in its employ, the law does require that an employer take prompt action to prevent such bigots from expressing their opinions in a way that abuses or offends their co-workers. By informing people that the expression of racist or sexist attitudes in public is unacceptable, people may eventually learn that such views are undesirable in private, as well. Thus, Title VII may advance the goal of eliminating prejudices and biases in our society.[13]

Sexually Themed Jokes. The Montana Human Rights Commission found a hostile environment based solely on off-color jokes and cartoons displayed in the workplace. None of the jokes were said specifically to the complainant; none referred to her; the cartoons were distributed by men and women alike, apparently once or twice a month over several years; the cartoons weren't even sexist or misogynistic. The Commission, however, was not amused. It concluded that the jokes "ha[d] no humorous value to a reasonable person," and "offended [complainant] as a woman."

The Commission ordered the city to pay damages, to "not ...permit, tolerate, or condone the sexual harassment of any employee" (apparently including such humor), and to "evaluate on an annual basis the performance of each department head on the basis of the quality and success of their efforts to implement and enforce the antidiscrimination policies."[14]

Similarly, the EEOC recently concluded that an employee's allegation that she was "sexually harassed by offensive jokes-of-the-day circulated to her and her co-workers, and by the Supervisor's praise [in a department meeting] of the co-worker circulating the jokes" was sufficient to state a claim under Title VII.[15] The New Jersey Office of Administrative Law likewise found one incident of 11 pages worth of jokes being forwarded by e-mail to the whole department to be "sexual harassment" creating an "offensive work environment"; the judge "f[ou]nd the 'jokes' degrade, shame, humiliate, defame and dishonor men and women based upon their gender, sexual preference, religion, skin pigmentation and national and ethnic origin" and were thus illegal.[16]

An official U.S. Department of Labor pamphlet likewise defines harassment as including cases where "[s]omeone made sexual jokes or said sexual things that you didn't like," with no requirement that the jokes be insulting or even misogynistic.[17] A Seattle Human Rights Department pamphlet gives "the secretary who was frequently told sexual jokes by her co-workers and supervisor" as an example of sexual harassment.[18] A Hanson, Massachusetts, harassment policy for city employees defines sexual harassment as "any unwelcome action, sexual in content or implication, in the workplace that includes...sex oriented 'kidding' or 'jokes' [and] sexually suggestive objects in the workplace."[19]

Employment experts have gotten the message and are passing it along to employers. Thus, they recommend, to avoid liability employers should purge workplaces of "blonde jokes" (on the plausible theory that they convey offensive attitudes towards women)[20] discussions of scenes from sex comedies such as *There's Something About Mary*[21] and Clinton-Lewinsky jokes.[22]

Speech Among Consenting Listeners.   In fact, speech can be punished as harassment even if it isn't overheard by anyone who is offended. Consider *Schwapp v. Town of Avon*, a Second Circuit case holding that "ten racially-hostile incidents of which [plaintiff] allegedly was aware during his 20-month tenure," of which only four occurred in his presence, were enough to create a potential harassment case. "The district court," the Circuit held, "erred in failing to consider the eight ...incidents that did not occur in Schwapp's presence," including one "made prior to Schwapp's employment" and "two comments made during Schwapp's employment [but outside his presence] that were hostile toward minority groups of which Schwapp is not a member....[T]he fact that a plaintiff learns second-hand of a racially derogatory comment or joke by a fellow employee or supervisor also can impact the work environment ...."[23]

This makes sense as a matter of substantive harassment law: For instance, if I (a Jew) know my coworker is a virulent anti-Semite, I might find it hard to work around him even if he's always polite to my face. Having to work around people who hate you (even politely hate you) might well create a "hostile, abusive, or offensive work environment." But this shows that harassment law provides no safe harbor even when one is talking to coworkers who one knows won't be offended—any bigoted statements made at work may lead to harassment liability.

Frequency.   Finally, the "severe or pervasive" requirement does not require that the offensive speech happen daily or weekly. Some cases have held that even a single incident of speech—for instance, one racial slur by a supervisor, or a "single incident of verbal abuse and negative comment concerning Japanese people"—may be "severe or pervasive."[24] *Brown Transport*, discussed above, was based on biweekly paychecks. *Dernovich* was based on sexually themed jokes that were distributed about every two weeks. *Schwapp* involved an average of one offensive statement every two months; if one counts only statements heard personally by the plaintiff, the rate was one every five months. *Danco, Inc. v. Wal-Mart Stores, Inc.*, a First Circuit case, affirmed a harassment finding based on three incidents: two personal slurs (one including a threat), plus the words "White Supremacy" spray-painted in a parking lot.[25]

Other cases have granted summary judgment against harassment claims based on single incidents, or even based on several incidents, on the grounds that they weren't "severe or pervasive" enough.[26] I don't suggest that single incidents or even biweekly or bimonthly incidents will always lead to the case going to the jury. But as one might expect, "severity or pervasiveness" is generally in the eye of the beholding judge and jury.

The Severity/Pervasiveness Requirement

If there is anything about harassment law that prevents liability based on this sort of speech, it has to be the severity/pervasiveness component: The fact-finder—judge or jury—must conclude not only that the speech was offensive, based on race, religion, sex, or some other attribute, but also that it was either "severe" or "pervasive" enough to create a hostile or abusive environment for the plaintiff and for a reasonable person. And if the outcomes in the above cases were, as one critic suggests, "bizarre judicial misapplications," "exception[s] to the rule" that should be ignored in determining the rule's true scope, it could only be because the speech in those cases didn't meet the severity or pervasiveness thresholds.[27]

But how exactly can we condemn the fact-finders here of being guilty of "bizarre judicial misapplications"? After all, nothing in the rule they were told to apply says that religious proselytizing, political commentary, or off-color jokes are insulated from liability. Perhaps you or I can say that a reasonable person ought not find Bible verses or the phrase "Men Working" or jokes about sexually graphic road signs to be "severe" or "pervasive" enough to create a hostile environment, but obviously other people, who probably thought themselves to be quite reasonable, have disagreed.

"Severe," "pervasive," "hostile," and "abusive" are mushy terms, as courts have specifically acknowledged.[28] I'm not completely sure what it means to say that people have "bizarre[ly] misappli[ed]" such terms. They might just have had a different notion of how offensive something must be to be "severe," or how frequent it must be to be "pervasive." Certainly courts have taken very different views of what these terms mean.

When we judge a rule, we can't judge it simply by how we would apply it ourselves, or by the best-case scenario of how it could be applied. As Justice Brennan warned, "If there is an internal tension between proscription and protection in the statute, we cannot assume that, in its subsequent enforcement, ambiguities will be resolved in favor of adequate protection of First Amendment rights."[29]

Rather, we must judge the rule by how we might expect the "ambiguities will be resolved" by the variety of fact-finders in our judicial system. And I imagine that in that system, quite a few fact-finders will conclude that various religious statements, political posters, "vulgar and degrading" jokes, and "indecent" art can indeed be "severe" or "pervasive" enough to create a hostile environment. Perhaps one can argue that this is acceptable, but one can't deny that this will happen.

How the Law's Vagueness Increases Its Breadth

So we see that, on its face, harassment law can suppress core protected speech. Whatever shelter there is for such speech must come from the "severe or pervasive" requirement. The heart of a defense of harassment law, I take it, would be an assertion that this requirement—despite the examples I gave above—will shield all protected speech except the most obnoxious.

Let's consider, though, how this would work out in practice. Imagine you're an employment lawyer, and an employer comes to you and says:

> Help me out. One of my employees is complaining that her coworkers' political posters and lunchroom conversations have created a hostile environment based on her [race / religion / sex / national origin / age / disability /military membership or veteran status / sexual orientation / marital status / political

affiliation / criminal record /occupation / citizenship status / personal appearance / tobacco use outside work / Appalachian origin / receipt of public assistance / dishonorable discharge from the military]. The speech sounds to me like normal political argument, and I don't want to suppress it. But I also don't want to be stuck with a big lawsuit.

What can you say in response? Saying "Well, you're OK if the speech isn't severe or pervasive enough to create a hostile or abusive environment" obviously gets you nowhere: The employer will just ask you "Well, is it severe or pervasive enough or isn't it?"

Your answer would probably have to be "We won't know until it gets to court." With vague words like "severe," "pervasive," "hostile," and "abusive," that's generally all you can say. As one state administrative agency frankly acknowledged, "one person's 'discussion' may be another person's 'harassment.'"[30] And because of this, the safe advice would be: "Shut the employees up." After all, the typical employer doesn't profit from its employees' political discussions; it can only lose because of them. The rational response is suppression, even if the lawyer personally believes that the speech probably doesn't reach the severe-or-pervasive threshold. In the words of an article entitled "Sexual Harassment: The Employer's Role in Prevention":

The practical advice for employers evaluating potentially harassing conduct [including speech] is to be as conservative as possible. If conduct might be construed as harassing, it has no place in the workplace. If an employee (and especially a manager or a supervisor) is not sure whether or not conduct will be unwelcome, the best advice is to avoid such conduct....I recognize the appeal in [an approach that tries to more warmly accommodate sexual banter and consensual supervisor-subordinate relationships]; as an employer, I might even make the decision to adopt it—risks and all. However, as a lawyer advising clients as to how to limit liability in an ever more litigious employment setting, I don't recommend it.[31]

If one takes at all seriously what the Supreme Court has said, this oversuppression is precisely the effect that vague laws have. Vagueness leads people "to 'steer far wider of the unlawful zone,' than if the boundaries of the forbidden areas were clearly marked. Those ...sensitive to the perils posed by ...indefinite language, avoid the risk ...only by restricting their conduct to that which is unquestionably safe."[32] Unless the Court was talking through its hat when it said this, the risk of employers "steer[ing] far wider of the unlawful zone" because of the rule's vagueness has to be considered in determining the true magnitude of the speech restriction. As the Court held in *Reno v. ACLU*, in determining the breadth of a law, we must look to whether "a speaker [could] confidently assume that [his speech] would not violate the CDA"; the "vague contours of [a law's] coverage" "present[s] a greater threat of censoring speech that, in fact, falls outside the statute's scope."[33]

In fact, consider the suggestion to employers given by Professor Deborah Epstein, who disagrees with my estimation of the breadth of harassment law. Contrary to the position I've just outlined, she argues that "an employer can easily create a narrow, speech-protective antiharassment policy that minimizes any chilling effect":

> One strategy is to explain to workers that they may make gender-specific or sexual comments until they receive an indication from a particular employee that such statements are unwelcome.... Once a worker has indicated that the speech is unwelcome, the speaker should be directed to either stop or set up a meeting with a designated EEO officer for advice.[34]

Employees can thus only say "gender-specific or sexual" things—and I assume this includes supposedly sexist political or social statements, sexually themed jokes, and so on—until one listener objects. At that point, they must either shut up or schedule a meeting with a "designated EEO officer" before speaking further.

Gone is any requirement that the speech be "severe or pervasive," or that it create a hostile or abusive environment, or that it even be offensive to a reasonable person. The policy

Professor Epstein suggests would bar any "gender-specific or sexual" speech so long as there's any objection, at least until one gets clearance from above. This is "a narrow, speech-protective antiharassment policy that minimizes any chilling effect"?

Of course, harassment law, like many other laws, is underenforced as well as overenforced. Many employers, because of ignorance or bigotry or whatever else, ignore the risk of liability and don't suppress speech or conduct that should be restricted. And though I have no idea whether "in the vast majority of cases, the judiciary is not engaging in overbroad enforcement, but instead is failing to impose liability," I'm sure this underenforcement happens in some cases, perhaps many cases.

But other employers pay attention to the risk and consequently suppress any speech that might possibly be seen as harassment, even if you and I would agree that it's not severe or pervasive enough that a reasonable person would conclude that it creates a hostile environment. Likewise, some fact-finders are imposing fairly low thresholds of severity or pervasiveness, even as other fact-finders are imposing higher ones. In those cases, the law may pose First Amendment problems regardless of whether it's underenforced in other situations.

The Maryland Commission on Human Relations puts it quite frankly, in a pamphlet entitled *Preventing Sexual Harassment: A Fact Sheet for Employees*: "Because the legal boundaries are so poorly marked, the best course of action is to avoid all sexually offensive conduct in the workplace." Hard to argue with logic like that.[35]

The Law's Effect on Individual Statements

The Inevitable Need to Suppress Isolated Statements

We see, then, that the "severe or pervasive" requirement is too vague to provide much protection for speech, and even the policy proposed by one of harassment law's leading defenders essentially eliminates this requirement. This, though, isn't some slight drafting flaw that can be corrected with a bit of tinkering: Harassment law by its nature restricts individual statements, even when they're clearly not severe or pervasive enough to generate a hostile environment.

Recall that a hostile environment can be created by many different employees, each making only one or a few offensive statements. Individually, the statements might not be "severe or pervasive" enough to create liability, but in the aggregate they may be actionable.

An employer can't just announce to its employees: "Say whatever you like, so long as the aggregate of all your statements and all the other employees' statements isn't so severe or pervasive that it creates a hostile environment." Most employees have no idea what their coworkers may have said days, weeks, or months ago. If the employer wants to protect itself, it must tell each employee what speech that employee must avoid.

The employer's only reliable protection is a zero-tolerance policy, one which prohibits any statement that, when aggregated with other statements, may lead to a hostile environment.

What Experts Advise Employers

In fact, many employment experts are recommending that employers suppress individual instances of offensive speech. One writes, in an article entitled "Avoid Costly Lawsuits for Sexual Harassment":

> Suggestive joking of any kind simply must not be tolerated...At the very least, you must insist that supervisors never engage in sexual joking or innuendo[; t]hat also goes for employees who hope to be promoted into supervisory positions..... Nip These Activities in the Bud....Don't let your employees [p]ost pin-up photographs on the walls[or t]ell sexual jokes or make innuendos.[36]

Another writes, in a piece called "Not Sure What Constitutes Sexual Harassment? Take a Look": "If you think there's any chance that what you are doing is unwelcome or offensive, knock it off." An article by an *Investor's Business Daily* reporter called "Watch What You Say, or Be Ready to Pay" says:

Be aware that offensive comments may translate into megabuck liability. Any disparaging comments or joking references concerning an employee's age, sex, race, religion or national origin can put your company on a fast track to court .... If you're an employer, have a strong written policy against a hostile work environment and harassment.[37]

An *Employee Relations Law Journal* article on religious harassment asserts:

[A]n employer's incentive to prohibit conduct and speech that might constitute harassment has increased based on the Civil Rights Act of 1991, which subjects employers to liability for emotional distress and punitive damages. To avoid liability, the prudent employer will proscribe all speech and conduct that may constitute harassment. The possibility of creating a "chilling effect" from prohibiting speech and conduct that may constitute harassment is outweighed by the risk of significant liability.[38]

The Sexual Harassment Prevention Game, a board game that is intended for use in employee training programs and that has been endorsed by the National Public Employees and Labor Relations Association, suggests the following:

A female janitor, offended by posters of partially clad female bodybuilders taped on the locker room wall, complains of sexual harassment. The pictures were hung by another female janitor using them as inspiration for pumping iron.

What should be done? [Answer:] Remove the posters that are found offensive...Confused about harassment?

Well, then follow [the game creator's] advice.

Don't say or do anything around an employee or co-worker that you wouldn't do around your spouse, your child, or dear old mom.[39]

Finally, consider the words of the EEOC itself: "While isolated incidents of harassment generally do not violate federal law, a pattern of such incidents may be unlawful. Therefore, to discharge its duty of preventive care, the employer must make clear to employees that it will stop harassment before it rises to the level of a violation of federal law."[40] Wise advice, and entirely consistent with the realities of harassment law—but it makes clear that harassment law does pressure employers into restricting speech even when it doesn't "rise to the level of a violation of federal law."

What Employers Are Actually Doing

Employers are in fact enacting such broad policies, and are indeed suppressing individual incidents of offensive speech. When a Florida city found that "frequent sexual jokes and innuendos among employees [created] a hostile work environment," the city announced "a 'zero-tolerance' policy on sexual humor."[41] Leavenworth, Kansas has enacted a policy that bans all sexual harassment, including even isolated incidents of "[o]ffensive comments, jokes, innuendos, other sexually oriented statements, and displaying sexually suggestive objects or pictures, cartoons, posters, or magazines.[42]

When a library employee complained about a coworkers' posting a *New Yorker* cartoon that used the word "penis"—with no sexually suggestive connotation at all—the library ordered that it be taken down.[43] When a professor at Penn State complained that a print of Goya's Naked Maja hanging in a classroom constituted sexual harassment, the school administration removed the painting, citing as one reason the risk of harassment liability.[44] When an employee at Murfreesboro (Tenn.) City Hall complained about a painting depicting a partly naked woman, the City Attorney had it taken down, saying:

I feel more comfortable siding with protecting the rights under the Title VII sexual harassment statutes than...under the First Amendment....We wouldn't permit that type of drawing or picture to hang in the fire hall. As far as I'm concerned, a naked woman is a naked woman.[45]

In both of the last two cases, the paintings probably couldn't have created a hostile environment by themselves, even in the view of jurors who most dislike nudes or who are most convinced that "nude or seminude photographs of women ...harm women by encouraging men to view them as sex objects." But surely the employers couldn't say to their employees: "Well, a nude here or there is fine, but if any of you puts up a picture that causes the aggregate to go over the severe-or-pervasive threshold, you'll be disciplined." To prevent liability, the employer has to suppress each individual picture; in the words of the Murfreesboro City Attorney, discussing the painting of the partly naked woman:

Though [the complainant] probably couldn't win a sexual harassment suit over the picture, Murfreesboro still has to protect itself against future lawsuits, [the City Attorney] said. If the city did nothing about the complaint about [the painting] or other complaints of harassment, a court could conclude the city was ignoring the rights of its female employees.[46]

At the University of Nebraska at Lincoln, a harassment complaint was filed against a graduate student who had on his desk a 5" x 7" photograph of his wife in a bikini. The employer ordered that the photo be removed.[47] And of course this is only to be expected: When the law tries to root out "pornography," especially using a definition as vague as "speech severe or pervasive enough to create a hostile environment for a reasonable person based on sex," attacks on legitimate art are sure to follow.

What Courts Are Forbidding Through Injunctions

This is also why many injunctions in harassment cases ban isolated statements. One court, for instance, has ordered an employer and its employees to "refrain from any racial, religious, ethnic, or other remarks or slurs contrary to their fellow employees' religious beliefs"[48]—no severe-or-pervasive threshold there. Another injunction prohibited, among other things, "derogatory bulletins, cartoons, and other written material" and "any racial, ethnic, or religious slurs whether in the form of 'jokes,' 'jests,' or otherwise."[49] A third ordered the employer and employees to "cease and desist from...racial harassment in the workplace including, but not limited to, any and all offensive conduct and speech implicating considerations of race."[50] Yet another prohibited all employees "from making sexually explicit remarks, jokes, language and engaging in such conduct [i.e., sexually harassing conduct] toward female employees."[51]

Another court barred any "sexually suggestive, sexually demeaning, or pornographic"[52] materials from the workplace, again without regard to whether they were severe or pervasive enough to create a hostile environment—a single Gauguin reproduction would have been a contempt of court. The injunction defined "sexually suggestive" as covering anything that "depicts a person of either sex who is not fully clothed ...and who is posed for the obvious purpose of displaying or drawing attention to private portions of his or her body." An amicus brief in the appeal of that case, signed by seventy-nine law professors (including, among others, Anthony Amsterdam, Erwin Chemerinsky, and Susan Estrich), explained that such a broad injunction against these "discrete acts" was necessary because "the court is both authorized and obligated to insure that the illegal activity will not recur."[53] The courts and the professors realize that you can't simply enjoin everyone from "acting in a way that's so severe or pervasive as to create a hostile environment": if you want to make an injunction stick, you have to ban each individual statement.

And if that's the way for courts to undo existing hostile environments, then it's also the way employers must act to prevent liability in the first place. Employers, after all, are also "obligated to insure" that harassment won't happen.[54] As the seventy-nine law professors point out, to prevent a hostile environment, even "discrete acts" must be banned, and this is as true for preventive policies as for remedial injunctions.

"It Is Necessary To Prohibit the Individual Actions"

Finally, consider the view of Professor Thomas Grey, a thoughtful and moderate scholar who was the architect of the Stanford Law School harassment restrictions. The restrictions barred even isolated incidents of grossly offensive speech, but, Professor Grey argued, this was necessary to prevent a hostile educational environment:

> [T]he injury of discriminatory denial of educational access through maintenance of a hostile environment can arise from single acts of discrimination on the part of many different individuals. To deal with a form of abuse that is repetitive to its victims, and hence constitutes the continuing injury of harassment to them, it is necessary to prohibit the individual actions that, when added up, amount to institutional discrimination.[55]

On this point, Professor Grey is absolutely right: To avoid the risk of a hostile environment, an institution can't, in practice, just restate the severity/pervasiveness test—it must "prohibit the individual actions [including speech] that, when added up, amount" to a hostile environment.

Conclusion: The Speech That Harassment Law Restricts

The scope of harassment law is thus molded by three facts:

1. On its face, harassment law draws no distinction among slurs, pornography, political, religious, or social commentary, jokes, art, and other forms of speech. All can be punished, so long as they are "severe or pervasive" enough to create a "hostile environment."

2. The vagueness of the terms "severe" and "pervasive"—and the fact that the law is implemented by employers, who have an incentive to oversuppress—means that the law may practically restrict any speech that an employer concludes

might be found by a fact-finder to be "severe or pervasive" enough.

3. Finally, because an employer is liable for the aggregate of all its employees' speech, wise employers will bar any sort of statement that might, if repeated by enough people, be "severe or pervasive" enough to create a hostile environment.

Putting all this together, harassment law potentially burdens any workplace speech that's offensive to at least one person in the workplace based on that person's race, religion, sex, national origin, age, disability, military membership or veteran status or, in some jurisdictions, sexual orientation, marital status, political affiliation, criminal record, occupation, citizenship status, tobacco use outside work, Appalachian origin, receipt of public assistance, dishonorable discharge from the military, or personal appearance, even when the speech is political and even when it's not severe or pervasive enough to itself be actionable.

The evidence I have set out—the best guess as to how a cautious employer would behave, the policies recommended by employment lawyers, the policies actually implemented by some employers, the injunctions issued by courts, the logic of the seventy-nine law professors' brief, the justification provided in the educational context by Professor Grey, even the recommended policy given by Professor Epstein, who claims that harassment law is a very narrow speech restriction -- all points towards this. The "regulatory reach" of harassment law is certainly not limited to the "most objectively extreme, persistent, and unwelcome" forms of conduct.

Of course, the speech-restrictive potential of harassment law won't be realized in every situation. Many employers will live dangerously—from prejudice, ignorance, or even a commitment to free expression. Many offended employees won't complain. Many fact-finders will apply high thresholds of "severity" and "pervasiveness" rather than low ones.

But this is true of all speech restrictions. Sexually themed literature wasn't completely suppressed by pre-1960s restrictive obscenity laws. Sedition laws are notoriously ineffective at suppressing sedition. Even the broadest libel laws would be vastly underenforced, and juries can exhibit unjustified hostility towards libel plaintiffs as well as unjustified sympathy.

To properly measure harassment law's impact on speech, we should ask: What restrictions would prudent, law-abiding employers—employers who heed the EEOC's statement that "Prevention is the best tool for the elimination of sexual harassment"—impose in trying to avoid liability?[56] The answer appears to be what I outline above: a broad prohibition on a wide range of isolated statements.

It's a mistake to hide behind the supposed shield of the severity and pervasiveness requirements. Harassment law puts at risk speech—including religious proselytizing, bigoted political statements, sexually themed humor, and sexually suggestive art—whether or not it's severe or pervasive. Whether this burden is justified is a matter that's been extensively debated elsewhere, but there should be no denying that the burden exists.

1. See, e.g., *Harris v. Forklift Sys., Inc.*, 510 U.S. 17, 21-22 (1993) (discussing harassment based on race, religion, sex, or national origin). This definition applies only to hostile environment harassment; I don't purport to deal with quid pro quo sexual harassment, in which a supervisor demands sex in exchange for favorable treatment.

    For citations to materials reflecting harassment based on the other grounds, from age and disability onward, see http://www.law.ucla.edu/faculty/volokh/harass/breadth.html A.

2. *Brown Transp. Corp. v. Commonwealth*, 578 A.2d 555, 562 (Pa. Commw. Ct. 1990).

3. *Hilsman v. Runyon*, Appeal Nos. 01945686, 01950499, 1995 WL 217486, at *3 (E.E.O.C. Mar. 31, 1995).

4. Dean J. Schaner & Melissa M. Erlemeier, "When Faith and Work Collide: Defining Standards for Religious Harassment in the Workplace," *Employee Rel. L.J.*, June 1, 1995, at 26.

5. EEOC Fact Sheet on Proposed Guidelines on Harassment Based on Race, Color, Religion, Sex, National Origin, Age or Disability 1-2 (1993).

6.   *Peck v. Sony Music Corp.*, 68 Fair Empl. Prac. Cas. (BNA) 1025, 1995 WL 505653 (S.D.N.Y. Aug. 25, 1995)

7.   *Tunis v. Corning Glass Works*, 747 F. Supp. 951, 959 (S.D.N.Y. 1990)

8.   Kentucky Comm'n on Human Rights, *Human Rights Report*, Spring 1994, at 2.

9.   *Pakizegi v. First Nat'l Bank*, 831 F. Supp. 901, 908 (D. Mass. 1993)

10. EEOC Letter of Determination, *Ozawa v. Hyster Co.*, Charge No. 380863519, at 1-4; Complaint at 3, *EEOC v. Hyster Co.*, No. 88-930-DA (D. Or. filed Aug. 15, 1988)

11. *Bowman v. Heller*, No. CIV.A. 90-3269, 1993 WL 761159, (Mass. Super. Ct. July 9, 1993), aff'd in part on other grounds, vacated in part, 651 N.E.2d 369 (Mass. 1995).

12. Advisory Opinion, Cases 27-CA-10941(P), 27-CA-10962(P), 27-CB-2741(P), 27-CB-2744(P), NLRB Off. Gen. Counsel, 1991 NLRB GCM LEXIS 11 (Jan. 31, 1991). The NLRB held that an employer was allowed to discipline employees who made such statements, because it might otherwise have been liable under Title VII.

13. *Davis v. Monsanto Chem. Co.*, 858 F.2d 345, 350 (6th Cir. 1988)

14. *Dernovich v. City of Great Falls*, Mont. Hum. Rts. Comm'n No. 9401006004 (Nov. 28, 1995).

15. *Rippey v. Danzig*, appeal no. 01983065, 1999 WL 302415, (Apr. 27).

16. *Olivant v. Department of Environmental Protection*, 1999 WL 450427 (N.J. Adm. Apr. 12).

17. U.S. Dep't of Labor, *Sexual Harassment: Know Your Rights* (1994).

18. Seattle Human Rights Dep't, Building for Equality 1 (1996).

19. Town of Hanson, Massachusetts Board of Selectmen, Policy Statement: "Sexual Harassment is Unacceptable Conduct in the Workplace and Will Not Be Condoned or Tolerated," Nov. 1997.

20. "Genevieve Buck, Sexual Harassment Rulings Hit Close to Home," *Chicago Tribune*, July 17, 1998, at C5.

21. Hector D. Cantu, "Something Funny About 'Mary'? Zip Your Lips," *Dallas Morning News*, July 24, 1998, at 1C.

22. See, e.g., Carol Smith, "Sexual Harassment Arena Is Broadened, Binding Employers," *Seattle Post-Intelligencer*, Oct. 30, 1998, at B1.

23. *Schwapp v. Town of Avon*, 118 F.3d 106, 111-12 (2nd Cir. 1997).

24. See *Taylor v. Metzger*, 152 N.J. 490 (single racial slur); *Leonard v. Metropolitan Life Insurance Co.*, 318 N.J. Super. 337 (App. Div. 1999) (two remarks about plaintiff's diabetes); *Reid v. O'Leary*, No. CIV. A. 96-401, 1996 WL 411494 (D.D.C. July 15, 1996) (single epithet);

Yabuki v. Department of the Army, EEOC Req. No. 05920778 (June 4, 1993) (single incident containing a personal abusive statement and a negative comment concerning Japanese people); *Nguyen v. Runyon*, EEOC Appeal No. 01963721, 1997 WL 40256 (Jan. 22, 1997) (single incident of "supervisor [speaking to plaintiff] in a disrespectful manner, ma[king] threatening gestures and insult[ing] him by using racial slurs in front of co-workers"); *Gamboa v. United States Postal Service*, EEOC Request No. 05890633 (Aug. 31, 1989) (single incident in which hearing-disabled complainant asked a supervisor who was speaking to move so she could read his lips, and the supervisor responded by "harshly order[ing complainant] to move to another area" and then "told her to move again," which led complainant to feel humiliated); *Daniels v. Essex Group, Inc.*, 937 F.2d 1264, 1274 n.4 (7th Cir. 1991) (stating that a single instance of racial harassment can be "severe or pervasive" enough). See also Maxine H. Neuhauser & Mark D. Lurie, "Extending the Scope of the Law Against Discrimination," *N.J.L.J.*, June 7, 1999, at 32 ("Even one angry outburst, ill-advised joke or insensitive comment holds the potential for litigation liability [under New Jersey law].").

25. 1999 WL 333406 (1st Cir. May 12).
26. *DeAngelis v. El Paso Mun. Police Officers' Ass'n*, 51 F.3d 591 (5th Cir. 1995).
27. Deborah Epstein, "Can a 'Dumb Ass Woman' Achieve Equality in the Workplace? Running the Gauntlet of Hostile Environment Harassing Speech," 84 *Geo. L.J.* 399, 417-18 (1996).
28. See, e.g., *Gallagher v. Delaney*, 139 F.3d 338, 347 (2nd Cir. 1998) (even though it was "doubtful that the allegations rise to the level of a hostile work environment ...reasonable jurors might disagree"; because "an Article III judge is not a hierophant of social graces [, e]valuation of ambiguous acts such as those revealed by the potential evidence in this case presents an issue for the jury").
29. *NAACP v. Button*, 371 U.S. 415, 437 (1963).
30. *Bissell v. Kaleidoscope, Inc.*, charge no. 1987CF3584, 1991 WL 698599 (Ill. Hum. Rts. Comm'n).
31. Mark I. Schickman, "Sexual Harassment: The Employer's Role in Prevention," *Compleat Lawyer*, Winter 1996, at 24-25, 28.
32. *Baggett v. Bullitt*, 377 U.S. 360, 372 (1964).

33.   117 S. Ct. 2329, 2344-46 (1997).

34.   Deborah Epstein, "Can a 'Dumb Ass Woman' Achieve Equality in the Workplace? Running the Gauntlet of Hostile Environment Harassing Speech," 84 *Geo. L.J.* 399, 419-20 (1996).

35.   Maryland Commission on Human Relations, *Preventing Sexual Harassment: A Fact Sheet for Employees* (1994).

36.   Phillip M. Perry, "Avoid Costly Lawsuits for Sexual Harassment," *Law Prac. Mgmt.*, Apr. 1992, at 18; see also Barry A. Hartstein & Thomas M. Wilde, "The Broadening Scope of Harassment in the Workplace," *Employee Rel. L.J.*, Mar. 22, 1994, at 639.

37.   Geanne P. Rosenberg, "Watch What You Say, or Be Ready to Pay," *Investor's Bus. Daily*, Nov. 6, 1996, at A1.

38.   Dean J. Schaner & Melissa M. Erlemeier, "When Faith and Work Collide: Defining Standards for Religious Harassment in the Workplace," *Employee Rel. L.J.*, June 1, 1995, at 7.

39.   Daryl Strickland, "Board Game Helps Workers Learn Do's, Don'ts of Sexual Harassment," *Seattle Times*, Mar. 1, 1996, at E1 (describing and quoting from the game). The game sells to employers for $600 for five copies.

40.   EEOC, Enforcement Guidance: Vicarious Employer Liability for Unlawful Harassment by Supervisors pt. V.C.1.a (following footnote reference 58) (June 18, 1999).

41.   Leanora Minai, "St. Pete Beach Cracks Down on Harassment, Sexual Humor," *St. Petersburg Times*, Feb. 8, 1997, at 4B.

42.   Leavenworth, Kansas personnel policy No. III-6 ("Sexual Harassment Policy") (1997).

43.   Cheryl Johnson, "The Latest in Offensive Workplace Items? A New Yorker Cartoon," *Minn. Star. Trib.*, Jan. 18, 1994, at 3B.

44.   Nat Hentoff, "Sexual Harassment by Francisco Goya," *Wash. Post*, Dec. 27, 1991, at A21.

45.   Jennifer Goode, "It's Art vs. Sexual Harassment," *Tennessean*, Mar. 1, 1996, at 1A.

46.   Catherine Trevison, "Court to Decide if Nude is Naughty," *Tennessean*, Feb. 13, 1997, at 1B.

47.   Nat Hentoff, "A 'Pinup' of His Wife," *Wash. Post*, June 5, 1993, at A21.

48.   *Turner v. Barr*, 806 F. Supp. 1025, 1029 (D.D.C. 1992).

49.   *Snell v. Suffolk County*, 611 F. Supp. 521, 531-32 (E.D.N.Y. 1985).

50. *Harris v. International Paper Co.*, 765 F. Supp. 1509, 1527 (D. Me. 1991).

51. *Sharpe v. Robert S. Biscan & Co.*, No. 3:94-0567, slip op. at 17 (M.D. Tenn. Dec. 1, 1995).

52. *Robinson v. Jacksonville Shipyards, Inc.*, 760 F. Supp. 1486, 1542 (M.D. Fla. 1991).

53. Brief Amicus Curiae of 80 Individual Law Professors and Lawyers on Behalf of Plaintiff-Appellant and Cross-Appellee at 21, *Robinson v. Jacksonville Shipyards, Inc.* (No. 91-3655) (11th Cir. Apr. 27, 1992).

54. *Stroehmann Bakeries, Inc. v. Local 776, International Brotherhood of Teamsters*, 969 F.2d 1436, 1442 (3d Cir. 1992) (employer has "obligation to prevent and sanction sexual harassment in the workplace"); *Newsday, Inc. v. Long Island Typographical Union*, 915 F.2d 840, 845 (2d Cir. 1990) (employer has "legal duty to eliminate sexual harassment in the workplace"); *Munn v. City of Savannah*, 906 F. Supp. 1577, 1584 (S.D. Ga. 1995) (employer has duty to prevent harassment); 29 C.F.R. § 1604.11(f) (1996) ("Prevention is the best tool for the elimination of sexual harassment.").

55. Thomas C. Grey, "How to Write a Speech Code Without Really Trying: Reflections on the Stanford Experience," 29 *U.C. Davis L. Rev.* 891, 907 (1996).

56. 29 C.F.R. § 1604.11(f) (1996) (the regulation covering sexual harassment).

Workplace Harassment and the First Amendment: A Reply to Professor Volokh

David Benjamin Oppenheimer

When the government assesses damages against an employer based on the speech of the employer's employees, the employer is entitled to the protections of the First Amendment to the United States Constitution. On this proposition Professor Volokh and I are in complete agreement. We disagree, however, on the question of whether current developments in the law of workplace harassment conflict with the right of free speech. As he has eloquently stated, he believes that recent decisions under Title VII of the 1964 Civil Rights Act [1] threaten our Constitutional right to be free from state interference with the expression of ideas.[2] I believe that Title VII law, while prohibiting much workplace harassment, has steered clear of any Constitutional violation. While Title VII imposes tort liability [3] on employers for sex and race-based on-the-job harassment, our traditional rules protecting freedom of speech remain intact.

Private employers are, of course; generally free to impose restrictions on employee speech without governmental interference. Thus, employers may insist that employees treat one another with courtesy and respect and refrain from uttering unwanted slurs, suggestive comments, or rude statements; such rules imposed privately by employers are of no interest to the state. The problem arises when employees who have been banned by harassment suffered on the job sue employers who have chosen to refrain from enacting or enforcing such rules. The state's involvement, and thus the concern of Constitutional law, is the enactment of legal standards and the operation of a legal system in which employers are ordered by the state to compensate employees injured by workplace harassment. Where the harassment is verbal, rather than physical, the state is in the position of restricting verbal conduct[4]; the potential for interference with freedom of expression is obvious.

Despite the potential for Constitutional infirmity, in reality employers are well protected. To begin with, Title VII prohibits workplace harassment only under circumstances where the harassment has verifiable effects on employees.[5] Title VII broadly prohibits employers from discriminating against individuals with respect to the conditions of their employment based on their race, color, religion, sex, or national origin. The Supreme Court has interpreted the Act to prohibit conduct, including solely verbal conduct creating a hostile work environment, only when the plaintiff can establish five elements. The elements are (1) that the conduct was unwelcome; (2) that it consisted of physical or verbal acts; (3) that the acts constituted sexual or racial intimidation, ridicule or insult; (4) that the acts were sufficiently severe or pervasive to alter the conditions of the plaintiff's employment, creating a work environment that the plaintiff subjectively experienced as abusive; and (5) that a reasonable person in the plaintiff's position would also have experienced the acts as sufficiently severe or pervasive to alter the conditions of his or her employment, creating an abusive work environment.[6] If any of these elements are absent, the government will not assess liability and damages.

It is, of course, axiomatic that the right of free speech is not absolute. Some speech simply falls outside the purview of the First Amendment. Obscenity, for example, is not protected. Blackmail, extortion, and fraud are carried out through words alone, yet those words have no Constitutional shield. The same is true for "fighting words"—words used to provoke violence. Some commentators describe these as categories of "no-value" speech. Workplace harassment, like fighting words, is conduct, or language, which provokes actual injury, in the form of an injurious and verifiably altered work environment. The wrong is not simply in engaging in the harassment, but in causing foreseeable injury to another—injury not only subjectively experienced by the plaintiff, but objectively injurious to a reasonable person. Unwelcome conduct, whether words or deeds, which constitutes intimidation, ridicule or insult and is objectively sufficiently severe or pervasive to alter the conditions of its workplace, making it abusive to employees, may be properly regarded as outside the protection of the First Amendment.

Moreover, even if verbal workplace harassment is entitled to some Constitutional protection under the First Amendment, protected speech is subject to government regulation. Some speech is considered to be sufficiently low in value that it may be regulated, although not altogether banned. The key to determining whether speech is "low-value" is a balancing test, in which the Court asks both how harmful the speech is, and how important it may be in promoting core democratic values.[7] Under this reasoning, speech deemed "indecent" might be banned from the airwaves at certain hours. During union election campaigns, the time, place and manner, and even the content of speech by employers may be regulated; certain speech during campaigns is simply prohibited. Persons deemed "captive audiences" such as public transit riders, school students, medical patients and persons enjoying the privacy of their own homes may be protected from unwanted speech, even when the speech is political, thus implicating the core values of the First Amendment.[8]

Women and minority group members in the workplace are a captive audience in much the same way as school students, medical patients, or employees facing a union election. For example, unlike the targets of street harassment, they cannot simply walk away from on-the-job harassment. They look to their employer to protect them, just as they expect protection from other unsafe working conditions. Having forfeited a certain amount of autonomy in exchange for their employment, they take in exchange an increased expectation of protection. It is because of this exchange that the law of torts describes the employer/employee relationship as a "special relationship"—one in which the employer has a higher duty of care than would a stranger.[9]

Professor Volokh complains, "One should explain just where the line is drawn between those captives who can't be protected and those who *can*." One response is that the Court has supplied that answer in *Gissell* and the cases that follow it, right through to the dicta in *R.A.V.* Workers may be protected from harmful speech within the workplace when it interferes with an important governmental policy, such as labor peace or equal employment opportunity. But to some extent Constitutional analysis simply doesn't permit such bright lines as Professor Volokh would impose. It is in the very nature of balancing competing important interests that the lines may be hard to draw. What is easy is the conclusion that the kind of speech condemned in Title VII decisions—speech that creates a sufficiently hostile or offensive work environment that it interferes with the right of women and minority group members to equality in the workplace—belongs in the category of no-value or low-value speech

Furthermore, the First Amendment is not the only Constitutional protection at stake when we consider the legitimacy of governmental regulation of workplace harassment. It is a sad truth that women and minority employees stand in much the same position as patients at an abortion clinic. Their rights are imperiled and require the state's protection. For African Americans and other racial and ethnic minority employees in particular, there is a well-established Constitutional, as well as a statutory, source of their right to be free from harassment. The Thirteenth Amendment, prohibiting slavery, has long been recognized to protect against not only slavery itself but also the badges and incidents of slavery,[10] such as racial discrimination in employment.[11] The prohibition applies not only to the States but to private persons as well. As a result, racial and ethnic minority group members have a particularly strong entitlement to the state's protection from harassment.[12]

Considering these traditional and well-recognized limitations, governmental regulation of workplace harassment should not be seen as breaking new ground. There are persuasive arguments that racial and sexual harassment, like obscenity and fighting words, is outside the scope of the First Amendment's protection; that even if harassment is entitled to protection in some environments, it may be banned in the workplace; and that countervailing Constitutional interests in protecting minority workers justify regulating harassment on the job.

Nor should the government's regulation of workplace harassment appear extraordinary. That the state is entitled to regulate such conduct as tortuous, even when it takes the form of speech, is well established. Many torts empower the government to assess liability for verbal conduct. The tort of assault, for example, can be carried out through words alone. A threat of violence, accompanied by the capacity to carry it out, is sufficient to impose liability even where no physical touching occurs. Nonetheless the state may award damages against the assault tortfeasor without violating his or her First Amendment rights. The same is true of the torts of intentional infliction of emotional distress, invasion of privacy, defamation, and misrepresentation.[13] In each case the defendants' speech alone may properly be the basis of a finding of liability.[14]

These traditional expressive torts are not entirely outside the protections of the First Amendment. Each is protected from abuse by the shield of Constitutional privilege.[15] As a result; the tortfeasor accused of a verbal tort is entitled to a requirement that the plaintiff prove actual fault and actual damages; strict liability may not be imposed, nor may damages be presumed. As I demonstrate below, the Supreme Court and Circuit Courts of Appeals have applied these requirements to limit the effect of hostile work environment law under Title VII, just as they have to defamation, invasion of privacy, and infliction of emotional distress.

It bears repeating that to prove a violation of Title VII the plaintiff must prove a good deal more than "mere words." She must prove that she suffered an actual injury and that a reasonable person would have similarly experienced the wrongful conduct as injurious. Despite these protections, Professor Volokh is concerned that over-careful employers will prohibit conduct, which falls outside the scope of Title VII, and thus censor speech that could not be regulated by the government. If we examine the practice of employment discrimination law, however, a different picture emerges.

Courts assessing Title VII workplace harassment claims consistently hold plaintiffs to a heavy burden in hostile work environment cases involving verbal harassment. Four cases from the U.S. Circuit Courts of Appeals illustrate just how difficult it is for a plaintiff to prove a verbal harassment case, and thus how well protected employers are from actions that abuse their First Amendment rights. These cases fall into two categories—those that find the harassment insufficiently pervasive to have affected the work environment, and those that find the employer insufficiently aware of the harassment to be held responsible.

An example of the first category is the decision in *Hicks v. Gates Rubber Company*,[16] a verbal harassment case in which the Tenth Circuit considered an appeal following summary judgment for the employer. An employee who referred to African Americans as "niggers" and "coons" supervised the plaintiff, a black security guard. In a comment directed specifically at the plaintiff, he referred to "lazy niggers and Mexicans." Another security guard referred to the plaintiff as "Buffalo Butt." The circuit court affirmed the district court's finding that the harassment was "essentially occasional and incidental," not raising to the level of pervasive harassment required to trigger a Title VII violation.[17]

Similarly, in *Rabidue v. Osceola Refining Co.*[18] the Sixth Circuit affirmed a defense judgment in a sexual harassment case in which there was substantial verbal harassment. Douglas Henry, a supervisor, with the knowledge of senior management, harassed Rabidue. The court described Henry as "an extremely vulgar and crude individual who customarily made obscene comments about women generally, and, on occasion, directed such obscenities to the plaintiff." He "routinely referred to women as 'whores,' 'cunt,' 'pussy' and 'tits.' " Regarding the plaintiff, "Henry specifically remarked 'all that bitch needs is a good lay' and called her 'fat ass.'" Nonetheless, the court found that the evidence did not demonstrate that Henry's "vulgarity substantially affected the totality of the workplace."

In a hostile work environment case, even when the harassment is found to be sufficiently pervasive to affect the conditions of employment, if the employer has not clearly been notified of the wrongful conduct it will escape liability.[19] For example, in *Kolcher v. Rosa and Sullivan Appliance Center*,[20] the Second Circuit rejected the plaintiff's argument that her employer was vicariously liable for harassment committed by its store manager under the law of agency. Store manager Herbert Trageser had sexually harassed the plaintiff and another woman employee, both of whom he directly supervised. He repeatedly commented on their breasts and other parts of their bodies and pretended to masturbate and ejaculate onto them. Although the court agreed that this conduct was actionable against Trageser, it refused to hold the employer responsible unless the plaintiffs could demonstrate that the employer failed to take adequate steps after being made aware of the harassment.

The First Circuit reached a similar result in *Klessens v. United States Postal Service*.[21] Klessens testified that shortly after she started working for the Postal Service, a co-worker began making sexually explicit remarks to her about her body and told her "if I don't get laid I'm going to take hostages." Another co-worker made sexually lewd statements to her, telling her she was a "nice piece of ass" despite her "small tits" and told her at length of his own sexual "exploits." She complained to her supervisor, who responded by making further "jokes" with her, in front of one of her antagonists, also about "getting laid." She then complained to her supervisor's supervisor, who declined to assist her but commented "OK, Bill has done this before, he wrote a letter to another female that worked there, saying that he wanted to slip his tongue so far up her ass...." The district court found the plaintiff failed to prove the existence of an offensive or abusive work environment. The circuit court found that this was a "close" question, but further found that Klessens clearly failed to notify the Postal Service of her harassment, thus requiring the dismissal of her claim.

Klessens and *Kotcher* illustrate an important distinction between hostile work environment claims and quid pro quo claims. In a quid pro quo case, where an employee's employment status is conditioned on her acceptance of sexual demands, employers are held strictly liable for the acts of their supervisors, even when the employer itself has done nothing wrong.[22] By contrast, in hostile work environment cases, the prevailing view is that employers should only be subjected to direct liability; vicarious (or strict) liability has been rejected. The justification for the distinction is based on an interpretation of the law of agency that only treats supervisors as agents, thus capable of binding their principals, if they are top management officials or if exercising their authority to hire, fire or promote subordinate employees. Although I believe this division is ill advised as a matter of agency law, it does have the effect of providing employers with substantial added protection from liability for verbal hostile work environment harassment.

The rejection of strict liability in hostile work environment cases, and the requirement that the harassment be sufficiently pervasive to actually have an effect on the conditions of employment, satisfy two of the three requirements mandated by the Supreme Court for defamation liability in *Gertz v. Robert Welch*, Inc. In *Gertz* the Court held that despite the protections provided by the First Amendment, injurious speech, even when it concerns an issue of public or general interest, might be the basis of civil liability.   But in order to protect the right of free expression, the Court limited liability by requiring findings of falsehood, fault and injury; strict liability in cases subject to a Constitutional privilege is not permitted, nor may any liability be assessed in the absence of proof of injury. Professor Volokh concedes "if harassment law confined itself to false statements of fact or to other similarly unprotected forms of speech [such as threats or obscenity or fighting words]. I'd have little difficulty with it. In other words, he has no objections to the existing exceptions, but would resist adding an analogous exception for harassment unless it was premised on false statements. Yet the falsity requirement of *Gertz* merely shifts the burden of proof of defamation law's defense of truth; it is the requirements of actual fault and injury that effectively protect the free speech interests in defamation cases.[23]

The *Meritor* case and the four cases from the Circuit Courts of Appeals illustrate how the second and third prongs of the *Gertz* rule have been applied, in effect, to verbal workplace harassment cases. The predicate of actual injury is satisfied by the requirement that the plaintiff prove the harassment was sufficiently severe or pervasive that it actually altered the conditions of her employment. Rejecting the imposition of strict liability on the employer requires fault. By satisfying the requirements of *Gertz*, the current law of hostile work environment harassment meets any legitimate concerns about the effect of Title VII on free expression. These cases also illustrate how difficult it is for a plaintiff to prevail in a workplace harassment case and how well protected employers are from non-meritorious harassment actions. Further, they demonstrate the courts' failure of vigilance on the issue; in each case liability could have been assessed without any impact on the right of free expression. They may thus help explain why on-the-job harassment continues to be a common problem, affecting many African Americans and other minority group members, and by some estimates over half of all working women.[24]

Professor Volokh relies on a few well-chosen stories and portions of a few district court and state court decisions to illustrate his arguments. Some of his anecdotes are distressingly incomplete. Consider, for example, his two illustrations concerning religious harassment. The first, the *Brown* case,[25] was largely concerned with the question of whether a Jewish employee was terminated because of his religion; the findings of harassment occupied a single paragraph. The second, the *Sapp 's Realty* case,[26] concerned an employee either fired or constructively discharged from her job[27] after she complained that her supervisor was constantly trying to convert her to his religion and constantly demeaning other religions.[28] In both of these cases the principle purpose of the evidence of harassment was to prove the motivation for the termination.

While I agree with Professor Volokh that the Murfreesboro City Hall story is outrageous, disputes over displays of public art pre-date concern about workplace harassment by many years. The censorship zealots will always find some rationale for their complaints, but the suggestion that Title VII required censorship of the painting is absurd. Neither the city attorney nor Professor Volokh can point to any court decision under Title VII in which an employer was found liable for displaying artwork. The closest he comes, in a case that merits further discussion, is the *Jacksonville Shipyards* case.[29]

In *Jacksonville Shipyards*, three women craft workers testified about pervasive on-the-job sexual harassment. The harassment included posting many pictures of nude women, in some cases engaged in intercourse or masturbation, taken from various magazines (*Playboy, Penthouse, Hustler, Cheri, Chic*); posting calendars depicting nude women displaying their genitals; leaving pictures of nude women at the women's work areas; making sexual statements to and about the women employees ("the more you lick it, the harder it gets," "black women taste like sardines"); making requests of them that they disrobe; solicitations for sexual acts ("lick me you whore dog bitch"); unwanted touching of various parts of their bodies (including the breasts); posting "Men Only" signs at the women's work areas; and failing to respond seriously to sexual harassment complaints (demanding that a woman apologize for using profanity in her complaint, responding to a complaint by putting an arm around the complainant and saying "Let me blow in your ear and I'll take care of anything that comes up," and demanding an apology be accepted as a resolution. The male workers performing traditionally male jobs vastly outnumbered the women; the ratio varied from 2 out of 960, to 7 out of 1,017. The shipyard had a longstanding policy of prohibiting employees from bringing newspapers or magazines to the workplace and of prohibiting the posting of any political or commercial materials. It made an exception, however, for posting depictions of nude women or possessing magazines which included depictions of nude women.

Plaintiff Lois Robinson, a welder, had missed many days of work due to the harassment, but because she could not specify which days were lost, her recovery was limited to $1.00 in nominal damages. It was in this context that the Court ordered the company to adopt an anti-harassment policy, which included a ban on sexually suggestive pictures in the work place, essentially requiring it to treat such materials in the same manner as it treated other pictures.

One may argue that this district court injunction was overbroad. But it is worth keeping in mind that it is the most draconian court decision under Title VII that Professor Volokh can muster. If this is the worst he can come up with, we should ask whether there is really a problem serious enough to require dismantling a significant portion of the 1964 Civil Rights Act.

In sum, Professor Volokh's concerns are not well founded. As applied by the courts. Title VII's prohibition on workplace harassment does not infringe on legitimate rights of free expression. And, given the high barriers imposed on Title VII plaintiffs, it should not have the effect of chilling permissible speech.

1. 42 U.S.C.A.§2000e -17 (West 1995).
2. See Eugene Volokh, "Thinking Ahead About Freedom of Speech and Hostile Work Environment," 17 *Berkeley J. Emp. & Lab. L.* 305 (1996).
3. For discussions of Title VII violations as torts, see *Price Waterhouse v. Hopkins*, 490 U.S. 228, 264 (1989) (O'Connor, J., concurring) (referring to Title VII as creating an employment tort); *Hirschfeld v. New Mexico Corrections Dep't*, 916 F.2d 572, 576 (10th Cir. 1990) (referring to sexual harassment as a tort). *Baker v. Weyerhaeuser Co.*, 903 F.2d 1342, 1346 (10th Cir. 1990) (same); *Miller v. Bank of America*, 600 F.2d 211, 213 (9th Cir. 1979) (same); Cheryl Kause Zemelman, "The After-Acquired Evidence Defense to Employment Discrimination Claims: The Privatization of Title VII and the Contours of Social Responsibility," 46 *Stan. L. Rev.* 175, 196 (1993) (discussing Title VII violations as tons); David B. Oppenheimer, "Negligent Discrimination," 141 *U. PA. L. Rev.* 899 (1993) (same); *Cf.* Gulian K. Hadfield, "Rational Women: A Test for Sex-Based Harassment," 83 *Cal.. L. Rev.* 1151, 1166 (criticizing current analysis of sexual harassment law as encouraging a "ton-like inquiry").
4. See *R.A.V. v. City of St. Paul*, 505 U.S. 377. 389-390 (1992) (dictum) (laws directed against conduct may be violated by words alone.) The Court points to Title VII and the EEOC's Guidelines on sexual harassment as an example of a permissible regulation of conduct (that incidentally sweeps up certain speech; the regulation is not impermissible because it is not directed at speech).
5. See *Harris v. Forklift Systems, Inc.* 114 S. Ct. 367 (1993).

6. *Harris*, 114 S. Ct. at 370; *Meritor Savings Bank v. Vinson*, 477 U.S. 57, 67 (1986).

7. *Young v. American Mini Theatre, Inc.*. 427 V.S 50, 62-63 (1976) (city may restrict location of "adult" book stores and theatres).

8. See *Lehman v. City of Shaker Heights*, 418 US. 298, 302 (1974), *Bethel School District v. Fraser*, 478 U.S. 675, 684 (1986), *Madsen v. Women's Health Center*, 114 S. Ct. 2516. 2526 (1994), *Frisby v. Schultz*, 487 U.S. 474, 484-485 (1988) (town ordinance completely banning picketing of residences not facially invalid under First Amendment).

9. Restatement (Second) of Agency § 492 (1957); *See. e.g.*, *Alcom v. Anbro Eng'g, Inc.*, 468 P.2d 216. 218-19 (Cal. 1970) (in permitting employee's action against employer for racial harassment by supervisor. California Supreme Court explains that "plaintiff's status as an employee should entitle him to a greater degree of protection from insult and outrage than if he were a stranger to defendants").

10. *Jones v. Alfred H. Mayer Co.*, 392 U.S. 409, 440 (1968).

11. *McDonald v. Santa Fe Trail Transp. Co.*, 427 U.S. 273, 288-290 (1976).

12. Professor Volokh and I disagree on the scope of the *Jones* decision. As I read it, it affirms the position that the Congress may prohibit the badges and incidents of slavery under the Thirteenth Amendment. While this does not operate as a "repeal" of the First Amendment, see Volokh, *supra* note 2. at 315. it does provide a heavy counter-balance when balancing First Amendment rights to engage in low value speech against Thirteenth Amendment rights to be free from racial discrimination.

13. See. e.g. *Hustler Magazine v. Falwell*, 485 U.S. 46 (1988) (permitting intentional infliction of emotional distress actions, but limiting them, at least in the case of public figures, to cases in which there is a false statement of fact made with actual malice.) *See also* Restatement (Second) of Torts § 46 (intentional infliction of emotional distress), § 652A (invasion of privacy), 8 558 (defamation). § 525 (misrepresent-ation).

14. A number of early workplace harassment cases were brought as common law tort claims, well before a cause of action under Title VII was recognized. See *Alcoro v. Anbro Eng'g, Inc.*, 468 P.2d 216, 218-219 (Cat. 1970) (employee brought intentional infliction of emotional distress claim against employer for racial harassment on the job), *Argarwall v. Johnson*. 603 P.2d 58 (Cal. 1979) (employee

racially harassed in his employment brought action for defamation and intentional infliction of emotional distress); *Poid v. Revion. Inc..* 734 P.2d 580 (Ariz. 1987) (employee sexually harassed on the job brought action for assault and battery and intentional infliction of emotional distress). *Cf. Monge v. Beebe Rubber Co.*, 316 A.2d 549 (N.H. 1974) (employee terminated in retaliation for refusing supervisor's sexual advances brought action for breach of contract); *Fisher v. Carrouiel Motor Hotel, Inc.*, 424 S.W.2d 627 (Tex. 1967) (African American restaurant patron removed from buffet line because of his race brought action for assault and battery).

15. See *Gertz v. Robert Welch. Inc.*, 418 U.S. 323. 347-350 (1974); *Hustler,* 485 U.S. 46 (1981).

16. 833 F.2d 1406 (10th Cir. 1987).

17. The court reversed the grant of summary judgment on a related claim of sexual harassment on evidence that there had been extensive unwanted physical touching

18. 805 F. 2d 611 (6th Cir. 1986).

19. See J. Hoult Veikeike, "Notice Liability in Employment Discrimination Law," 81 *Virginia L. Rev.* 273 (1995). As I have previously written. I believe the justifications usually offered for this rule are unsatisfactory. See David B. Oppenheimer, "Exacerbating the Exasperating: Title VII Liability of Employers For Sexual Harassment Committed by Their Supervisors," 81 *Cornell L. Rev.* 101 (1995).

20. 957 F. 2d 59 (2nd Cir. 1992).

21. No. 93-1823, 66 Fair Empl. Prac. Cas. (BNA) l630 (1st. Cir. 1994) (LEXIS, Labor Library, BNA LRR Fair Employment Practice Cases ft. Vol. 1).

22. See *Meritor Savings Bank v. Vinson*, 477 U.S. 57, 72 (1986).

23. If the critical issue in harassment cases became the truth or falsehood of the harasser's speech, the supervisor in the *Rabidue* case could defend himself by proving that Ms. Rabidue really did need "a *good* lay." Such a test is patently ridiculous.

24. See Barbara A. Gutek, *Sex and the Workplace* 46 (1985) (reporting that 53.1% of working women have experienced sexual harassment), Alex Kozinski, *Foreword* to Barbara Lindemann & David D. Kadue, *Sexual Harassment in Employment Law* at v. (1992) (asserting that every woman who has spent substantial lime in the work force has been the object of sexual harassment).

25. *Brown Transportation Corp. v Commonwealth of Pennsylvania*, 578 A.2d 555 (Commonwealth Court 1990).
26. *Sapp's Realty, Ore. Comm'r of Bureau of Labor and Indus.*, Case No. 11-83 (Jan. 31, 1985).
27. When told she was fired, she responded that he couldn't fire her because she quit. The supervisor insisted she couldn't quit because she was fired. *Sapp's Reatly* at pp. 42-43.
28. For example, he told her that Catholic nuns were used as harems for priests, that the children of nuns were killed at birth, and that the Catholic Church was the devil, *id.* at 29.
29. *Robinson v. Jacksonville Shipyards, Inc..* 760 P. Supp. 1486, (M.D. Fla. 1991).

Men, Women, and Sex at Work

Caroline A. Forell and Donna M. Matthews

Is there such a thing, in life or in law, as reasonable people, or only men and women, with all their differences?

—Susan Estrich, "Rape"

The concept of a no gendered reasonable person is sometimes a non sequitur. The reasonable person assessing sex at work is a prime example. Psychology professors Barbara Gutek and Maureen O'Connor note that the prevalent view that men and women perceive sex in the workplace differently has "a basis in both common sense and empirical fact." These gendered perceptions have real consequences. Social science research, such as that conducted by Weiner and his colleagues, confirms what common sense tells us: sexual conduct in the workplace that many men view as harmless and enjoyable, is experienced by many women as harmful and degrading. Because of this discrepancy, it is simply unrealistic to believe that a truly genderless standard can be used for determining whether conduct is sufficiently egregious to justify liability. In practice, when asked to assess the conduct of an actor accused of creating a hostile sexual environment, the decision maker will either explicitly (reasonable man or reasonable woman) or implicitly (reasonable person) adopt a gendered perspective.

The 1991 Senate confirmation hearings for Supreme Court nominee Clarence Thomas highlighted the different perspectives of men and women. The hearings presented the fundamental problem of how to convince decision makers (ninety-eight male and two female senators) that conduct which many women view as sexual harassment merits serious consequences for the harasser. In the case of Clarence Thomas, the stakes were extremely high: life tenure on the most powerful court in the country. Not only sex but also race and politics shaped the perspectives brought to the hearings. Nevertheless, the conduct that Anita Hill described exemplifies the fault line between men and women's perspectives about what constitutes a hostile work environment. The hearings galvanized women around the issue of sexual harassment and gave new meaning to the phrase "they just don't get it."

Many of the senators hearing Hill's testimony believed that the conduct she described was not and should not be actionable as sexual harassment or discrimination, even if she was telling the truth. Nor did they think it should interfere with Thomas's confirmation. Senator John B. Breaux said, "I think the charges are *not of a sufficient nature* to either not support [Thomas] or delay the vote" (emphasis added). As Senator Paul Simon put it: "Many men were stunned to learn what women regard as sexual harassment. 'He didn't even touch her!' one of my Senate colleagues commented … when the issue first arose."

Some of these reasonable men did not believe a reasonable *person* would have found that Thomas's conduct created a hostile work environment. After all, it wouldn't have felt like sexual harassment to *them*.

Polls indicated that at first, male or female, black or white, a majority of Americans didn't believe Anita Hill's version of "he said/she said." This is not surprising; as Catharine MacKinnon in *Feminism Unmodified* points out, most people find it difficult to believe women's "accounts of sexual use and abuse by men," particularly by powerful men. Interestingly, a year after Thomas was confirmed as a member of the Supreme Court, polls showed that public perceptions had changed dramatically: more people believed Hill than Thomas. Setting aside the issue of credibility, if Anita Hill had brought a timely sexual harassment action against Clarence Thomas, and if she had been thought credible at the time, would *any* standard of care have assured that his conduct would be judged sufficiently severe and pervasive to constitute illegal sexual harassment? Only under a standard that explicitly considered female perspectives would Thomas's conduct likely be viewed as sufficiently egregious to merit liability. Applying a reasonable woman standard, by requiring decision makers to consider how pressuring a subordinate for dates and subjecting her to graphic sexual stories is disrespectful and intimidating, enables them to comprehend the harm in such conduct.

The Evolution of Hostile Environment Sexual Harassment

Sexual harassment's recent appearance and rapid development as a legal claim is more her-story than history. Men have sexually harassed women for thousands of years, but the conduct wasn't given a name until 1975, when a group of feminists in Ithaca, New York, held a meeting called "Speak-Out on Sexual Harassment." It took years of concerted effort by feminist lawyers and clients to establish a legal identity and remedy for such conduct. The breakthrough came in 1976, when the federal circuit for the District of Columbia heard two cases about retaliation against a female employee for refusing her supervisor's sexual advances. The court held in both cases that this was actionable sex discrimination under Title VII of the Civil Rights Act. Before these two path-breaking decisions, punishing women workers who rejected sexual advances did not constitute employment discrimination on the basis of sex.

In 1979, Catharine MacKinnon published her influential book *Sexual Harassment of Working Women*, in which she defined sexual harassment as "the unwanted imposition of sexual requirements in the context of a relationship of unequal power." In MacKinnon's view, the power disparities between employer and employee and men and women lie at the core of sexual harassment. Her book treats sexual harassment as sex discrimination and outlines two basic forms: *quid pro quo* and hostile work environment. In the twenty years since MacKinnon's book was published, courts around the world, including the U.S. Supreme Court, have adopted her views and categories concerning sexual harassment.

The courts first recognized *quid pro quo* sexual harassment, which involves sexual coercion related to the terms or conditions of employment: offering rewards for granting sexual favors or threatening punishment for refusal. In the breakthrough cases, the plaintiffs lost jobs or other tangible job benefits when they refused to submit to their supervisors' sexual advances. After the first cases a consensus gradually arose, finding that *quid pro quo* harassment is unreasonable, harmful, and discriminatory. Thus, in most *quid pro quo* cases unreasonableness and injury are easily established, no matter which standard of care or whose point of view is adopted. In 1998 the U.S. Supreme Court decided *Burlington Industries, Inc. v. Ellerth,* holding that because tangible economic harm is involved, employer liability for *quid pro quo* sexual harassment is vicarious and strict—if the plaintiff proves *quid pro quo* sexual harassment, the employer is liable.

Courts took longer to recognize the more controversial hostile environment sexual harassment as a form of discrimination. Hostile environment sexual harassment is sex-based conduct that interferes with a person's job performance, even if it has no tangible or economic job consequences, and even if the interference is unintentional. Supreme Court Justice Ruth Bader Ginsberg in *Harris v. Forklift Systems, Inc.* has described this form of harassment simply as "discriminatory conduct [that makes] it more difficult to do the job." It may involve purely sexual conduct (e.g., groping breasts or pressuring for dates) or purely sexist/antiwoman conduct (e.g., saying, "You're a woman, what do you know") but often involves both. As the reaction to Anita Hill's allegations demonstrated, there is little consensus about what constitutes hostile environment sexual harassment. Therefore, unlike *quid pro quo* cases, perspective often controls the outcome.

Hostile environment sexual harassment did not emerge as a recognized claim until the early 1980s. Its status remained uncertain until 1986, when the Supreme Court's first sexual harassment case, *Meritor Savings Bank v. Vinson*, recognized hostile work environment as a form of sex discrimination. The Court noted that unwelcome sexualization of the work environment, as long as it was "sufficiently severe or pervasive 'to alter the conditions of [the victim's] employment and create an abusive working environment,' is actionable sex discrimination" under Title VII. Furthermore, the Court noted that if the conduct has that effect, liability can be found even if the actor did not intend to sexually harass the victim.

The harassing conducts alleged in *Meritor*, which included multiple instances of rape, was clearly intentional and egregious. Once the Court recognized hostile work environment as a legal claim, the *Meritor* conduct created an obviously abusive work environment—under any standard. Consequently, the Court did not address whose perspective or what standard determines whether someone has "creat[ed] an intimidating, hostile, or offensive working environment," or even what kind of injury must be proved.

However, most hostile work environment claims are not as clear-cut as *Meritor*. Usually, alleged harassers assert that they did not intend to sexually harass the target; plaintiffs respond that the behavior had the *effect* of creating a hostile environment, regardless of *intent*. In these cases, the standard of care applied often determines the outcome. The issue of whether the conduct was "sufficiently severe or pervasive" to make it unreasonable requires a normative assessment of severity and pervasiveness about which men and women may, and often do, differ.

The Supreme Court has continued to play a crucial role in the development of hostile environment sexual harassment. In 1993 the Court decided *Harris v. Forklift Systems, Inc.*, which focused on what kind of harm must be shown. *Harris* is important in part because most of the abusive conduct at issue was *sexist*, not sexual. Much of the harassment women experience is not sexual as such but it is sex-based, which has tended to get lost in the common perception of what "sexual harassment" means. A better term for the discriminatory conduct would be *sex-based harassment*, as Professor Vicki Schultz sets out in her article "Reconceptualizing Sexual Harassment." However, the Supreme Court continues to use the term *sexual harassment*, so we do too.

Justice Sandra Day O'Connor's opinion for the unanimous Court in *Harris* declared: "So long as the environment *would reasonably be perceived, and is perceived,* as hostile or abusive, ... there is no need for it also to be psychologically injurious" (emphasis added). By making clear that neither tangible nor psychological harm was required, the *Harris* Court made the reasonableness of the conduct the critical issue. However, the Court was silent about whether reasonableness can be explicitly gendered.

The Court issued another unanimous decision, *Oncale v. Sundowner Offshore Services, Inc.*, in 1998, which appeared to endorse a standard of care that assesses the alleged harasser's conduct from the perspective of the injured party. Justice Antonin Scalia, writing for the Court, held that male-on-male heterosexual sexual harassment creates a viable claim under Title VII if the plaintiff proves that the harassment occurred because of his sex. He noted that "the objective severity of harassment should be judged from the perspective of a reasonable person in the plaintiff's position, considering 'all the circumstances.'"

If the phrase "in the plaintiff's position" includes gender as part of his or her position, or if gender is intended to be included by "all the circumstances," then Justice Scalia's standard might substantively equate to a reasonable man standard when the injured party is male and a reasonable woman standard when the injured party is female. This interpretation is especially plausible in light of his emphasis on the "because of such individual's ... sex" requirement in Title VII, and his additional statement that all sexual harassment cases require "careful consideration of the social context in which the particular behavior ... is experienced by its target."

That the Court might find a woman-based standard appropriate when the target in a hostile environment sexual harassment suit is female represents tremendous progress. However, we believe the law must go further to achieve equality and justice for all. [T]he reasonable woman standard should apply in all cases of hostile environment sexual harassment, regardless of the gender of either party.

Why Courts Should Adopt the Reasonable Woman Standard

Applying a reasonable woman standard in hostile environment sexual harassment cases alters expectations of both legal and employment decision makers about sexual and sexist conduct in the workplace. The more male dominated the workplace, the more expectations change. Through the reasonable woman standard, our legal system can better achieve its important goals, including reducing the harm people inflict on others, compensating those harmed, and achieving substantive equality for all Americans. For claims of sexual harassment, the reasonable woman standard is a better vehicle than other standards for achieving these goals.

Working women are sexually harassed far more often than working men, and men are far more likely to sexually harass other workers. In part this can be attributed to the tendency of men to view a wider range of women's workplace behavior as sexual and welcoming, and therefore to assume they have permission to respond sexually. As psychology professor Barbara Gutek notes in *Sex and the Workplace*, "men [are] more likely than women to label any given behavior as sexual. Thus a normal business lunch seems to be labeled a 'date' by some men just because the luncheon partner is a woman."

Another reason women are sexually harassed at work more often than men is that traditional views of masculinity encourage dominating conduct—the exercise of power over someone else—and men often use sex as a means of asserting dominance. This explains why, if there are no women in the workplace, other men may be sexualized—treated like women—despite all the parties asserting heterosexuality. As Catharine MacKinnon argued in a "friend of the court" (amicus) brief in *Oncale*, the 1998 Supreme Court case concerning a man who had been sexually assaulted by his all-male coworkers: "Oncale's attackers were asserting male dominance through imposing sex on a man with less power. Men who are sexually assaulted are ... feminized: made to serve the function and play the role customarily assigned to women as men's social inferiors."

In addition, men may sexually harass women more often because women's typically subordinate positions in the workplace tend to sexualize them. According to the *Oxford Dictionary of Quotations*, Henry Kissinger said, "power is the great aphrodisiac." For some male supervisors, having power over a female employee *makes* her sexy. A 1995 study by John Bargh and colleagues entitled "Attractiveness of the Underling" indicated that for men whose values make them likely to sexually harass women, having power over a woman enhances the sexual attraction. The aphrodisiacal quality of power also affects these men's perception: they interpret women subordinates' neutral or merely friendly actions as flirtations or seductive.

The sexual thrill of domination, rather than romantic feelings, frequently motivates a sexual harasser to abuse his power. As a rule, men possess social, organizational, and physical power over women. Thus, when people abuse power through sex, the person abused is usually a woman. For men, being supervised by a woman is a rare experience, while for women it is the norm to be supervised by a man. Even in such traditional "women's" work as primary and middle school teaching, principals and superintendents are usually men. In traditional "men's" work, such as construction or engineering, supervisors are almost certainly male and often are openly contemptuous of women workers.

Vicki Schultz, in her article "Reconceptualizing Sexual Harassment," provides another important reason why women are so frequently harassed in the workplace. In arguing that hostile environment should be viewed from a "competence-centered" paradigm, she asserts that harassment of women workers is not about sexuality as much as it is about "reclaim[ing] favored lines of work and work competence as masculine-identified turf—in the face of a threat posed by the presence of women (or lesser men) who seek to claim these prerogatives as their own." Schultz notes that the stakes are high for men:

> Motivated by both material considerations and equally powerful psychological ones, harassment provides a means for men to mark their jobs a male territory and to discourage any women who seek to enter. By keeping women in their place in the workplace, men secure superior status in the home, in the polity, and in the larger culture as well.

Women also suffer greater injury: they much more frequently lose their jobs or suffer other tangible work detriment as a result of sexual harassment. Studies of sexual harassment of men show that some sexual conduct that women find harmful men view as perhaps annoying but not upsetting. Expert witness Susan Fiske testified in *Robinson v. Jacksonville Shipyards* that "when sex comes into the workplace, women are profoundly affected ... in their ability to do their jobs." By contrast, Fiske notes that the effect of sexualization of the workplace is "vanishingly small" for men. According to Barbara Gutek in *Sex and the Workplace*, the men she surveyed reported "significantly more sexual touching than women" and were more likely "to view such encounters positively, to see them as fun and mutually entered." Men apparently suffer no work-related consequences of sexual behavior at work, although they report more sexual behavior both directed at them specifically and in the workplace atmosphere generally. Even sexual conduct that does not meet the existing standards for sexual harassment lowers women's job satisfaction, while it has little or no negative effect on men.

One reason for the gendered reactions to and experiences with sex in the workplace may be that women have more to fear from sex. In our society, women are usually the targets of sexual violence. Except in all-male environments—where some men are "treated like women"—it is women who are raped and sexually assaulted. Because sex can be dangerous for women, when a workplace becomes sexualized, women are more likely to feel discomfort, fear, humiliation, or anger.

Women also prefer to keep sex out of the workplace more than men do because, when sex and work are combined, women are the ones objectified. Sex-role spillover partly explains this: societal gender expectations that sexualize and objectify women and assume men are asexual subjects carry over into the workplace from the broader culture. In "Understanding Sexual Harassment at Work," Gutek found that when men view women as sex objects rather than as serious workers, it undermines the women's credibility and job satisfaction. For example, in an article by Marian Swerdlow, a woman rapid-transit system worker described her arrival in the male-dominated workplace and how she quickly became aware of what it meant to be a woman in that environment. Shortly after her arrival, she realized that "a woman in the crew room" had heretofore meant "something utterly forbidden, but more than that, something sexual ... a woman's presence in the workplace had already been defined as having, above all, a sexual connotation." As the woman transit worker put it:

> A new woman was immediately viewed sexually. The first information men sought about a new woman were her marital status, usually under the flimsy cover, "What does your husband think of you taking the job?" Our looks were the talk of the crewrooms. We were propositioned... endlessly.

This common experience of workingwomen highlights the need to impose a woman-based standard on workplace sexual behavior in order to foster equality. Sexual harassment makes women appear and feel unequal. As Kathryn Abrams notes in her article "Gender Discrimination and the Transformation of Workplace Norms," sexualized behavior in the workplace creates both directly and by implication a radical inequality:

A woman struggling to establish credibility in a setting in which she may not be, or may not feel, welcome, can be swept off balance by a reminder that she can be raped, fondled, or subjected to repeated sexual demands....Sexual inquiries, jokes, remarks, or innuendoes sometimes can raise the spectre of coercion, but they more predictably have the effect of reminding a woman that she is viewed as an object of sexual derision rather than a credible co-worker.... Treatment that sexualizes women workers prevents them from feeling, and prevents others from perceiving them, as equals in the workplace.

Sexual harassment in the workplace keeps women "in their place"—which is why sexual harassment is sex-based discrimination. Women are often economically vulnerable. U.S. Department of Labor statistics show that women are disproportionately represented among the working poor in our society. Women's economic vulnerability makes it harder to resist sexual harassment. Many women cannot afford to risk losing their jobs or job benefits by complaining about, or even resisting, harassment. Unless employers know that courts will impose liability for sexual conduct that women find unreasonable, and therefore have incentive to prevent it, working-class women will have to endure not only low pay and low status but also sexual harassment.

Even in professions that are not female dominated, women are often paid less than similarly situated men. In part this can be attributed to the additional burden sexual harassment imposes on women. Sexual harassment diminishes a woman's professional credibility. Women may miss more days of work or have greater difficulty doing their jobs because they are being harassed. This often results in poor job evaluations that negatively affect compensation and advancement. Leaving a job because of sexual harassment may make it harder for a woman to get an equivalent job, particularly if she filed a claim of sexual harassment—regardless of the legal outcome. And many women simply rule out working in certain male-dominated workplaces because sexist behavior and sexual hostility from supervisors and coworkers are virtually inevitable.

People in charge set the tone of the workplace, including the level of sexualization that is tolerated. Supervisors tend to accept what seems "reasonable" to them. This may include harassment that comes solely from coworkers. When a male employer or supervisor engages in harassment himself or turns a blind eye on peer harassment, women workers don't thrive professionally—they experience their difference from men as inequality. Unless norms that are respectful of women are imposed from the outside, this male gaze will control.

To assure equal opportunity for professional growth and achievement, women's view on sex in the workplace—that there should be less of it—should be adopted for all workplaces. Men should be held to a woman-defined standard of behavior based on how a woman would treat a coworker. This does not mean that sex must be kept completely separate from work or make politely asking a coworker for a date (and respecting her response) unreasonable conduct. However, under the reasonable woman standard of care, behavior that many more men than women consider "reasonable," such as not taking no for an answer and gratuitous sexual comments or portrayals, would be sexual harassment. The credible threat of liability for allowing such conduct to continue would lead employers to require that their employees comply with the standards of a reasonable woman.

From Reasonable Man to Unreasonable Victim?: Assessing *Harris v. Forklift Systems* and Shifting Standards of Proof and Perspective in Title VII Sexual Harassment Law

David Schultz

Introduction

Recent litigation, including the decision of the Supreme Court of the United States in *Harris v. Forklift Systems, Inc.*,[1] has drawn the federal courts deeper into the difficult problem of determining if and when sexist language and sexual conduct in the workplace constitute a form of sex discrimination, thereby violating Title VII of the 1964 Civil Rights Act.[2] Among the numerous problems that arise when ascertaining whether specific language or conduct is discriminatory and violates Title VII is defining the perspective from which to judge the speech and conduct. A number of courts have held that sexual harassment constitutes a Title VII violation where there is "conduct which would interfere with [a] hypothetical reasonable individual's work performance and affect seriously the psychological well-being of that reasonable person under like circumstances."[3]

The reasonable person standard has been under attack and new standards of perspective and proof are emerging.[4] Lower courts judges are increasingly arguing for either a reasonable woman or reasonable victim test when evaluating sexual harassment claims under Title VII.[5] Courts adopting this new standard have reasoned that the reasonable person standard is not neutral but male-biased and patriarchal, that it tends to validate the aggressor's perspective and not the victim's, and that it fails to appreciate the perspective of women, which clearly differs from men.[6]

While no one endorses or seeks to encourage unwanted sexist speech and conduct in the workplace, efforts to silence or regulate it pose serious free speech issues under the First Amendment to the United States Constitution.[7] When do efforts to sue individuals for sex discrimination because they displayed nude pinups, made demeaning sexual remarks about women generally, or referred to women by vulgar names, violate their rights to free speech? Legal theorists, such as Catharine MacKinnon and Andrea Dworkin, as well as other antipornography advocates, contend that such sexist speech is not constitutionally protected, claiming that those who would protect it "value speech in the abstract more than they value people in the concrete."[8] These current efforts to address sexist speech in the workplace parallel MacKinnon's previous efforts to outlaw pornography as a form of discrimination against women. [9] These efforts led to the passage of an Indianapolis ordinance declaring that pornography is a form of discrimination against women.[10] The court, however, declared that ordinance unconstitutional as a form of viewpoint censorship.[11] The Supreme Court recently invalidated a city ordinance prohibiting hate speech because it discriminated on the basis of viewpoint. [12] Efforts to ban sexist speech may meet a similar fate. [13]

Many anticipated that the recent Supreme Court case of *Harris v. Forklift Systems, Inc.* would resolve the dispute regarding the appropriate standard of perspective courts should use in Title VII sexual harassment claims.[14] The Court, however, failed to address the reasonable man, person, or woman controversy. Instead, Justice O'Connor's majority opinion passed over this issue and addressed the issue of the threshold level of injury necessary to support a sexual harassment claim under Title VII. "[A]ny conduct that is merely offensive" would not invoke Title VII, yet "Title VII comes into play before the harassing conduct leads to a nervous breakdown."[15] Moreover, to ascertain when a work environment was hostile and violative of Title VII, the Court stated that one must consider all of the circumstances, including the frequency and severity of the discriminatory conduct, whether it was physically threatening, humiliating, or merely offensive, and whether it unreasonably interfered with the employee's work performance.[16] Thus, the Court left unresolved whether reasonableness would be judged from a woman's, man's, or some other viewpoint.

In light of the Court's failure to directly address the appropriate standard of reasonableness in *Harris*, this article evaluates the impact of the reasonable woman or victim standard as it has emerged in Title VII sex discrimination jurisprudence. The first section of this Article examines the prevalence and impact of sexist speech in the workplace and provides some definitions and topologies regarding sexist speech. The next section reviews Title VII sexual harassment law, focusing on the emergence of the reasonable person standard and the subsequent shift toward the reasonable woman standard. This section also addresses arguments regarding the inability of a reasonable person standard to appreciate the perspective of women in the workplace. The third section discusses arguments for and against the reasonable victim or reasonable woman standard. Among other issues, this section addresses the tension between eliminating sex discrimination and protecting free speech.

The last section concludes by proposing to confine or abandon the reasonableness test. I argue that all current reasonableness standards are conceptually empty and fraught with numerous legal, epistemological, and political problems. In their place, I advocate a balancing of interests test as a better means to balance free speech and the victim's sensitivity.

I also address the intersubjective[17] difficulties surrounding use of the current reasonableness tests. A balancing of interests test would-shift the emphasis to conditions necessary to create a non-hostile work environment that enhances worker participation and preserves free speech.

Sexist Speech and Conduct in the Workplace

Sexist speech and unwanted sexual behavior are prevalent in the workplace. A number of surveys conducted in the 1970's and 1980's reveal that a significant proportion of female workers are victims of abusive language, ranging from sexual comments, innuendos or jokes to explicit sexual invitations. Women are called "cunt," "pussy" and "bitch." Men wager on women's virginity and the frequency with which they engage in sexual activity. Millions of women endure whistles, catcalls and references to breast size. [18]

In *Harris v. Forklift Systems, Inc.*, one of the plaintiff's coworkers, a receptionist, testified that "lots of people make comments about my breasts."[19] Her remarks do not reflect on isolated experience but evidence the well-documented proliferation of sexist language and harassment at work which is predominantly directed at women.

A 1975 survey done by *Redbook* and *Harvard Business Review* found that of 9,000 women who returned surveys, ninety percent indicated that they had been sexually harassed.[20] A poll conducted for the National Association for Female Executives found that fifty-three percent of its members knew someone who was sexually harassed or were themselves harassed.[21] A 1988 government report indicated that forty-two percent of female federal employees claimed to have been sexually harassed, compared to sixteen percent of their male counterparts.[22] Other reports confirm that women are much more likely than men to be sexually harassed at work. [23] Similarly, recent studies have found sexual harassment to be a major problem in the schools as well as on the street.[24]

Studies indicate that, in addition to litigation costs, sexual harassment costs millions, if not billions, of dollars in lost productivity, decreased worker performance, increased health care costs to treat depression, and other related losses in personnel investment as victims quit or reduce their work performance.[25] Overall, the impact of sexual harassment on both victim and society is enormous.

Since sexist speech and conduct are widespread in society, it is important to isolate what constitutes sexual harassment in the workplace. The Equal Employment Opportunity Commission (EEOC) defines sexual harassment as follows:

Harassment on the basis of sex is a violation of section 703 of title VII. Unwelcome sexual advances, requests for sexual favors, and other verbal or physical conduct of a sexual nature constitute sexual harassment when
(1) submission to such conduct is made either explicitly or implicitly a term or condition of an individual's employment,
(2) submission to or rejection of such conduct by an individual is used as the basis for employment decisions affecting such individual, or
(3) such conduct has the purpose or effect of unreasonably interfering with an individual's work performance or creating an intimidating, hostile, or offensive working environment.[26]

One commentator has identified four categories of sexist speech:
"(1) speech demanding or requesting sexual relationships;
(2) sexually explicit speech directed at the woman;
(3) degrading speech directed at the woman; and
(4) sexually explicit or degrading speech that the woman employee knows exists in the workplace, even though it is not directed at her."[27]

This definition is broader than the EEOC guidelines and includes a greater variety of sexist language found at the workplace. The EEOC definition appears to address the first three types of speech because they involve activity clearly directed at the victim, yet it is arguable whether the EEOC guidelines address undirected generic sexist language which may also intimidate a woman and affect her workplace performance. The third form of sexist speech, involving undirected sexist and demeaning speech, is the major source of controversy in recent debates surrounding the emergence of a reasonable victim or woman standard.[28] Does sexist speech that is not directed at any particular person constitute a form of actionable harassment under Title VII? Should speech that a reasonable woman would find offensive and degrading be a violation of Title VII, even if a reasonable man would believe it harmless? To understand how the reasonable woman perspective impacts this issue, some attention to the development of sexual harassment law is necessary.

Evolution of Title VII Sex Discrimination Law

Hostile Environment and the Reasonable Person

Section 703 of the 1964 Civil Rights Act makes it unlawful for an employer, employment agency, or labor union to refuse to hire or otherwise discriminate against women on the basis of their sex.[29] Because Virginia Representative Howard Smith introduced sex at the last minute during the debates on the 1964 Civil Rights Act in an effort to defeat the bill, there is little legislative history to clarify what Congress intended this clause to prohibit.[30] Nevertheless, sexual harassment has come to be included within the meaning of sex discrimination under Title VII.

Three major events were instrumental in this development. In 1979, Catharine MacKinnon advanced the argument that "sexual harassment of women at work is sex discrimination in employment."[31] MacKinnon defined "sexual harassment" as the "unwanted imposition of sexual requirements in the context of a relationship of unequal power. "[32] Professor MacKinnon identified two possible forms of sexual harassment: quid pro quo, where direct sexual requests are made as a condition of employment or benefits, and hostile environment, where the conduct is not directly tied to any benefit, yet creates an unbearable atmosphere.[33]

MacKinnon, grounding her legal arguments both in the Equal Protection Clause of the Fourteenth Amendment and Title VII of the 1964 Civil Rights Act, sought to show how harassment was not simply an isolated act of sexual demands, but instead a more systematic use of power to enforce female subordination to men.[34] MacKinnon claimed that courts should view the issue of harassment from the perspective of women and understand that this conduct is a form of discrimination under Title VII.[35]

MacKinnon's arguments quickly influenced the EEOC's 1980 guidelines and interpretation of Title VII. Like MacKinnon, the EEOC recognized two forms of sexual harassment as violations of Title VII: expressly conditioning employment or benefits on submission to sexual advances and sexual conduct that creates a hostile environment.[36] The EEOC adopted a case-by-case approach to determine when conduct constitutes sexual harassment but did not state what standard should be used to ascertain this. [37]

The EEOC guidelines were critical to the third event that established sexual harassment as employment discrimination. In *Mentor Savings Bank FSB v. Vinson*,[38] the Supreme Court of the United States approved the EEOC guidelines and held that sexual harassment which created a hostile environment violated Title VII. [39] The plaintiff in that case was a bank employee who alleged that her supervisor coerced her into having sexual intercourse forty to fifty times.[40] Justice Rehnquist, writing for the Court, concluded that "[w]ithout question, when a supervisor sexually harasses a subordinate because of a subordinate's sex, that supervisor discriminate[s]' on the basis of sex."[41]

The Court stated that "[s]exual harassment which creates a hostile or offensive environment for members of one sex is every bit the arbitrary barrier to sexual equality at the workplace that racial harassment is to racial equality."[42] Yet the Court made two important qualifications in its ruling regarding the determination of what constitutes a hostile environment and the scope of employer liability. First, not every sexual utterance or epithet is a violation of Title Vll.[43] Instead, the harassment must be "sufficiently severe or pervasive 'to alter the conditions of [the victim's] employment and create an abusive working environment.' "[44]

Endorsing the EEOC's "totality of circumstances" approach, the Court stated that evidence of an alleged victim's sexually provocative conduct is not irrelevant, as a matter of law, to the issue of whether sexual advances were unwelcome.[45] Some type of judgmental or nonobjective criteria would be employed to determine if, in a particular case, the "totality of circumstances" created a Title VII hostile environment.[46]

The Court declined to announce a rule that employers are not "absolutely liable" for sexual harassment by their supervisors.[47] Instead, in hostile environment cases, a more particular case-by-case rule is necessary.[48] In dissent, Justice Marshall, joined by Justices Brennan, Blackmun, and Stevens, rejected this limit on employer liability in hostile environment disputes.[49] They responded by asserting that neither language in the EEOC guidelines nor Title VII supports this type of exception.[50]

While *Mentor Savings Bank* was an important ruling for Title VII sexual harassment cases, the Court left unresolved the major issue of whose frame of reference should be used when evaluating a hostile environment claim. What standard of judgment was required to ascertain if the harassment was "sufficiently severe and pervasive?" A series of lower court cases that followed *Mentor Savings Bank* addressed this issue.

In *Scott v. Sears, Roebuck & Co.*,[51] the court addressed a Title VII claim raised by a woman who was employed as an automobile mechanic.[52] Scott indicated that her supervisor and male coworkers propositioned her, slapped her on her buttocks, and made sexually suggestive comments.[53] Despite her supervisor's conduct, Scott admitted that she considered him to be a friend. [54] Scott was dismissed allegedly because she worked more slowly than the male employees.[55]

Employing the hostile environment analysis similar to that found in *Meritor Savings*, the district court ruled against Scott. The court of appeals upheld the district court's finding that the conduct was not sufficiently severe or pervasive to constitute a hostile environment under Title VII.[56] The court stated that "[a]ssuming all of the conduct Scott complains of is true, her claim still falls short of what is necessary to maintain an action" under Title VII.[57] While acknowledging the sexual comments, innuendos, and propositions, the court concluded that the conduct was not "so intimidating, offensive, or hostile that it affected" the terms and conditions of Scott's employment.[58] This author reads this decision as suggesting that the court looked to mainly "objective" factors rather than any subjective criteria to determine what constituted a hostile environment.[59] Moreover, when seeking to examine these objective criteria within the totality of the circumstances, the court adopted a perspective other than the victim's.[60]

The Sixth Circuit Court of Appeals, in *Rabidue v. Osceola Refining Co.*,[61] directly addressed the standard for judging whether conduct created a hostile environment.[62] In *Rabidue*, a discharged female employee brought a Title VII sex discrimination claim against Osceola Refining Company.[63] Rabidue claimed that a supervisor's vulgar, sexual remarks about women generally, and occasionally towards Rabidue, along with other male employees displaying sexually graphic pictures of women in the work area, were offensive and created a hostile environment.[64] The court articulated a five-step frame of analysis:

> [T]his court concludes that a plaintiff, to prevail in a Title VII offensive work environment sexual harassment action, must assert and prove that:
> (1)   the employee was a member of a protected class;
> (2)   the employee was subjected to unwelcome sexual harassment in the form of sexual advances, requests for sexual favors, or other verbal or physical conduct of a sexual nature;
> (3)   the harassment complained of was based upon sex;
> (4)   the charged sexual harassment had the effect of unreasonably interfering with the plaintiff's work performance and creating an intimidating, hostile, or offensive working environment that affected seriously

the psychological well-being of the plaintiff; and
(5)   the existence of respondeat liability.[65]

The Sixth Circuit clarified the frame of reference for determining what constituted a hostile environment, stating:

> [T]he trier of fact, when judging the totality of the circumstances impacting upon the asserted abusive and hostile environment placed in issue by the plaintiff's charges, *must adopt perspective of reasonable person's reaction* to a similar environment under essentially like or similar circumstances. Thus, in the absence of conduct which would interfere with that hypothetical reasonable individual's work performance and affect seriously the psychological well-being of that reasonable person under like circumstances, a plaintiff may not prevail on asserted charges of sexual harassment anchored in an alleged hostile and/or abusive work environment ....[66]

The court stated that in addition to showing that a reasonable person would be offended and the conduct would affect a reasonable person's job performance, a plaintiff must show that she was offended and that she suffered some injury as a result of the conduct.[67] The court further stated that the environment should be judged using a combination of objective and subjective factors, including the nature of the conduct, the employees' and supervisors' background and experience, the physical layout of the workplace, the type of obscenity used in the workplace, and the plaintiff's reasonable expectations upon entering the workplace.[68]

Employing a reasonable person standard, the court rejected Rabidue's claim, noting that the supervisor's vulgarity did not pervade the work atmosphere and reasoning that sexual jokes, sexual comments, and sexually explicit magazines are present in many workplaces.[69] The court stated that Title VII simply was not intended to change this type of conduct.[70]

In Broom v. Regal Tube Co.,[71] the United States Court of Appeals for the Seventh Circuit also adopted the reasonable person standard to judge hostile environment claims.[72] *Broom* involved an African-American woman whose supervisor repeatedly made racial and sexual comments to her, showed her sexually explicit photographs, and threatened her.[73]

The plaintiff claimed that she was constructively discharged and suffered a breakdown as a result of the supervisor's conduct.[74] Adopting *Rabidue's* objective and subjective approach, the court concluded that the supervisor's conduct would have interfered with a reasonable person's job performance and would have seriously affected a reasonable person's psychological well-being.[75] As to the subjective component, the court of appeals affirmed the district court's findings that the supervisor's conduct actually did interfere with the plaintiff's job performance and that it caused an identifiable injury.[76]

Hostile Environment and the Reasonable Woman

While the articulation of a reasonable person standard to determine hostile environment claims could be seen as an important victory in sex discrimination law, criticism of the reasonable person test emerged quickly. In his dissenting opinion in *Rabidue,* Judge Keith rejected the majority's enunciation of a reasonable person standard to judge hostile environment claims.[77] Urging a reasonable woman standard, Judge Keith concluded that while sexual language and sexually explicit poster might not offend men, they could offend a reasonable woman and affect her job performance.[78] Judge Keith reasoned that men and women tend to have different world views and perceptions and that adopting a reasonable person standard, rather than that of a reasonable woman, fails to recognize these differences.[79] The Sixth Circuit subsequently endorsed Judge Keith's reasoning when it held that the standard for judging whether an alleged victim of sexual harassment was constructively discharged is whether a reasonable woman in similar circumstances would feel compelled to resign.[80]

The District Court for the Middle District of Florida also followed Judge Keith's reasoning in *Robinson v. Jacksonville*

Shipyards, Inc. [81] The plaintiff in *Robinson* was a welder and one of very few women employed as a skilled craftsperson in a shipyard.[82] Over a period of several years she was continuously subjected to direct sexual comments and vulgar propositions, was referred to by numerous sexually derogatory names, and was constantly confronted with depictions of nude women posted around the worksite.[83] In particular, one coworker circulated a picture illustrating a nude woman with long blonde hair wearing high heels and holding a whip.[84] Robinson found this picture particularly offensive since she had long blonde hair and used a welding tool known as a whip. [85]

Robinson claimed that this conduct constituted sex discrimination under Title VII.[86] *The Robinson* court, noting the five-part analysis outlined in prior case law, indicated that whether the allegedly discriminatory conduct affected a "term, condition, or privilege of employment" must be evaluated under both objective and subjective standards.[87] Disagreeing with the *Rabidue* majority, the *Robinson* court opted to use the reasonable woman standard rather than the reasonable person standard to evaluate the objective component.[88] Contrary to the *Rabidue* majority's claim that Title VII could not remove sexual jokes and humor from the workplace, *the Robinson* court stated that this type of behavior would be insulting and intimidating to a reasonable woman.[89] While men may not find such conduct offensive, it could be construed as creating a hostile environment for women.[90]

The Ninth Circuit Court of Appeals, in *Ellison v.* Brady,[91] also rejected the *Rabidue* standard and questioned the ability of the reasonable person standard to reflect the differing perspectives of men and women.[92] The plaintiff in *Ellison* was a female employee of the Internal Revenue Service who received several unsolicited romantic overtures from a coworker.[93]

After speaking to both her supervisors and the coworker in an effort to terminate the conduct, Ellison filed an internal sexual harassment claim.[94] The Treasury Department rejected Ellison's claim, concluding that the conduct did not meet the EEOC guidelines.[95] The district court affirmed this ruling, but the Ninth

Circuit Court of Appeals overturned.[96]

The Ninth Circuit, noting its disagreement with the reasonable person standard, employed the victim's perspective to determine whether conduct was sufficiently severe and pervasive to create a hostile or abusive environment.[97] The court reasoned that using a reasonable person standard would simply reinforce the status quo.[98] Furthermore, the court acknowledged that men and women perceive conduct differently.[99] Even more significant was the court's disregard of the reasonable woman's view in favor of the adoption of the reasonable victim's perspective in all harassment cases.[100]

The *Robinson* and *Ellison* courts, as well as the dissenter in *Rabidue,* laid a foundation challenging the neutrality of the reasonable person standard and questioned whether such a standard could fairly reflect the perspective of women or any victim in Title VII cases. At the core of these claims is the assertion that men and women perceive the world differently. One must, therefore, determine whether there is a foundation for this assertion.

Reasonable Persons and Reasonable Women

The *Ellison v. Brady* court, noting the differences between men's and women's perceptions of social interaction, stated that the use of a reasonable person standard is not neutral and instead embodies the aggressor's perspectives.[101] The court noted that this empirical claim is supported, in part, by claims that the notion of reason and the typology of the reasonable person is a fiction and not applicable to women. [102]

Sociologist Carol Gilligan has noted significant differences between the moral reasoning that men and women employ.[103] For example, while men see the world in a hierarchial, rights-orientated, individualistic fashion, women are more likely to view the world in an egalitarian, duty-bound, socially-connected fashion.[104] As a result, men and women view their social environments differently. Legal commentators have argued that these gender differences explain Justice O'Connor's opinions,[105] feminist versus feminine views of the law,[106] the emergence of male liberal values as defining the contour of American law, [107] and the epistemology informing a female view of the legal process.[108]

Other authors have also recognized the differences between the way men and women perceive the world, but they further argue that women learn differently from men and, as a result, have developed their own unique epistemology influenced by experiences unique to women instead of by traditional male-dominated types of reason.[109] Others have attributed the differences between men and women to cultural or other forces in the epistemology and cognitive structuring of the world.[110] Some have argued that the law, because it embodies a uniquely male view,[111] excludes female experiences, rendering women invisible or politically powerless.[112] For example, Professor MacKinnon argues that current sexual harassment jurisprudence has failed to appreciate female experiences and that efforts toward Title VII reform reflect women defining for themselves what constitutes injuries to women.[113] The varying world perceptions between men and women have been attributed to cultural differences, the exclusion of women from the legal-political process,[114] the development of uniquely female experiences due to maternal or household duties, and men's rigid definition of "women's behavior."[115]

These commentators suggest that men's and women's perceptions of the world may vary so greatly that, in defining a hostile environment under Title VII, the difference in a reasonable person standard and reasonable woman standard is significant. A reasonable person standard which embodies a particularly white male perspective of the world fails to incorporate the experiences of women. The Ninth Circuit noted that there is a particular set of views that women share such that a common set of perceptions exists that can be included in a reasonable woman standard.[116]

Whether a court employs a reasonable person or reasonable woman standard may make a significant difference in the outcome of a case. The *Rabidue* court, employing a reasonable person standard, held that sexually graphic language and nude pinups did not constitute a hostile environment.[117] Yet the *Robinson* court, employing a reasonable woman standard, held that similar items did violate Title VII.[118] Presumably, the shift from a reasonable person to a reasonable woman standard accounts for the difference in these rulings.

From Reasonable Woman to Reasonable Victim

Rabidue, Robinson, and *Ellison* have had a significant and increasingly important impact on Title VII sex discrimination cases. Those and subsequent cases demonstrate that: (1) the reasonable woman standard is gaining acceptance; (2) the reasonable woman standard may make a difference, but only when a woman can show that the conduct affected her mental health or work performance; and (3) the reasonable woman standard is being transformed into a generic reasonable victim standard applied on a case-by-case basis.

Many lower courts are now using the reasonable woman standard.[119] In most instances, where the court has adopted a reasonable woman standard, the court has tended to rule in favor of the woman. Although this is not proof, it suggests that the use of a reasonable woman standard makes some difference in Title VII cases. One exception to this tendency, however, is the decision of the district court in *Harris v. Forklift Systems, Inc.*[120] There, the court adopted a reasonable woman perspective and found that the conduct the victim experienced was offensive.[121]

Nevertheless, the court ruled against the plaintiff, indicating that the harassment was not so severe as to affect the "plaintiff's psychological well-being.[122] The court concluded that although a reasonable woman would have found the conduct to be offensive, the conduct would not have interfered with her work.[123] The reasonable woman standard may make a difference, but the court still appears to demand a demonstration of harm or interference with the work performance of the victim before it will rule that a violation of Title VII has occurred. This is consistent with the Supreme Court's *Meritor Savings Bank* decision.[124]

The third trend emerging is the further fragmentation of the reasonable person standard into reasonable victim standards. This fragmentation may be the result of recent postmodern assaults on reason or rationality as an architectonic and universal category of experience and intersubjectivity.[125] Theorists argue that the perspective of the "other" presently cannot be recognized within the law and further, that traditional notions of reason and reasonableness are exclusionary and fail to appreciate the perspective of the excluded, a category which includes women.[126]

This criticism, as manifested in Title VII sex discrimination cases, is presented in *Ellison v. Brady*.[127] The court noted that "where male employees allege that co-workers engage in conduct which creates a hostile environment, the appropriate victim's perspective would be that of a reasonable man."[128] In *Harris v. Forklift Systems, Inc.*, the district court further qualified the reasonable woman standard to that of a "reasonable woman manager."[129] In *Harris v. International Paper Co.*,[130] the court contended that "[t]o give full force to this basic premise of antidiscrimination law...the standard for assessing the unwelcomeness and pervasiveness of conduct and speech must be founded on a fair concern for the different social experiences of men and women in the case of sexual harassment, and of white Americans and black Americans in the case of racial harassment.[131] Hence, a reasonable white or African-American victim appears to be necessary for Title VII adjudication.

Disaggregation of the reasonable person standard as a universal objective perspective was made even more explicitly in *Stingley v. Arizona*.[132]

> The proper perspective from which to evaluate the hostility of the environment is the "reasonable person of the same gender and race or color" standard. In the sexual harassment case of *Ellison v. Brady*, 924 F.2d 872, 878-79 (9th Cir. 1991), the court held that the proper reference for evaluating the "severity and pervasiveness" of the harassment is from the perspective of a

reasonable victim of the same gender…*Ellison's* reasoning may be applied seamlessly to racist environment claims, and at least one district court has done so. Based on *Ellison*, a "reasonable person of the same gender and race or color" standard will be applied in deciding this Motion.[133]

Thus, some courts assessing Title VII claims will adopt a reasonable victim perspective that considers race, sex, occupation, or other characteristics of the victim. The result is that judges and juries are asked to place themselves in a variety of perspectives which may differ from their own, which they may be unable to *do*.[134] This raises numerous intersubjective, epistemological, and legal problems as the categories of reasonableness or perspective are ascertained. [135]

Current litigation in Title VII sexual harassment cases, then, is quickly changing towards adoption of multiple perspectives to determine when the "totality of circumstances" constitutes discrimination. While this change in the law has benefits, it is not without problems.

Evaluating the Reasonable Woman/Victim Standard

Arguments in Favor of the New Standard

The Reasonable Person Perspective Is Male Biased

The courts have come to recognize that there are many perceptual differences between men and women, whites and blacks.[136] Attitudes and perceptions may be grounded in class, race, and a number of other immutable factors such that there is an intersubjective limit to the ability of a person of one race or gender to understand what a person of another race or gender finds offensive. For example, a white person may not be as offended by a picture of a black person with a noose around his neck as might an African-American person. Additionally, a sign that says "Whites Only" may elicit different sentiments among different races.

Given these differences in perception, a reasonable person perspective fails to capture the viewpoints of minority groups or those who are the victims of harassment. The apparent neutrality of the reasonable person standard masks its male bias, and the adoption of a reasonable woman standard allows for women to be recognized and to participate with men on equal footing in the workplace.[137]

Workplace Discrimination Is Real and Women Are Trapped by It

Numerous studies have noted that a large percentage of the female workforce has been sexually harassed.[138] One commentator argues that this harassment reinforces a series of power hierarchies at work which subordinate women to men and maintain female positions of powerlessness.[139] As long as women are subjected to this harassment, they will be unable to participate meaningfully in employment. The reasonable woman perspective empowers women, allowing women to define what constitutes harm to them.[140] It also permits women to use the power of the state to challenge male prerogatives and authority. [141]

The Reasonable Woman Standard Establishes a Balanced Means to Judge Discrimination

One criticism of the reasonable woman standard is that it may be too subjective, allowing the hypersensitive woman's or hypersensitive victim's attitudes to silence or override the free speech of coworkers. [142] A person who is overly sensitive to sexist speech may employ Title VII as a "heckler's veto," meaning that the threat of heckling or even violence will enjoin the free speech of workers.[143] The requirement that the victim or woman be "reasonable" is intended to establish some threshold to combat the possible unreasonableness of the overly sensitive.[144]

The reasonableness requirement seeks to ensure some standard of consistency, stability, and predictability that would otherwise be lost if liability arose for whatever shocks or bothers a sensitive person. Moreover, the requirement that victims demonstrate that the conduct unreasonably caused some real harm to their work performance mitigates the subjectivity of the reasonable woman test.

The Reasonable Woman/Victim Standard
Protects a Captive Audience

Some argue that the free speech rights of workers should be respected and that the remedy for sexist speech is counter speech.[145] However, worksites are not like political marketplaces where ample opportunity exists to offer speech to counter sexist or racially demeaning remarks. Women at work are a captive audience, frequently in a relatively weak position, and have no ability to escape from sexist speech.[146] Utilizing the reasonable woman or reasonable victim standard to adjudicate harassment is not subjective, nor does it constitute censorship. Rather, such a standard provides a means to ensure that women are neither driven from nor kept out of the worksite because of sexist language. The reasonable woman standard, then, seeks to rectify power imbalances at work and to protect a captive audience from being subjected to unwanted and derogatory speech. [147]

There is a strong case for adopting the reasonable victim perspective. Such a standard balances the inequalities of the power relationships in the workplace by using a combination of subjective and objective factors to adjudicate Title VII harassment claims. There are, however, numerous criticisms of the adoption of the victim's perspective.

Arguments Against the New Standard

The Reasonable Victim Standard Establishes Different
Standards of Conduct for Men, Women, and Other Opposing
Groups

One justification for the reasonable woman standard is based on the recognition that the intersubjective gulf between the sexes renders the reasonable person standard inapplicable to women. If, in fact, sensibilities between men and women vary and men are more tolerant of, or at least less offended by, sexually suggestive speech or conduct, there is a potential difference in the conduct and speech that will result in liability under Title VII.[148] For example, if women are more offended by sexually suggestive comments than men, a reasonable woman standard would permit far less of this type of speech than a reasonable male perspective would allow. A reasonable woman standard, therefore, might permit far less of certain types of speech than would a reasonable person standard. Similarly, under a gender-based standard, a male victim of harassment would be afforded less protection and be forced to endure more abuse than a female victim.[149] Hence, different standards of reasonableness would not only dictate different types of permitted speech but also the levels of the types of speech permitted.

If different standards are to be used, the problem arises as to how an employer or coworker knows what will be offensive to the victim. If there is an intersubjective gulf between men and women, it may be impossible for men to know what will be offensive to women. Thus, it may be impossible for those who do not share the victim's perspective to know what will be offensive to the victim. Because people should know what type of conduct is permissible prior to being held culpable for their actions, the inability to know what is offensive produces some unfairness.

One solution may be for employers to hire people with different backgrounds and perspectives to inform employers and other employees what constitutes offensive speech and conduct. Unless this participation seeks to reach genuine consensus, however, censorship will still present a potential problem. There are so many different things that may offend so many different people that worksite speech may be generally silenced.

Yet another aspect of the intersubjective problem involves adjudication of Title VII disputes by judges or juries. If the perspectives of men and women are different, could a jury composed of men effectively adjudicate a Title VII dispute from a reasonable woman's perspective? Could a male judge? How could male juries or judges truly be able to know what offends a reasonable woman? Although several male judges have employed reasonable woman standards and ruled in favor of women, how can we be sure that the altered standard was the reason for the decision or that the judge accurately employed this alternative standard? A judge could employ the reasonable woman perspective but conclude that no Title VII violation occurred.[150]

Even where a judge purports to use a reasonable person standard, one could argue that the standard was used incorrectly or that the judge misunderstood the standard. "[T]he reasonable woman construct itself does not constrain judges' discretion"[151] because the term is vacuous,"[152] can be imbued with meaning according to a judge's preconceptions, and can be employed without methodological rules to structure its employment.

Finally, if the intersubjective gulf between men and women is real, there may be an argument that juries need to be of a certain gender or race if they are to faithfully understand the victim's perspective. Such an argument would counter recent decisions regarding jury selection and discrimination[153] and create a host of new problems in Title VII trials.[154]

The Reasonable Victim Standard May Make It Difficult to Stipulate Whose Reasonableness to Use

Let us suppose that an African-American woman is subjected to sexually explicit material depicting black women in demeaning positions.[155] Furthermore, several traditional stereotypes of black women are invoked at her workplace, including those of black women as Jezebels and as sexually "loose and easy." This woman files a Title VII case. Should the dispute be adjudicated from a female or black-female experience? Given the unique experiences of black women, the Jezebel references might be more offensive to black women than to white women. The question of what standard is appropriate when the victim is both black and female has already presented a problem in the context of class certification of Title VII plaintiffs.[156] The stipulation of the appropriate perspective creates a concern regarding the adoption of the reasonable victim standard.

Since the victim's unique history and other circumstances may be important in ascertaining what offends the victim, definitions of the appropriate characteristics of the victim are clearly important. If the reasonable person standard fails to incorporate the perspective of all people, however, there is no reason to expect that a reasonable woman standard will be able to incorporate the perspective of all women.

Contemporary feminist jurisprudence is grounded in the experiences of white, middle class, heterosexual women, and it may not reflect the concerns of other female groups, such as lesbians.[157] Not all women share similar experiences or can be categorized in one group. [158] The category of reasonable woman, therefore, is no more able to reflect the experiences of all women than the reasonable person category is able to reflect the experiences of both men and women.

Until empirical data is gathered, concepts or categories are meaningless. Furthermore, raw empirical data is of no use until it is synthesized under some conceptual apparatus. [159] This suggests that the category of "reasonable" should remain empty until experiences or backgrounds of particular groups inform what would constitute a reasonable member of that group. Different experiences would give the concept a different meaning such that the entire notion of reasonable would be group specific. What is reasonable to one group may not be to another, and when seeking to determine the appropriate category for a victim in a sexual harassment case, there is a splintering of the category of reasonable person to reasonable woman, reasonable black woman, reasonable white lesbian, ad infinitum.

The result may be that a reasonable victim approach leads to problems of [160] in defining the appropriate perspective and raises the question of whether what is actually being measured is reasonableness, and not simply the sensitivity of a particular group reacting to a particular type of speech or conduct. Reasonableness will, in effect, have lost its meaning. We return, therefore, to the problem of distinguishing the extra-sensitive victim from a reasonable victim, whatever that is.[161] Finally, there may be problems selecting juries or judges to fit the particular perspective of the victim.

The Subjective Victim Standard Censors or Chills Speech

Judging offensiveness by a purely subjective standard that relies upon a victim's perspective alone could be used to censor speech that is distasteful to the victim. While sexually explicit speech may be offensive to some, it is nevertheless a form of communication deserving of legal protection as it may contribute to political discourse, workplace efficiency, a sense of self-efficacy, or some other goal. [162] A limitation on this particular speech is a form of content-based censorship where the victim is allowed the power of a heckler veto, prohibiting another individual from speaking.[163] Seeking to limit sexually suggestive speech at work is analogous to efforts by Indianapolis, Indiana, to make the display of certain types of pornography an actionable civil rights claim. [164] In striking down the Indianapolis ordinance, the court held that the ordinance represented pure content-based censorship. [165]

Moreover, companies and businesses, fearing Title VII liability, may cut off workplace speech, impose anti-fraternization rules for workers, limit what may be posted on bulletin boards, or otherwise regulate speech and conduct. This type of censorship should be viewed with alarm, given the limits companies have already placed on workers, including mandatory drug tests and other restrictions on personal freedoms.[166] Further, it appears to work against a wiser policy of encouraging workers and companies to discuss the problems of sexual harassment and discrimination at work. If, in fact, there is an intersubjective gap between the perceptions of men and women, increasing the amount of speech at work is a more appropriate way to foster intersubjective understandings of others' thoughts and emotions.

In the long run, encouraging shared communication and discussion in the workplace regarding what constitutes harassment will defuse harassment to a greater degree than simply seeking to suppress it will.

A Reasonable Woman or Victim Standard May Reinforce Stereotypes of Women as Helpless

Some commentators suggest that American law has embodied a patriarchal attitude towards women, often viewing them as helpless and dependent.[167] To use the power of the state in the form of Title VII to cleanse the worksite of all sexist language with the goal of protecting women may reinforce the image of women as the weaker sex, unable to protect themselves at work. According to Feminists for Free Expression, "the specter of paternalistic over-regulation of every nuance of interpersonal relations fosters a climate of mutual distrust and resentment between male and female co-workers, rather than an environment in which women and men can work constructively toward common understanding and equality."[168] Overregulation of the work environment, therefore, would once again employ the power of the state to protect women who, it is presumed, lack the ability to protect themselves.

In response, supporters of more strict enforcement of Title VII discrimination claims contend that women are in a hostile environment, relatively powerless to defend themselves in some situations, and possibly unable to escape an environment permeated with sexual harassment.[169] The argument has merit, especially in workplaces where women have been traditionally outnumbered by men or excluded entirely.[170] Not all workplaces, however, are equally coercive or place women in the same position of powerlessness. In many situations, women or other victims are able to complain about offensive speech or conduct or use grievance procedures to resolve disputes. Making all offensive conduct violative of Title VII seems overly broad. To use analogies from political speech, there may be messages or means of conveying ideas that are offensive.[171] Yet in the marketplace of ideas, this offensiveness may be crucial to stimulating debate. [172]

The Supreme Court has declared that broad restrictions on constitutionally protected speech are not permitted.[173] Instead, the state must articulate an important or substantial interest which the restriction is narrowly tailored to serve.[174] Critics of a broadly defined notion of hostile environment under Title VII make this analogy to political speech and urge that speech restrictions in the workplace should be narrowly defined. [175] Considering all of these factors, epistemological and legal problems weigh more heavily against the adoption of the victim's perspective than those factors which weigh in favor of it.

Conclusion: Defining a New Standard to Judge Title VII Claims

Strong arguments both support and oppose the introduction of the reasonable woman or victim standard for adjudicating Title VII claims. It may be possible for courts to adopt a purely subjective standard and hold that sexually demeaning speech is a violation of Title VII without a showing of either harm or speech directed towards the victim. There are some who suggest that either a "woman's description of her experience" of harassment[176] or a sense of "subjective hostility should at least make out a prima facie hostile environment case."[177] Referring to Strauss' fourfold definition of sexist speech, this would permit recovery under Title VII for the fourth category of speech, the presence of sexually explicit or degrading speech at work not directed at a particular employee. [178]

A rigid standard requiring that the speech be directed at the victim and the victim show harm as a result of the speech is too strict and fails to recognize the power dynamics and captured-audience position of many women at work. Women are often in a minority, in positions of relative weakness, and lack the real opportunity to combat the sexist speech with counter speech of their own. Conversely, a purely subjective standard which would recognize sexist speech that was not directed at a particular individual as a form of group harm is too broad and is probably unconstitutional. [179] Relying only upon the subjective standards of a reasonable victim creates the danger of mere offensiveness determining the speech content and rights of coworkers. Neither of these two extremes seems acceptable.

A possible alternative is to follow a course that uses both objective and subjective factors. There must, however, be some further specification regarding the employment of the subjective component to determine hostility. The reasonable woman standard employed in the determination of hostile environment claims emerged from a recognition that the reasonable person standpoint suffered from an apparent intersubjective gulf between the perceptions and attitudes of men and women. Similarly, the reasonable victim standard is the result of even greater intersubjective gulfs that render the reasonable person standard inapplicable to most victims. Instead of capitulating to purely subjective standards, there are ways to offer more structured guidance to the employment of the subjective judgment standard while simultaneously working to overcome the intersubjective gap that separates men, women, and other victims.

Specification of the use of subjective criteria could come from drawing a contrast between a hostile and non-hostile workplace, constructing rules to determine when a worksite departs from the ideal non-hostile environment. Alternatively, courts could employ a balancing of interests test to ascertain the First Amendment protection of sexist speech in the workplace.[180] This test would also impose rules to guide the subjective judgments that determine a hostile environment.[181] Both of these measuring sticks recognize the prevailing need to employ objective criteria to adjudicate Title VII sexual harassment claims. To preclude a balancing of interests test from being abused, however, there must be a constrained or more clearly guided use of subjective criteria.

These guidelines, as well as current Title VII analysis, indicate that judgments of hostile environment should include several criteria. First, any employee must show that speech or conduct in the workplace caused real harm to the employee's work performance. Mere offensiveness fails to justify the limitation of coworkers' free speech rights, and mere offensiveness should not be enough to implicate Title VII. Second, the complainant would need to establish a nexus between the harm and the speech in the workplace. Third, the determination of a hostile, in contrast to merely offensive, worksite would be ascertained, not by a vague reasonableness test, but by a balancing of interests where several criteria would be considered. On one side the court would consider the type and pervasiveness of sexist speech in the worksite, whether the speech is directed at the employee, and the employer's role in fostering or discouraging the speech. On the other side would be consideration of the number of women employees and their ability to offer counter speech to the sexist speech. This balancing test considers whether the worksite offers a genuine opportunity to speak out against the sexist speech, whether it affords women a genuine ability to participate in company policymaking regarding sexist speech and harassment, and whether it gives women meaningful options to inform others that certain conduct is offensive without rendering these women vulnerable to potential retaliation.[182]

Employing these criteria, among others, in a narrowly tailored balancing of interests test, would reveal whether the workplace was truly hostile and precluded advancement and participation of women, or whether it allowed women the opportunity to bring about changes in the environment. Presumably, the greater women employees' ability to bring about change, the less likely it is that the workplace is hostile. Conversely, the less ability there is to bring about change, the more likely it is that sexist speech is used to impede the empowerment of women by maintaining a hostile environment.

This balancing of interests test achieves several important advantages over current reasonableness tests. One, the test recognizes that worksites are not all or nothing propositions where they are either hostile or not. Instead, there are degrees of hostility and some sites are more hostile than others. Current Title VII analysis fails to appreciate this continuum. This balancing of interests analysis tailors the remedy to the degree of hostility present and the ability of women and other victims to effect a non-hostile environment. Moreover, the focus shifts away from perspectival disputes between victims and aggressors and toward evaluating the ability of employees to bring about the conditions necessary for the maintenance of a non-hostile working environment. This test accomplishes that goal by seeking not to limit free speech in the workplace but by encouraging more speech and discussion in the workplace.

Increase in workplace communication, in addition to fostering worksite efficiency, also helps to break down the intersubjective gulf between men and women that is the impetus for the splintering of the reasonable person standard. Presumably, an increase in workplace communication would be directed towards creating clear rules of conduct regarding what is acceptable conduct, thus eliminating the problem of vagueness when workers seek to ascertain what constitutes permissible behavior.

This new test also recognizes, consistent with Professor MacKinnon's arguments, that sexual harassment grows out of power imbalances and inequalities between men and women in the workplace.[183] It seeks to rectify those imbalances by evaluating the access women have to decisionmaking in the workplace and not by seeking to pit the free speech rights of male coworkers against female coworkers. Moreover, it links the empowerment of women to general worker empowerment and workplace democracy, instead of pitting one group against another. This results in a more democratic, efficient, and productive worksite, revealing how support of women's rights is in the interest of all coworkers.[184]

Finally, a balancing of interests test, while still employing a subjective weighing of criteria, operates with a more bounded rationality. The current concept of reasonableness for any particular victim is empty, lacking definition of what it means to be a reasonable woman, black woman, or lesbian. A balancing of interests test offers criteria for judgment while stipulating some reference point of a non-hostile worksite where women and men can reach consensus regarding the acceptability of types of speech and conduct that should occur in the worksite. This approach, emphasizing participation, consensus, and conditions that make both possible, mirrors arguments offered by Jurgen Habermas in his analysis of the conditions necessary to bring about democracy.[185] The determination of a hostile environment should be part of a transformative process which seeks to alter the worksite to foster conditions less hostile for all, while including greater workplace democracy and speech.

1. 114 S. Ct. 367 (1993).
2. See 42 U.S.C. § 2000e-2 (1988 & Supp. Ill 1992) (prohibiting employment discrimination on basis of gender).
3. *Harris v. Forklift Sys., Inc.*, No. 3-89-0557, 1991 WL 487444, at *6 (M.D. Tenn. Feb. 4, 1991) (quoting *Rabidue v. Osceola Refining Co.*, 805 F.2d 611, 620 (6th Cir. 1986), *cert. denied*, 481 U.S. 1041 (1987)), *affd*, 976 F.2d 733 (6th Cir. 1992), *rev'd*, 114 S. Ct. 367 (1993); accord *Brooms v. Regal Tube Co.*, 881 F.2d 412, 420 (7th Cir. 1989) (quoting *Rabidue*, 805 F.2d at 620).
4. See infra notes 77-100 and accompanying text (discussing emergence of reasonable woman standard); c/. Wayne R. LaFave & Austin W. Scott, Jr., *Criminal Law* 464-65 (2d ed, 1986) (examining standard by which justifiability of third party's use of force on behalf of another is judged); *State v. Fair*, 45 N.J. 77, 92-93, 211 A.2d 359, 367-68 (1965) (considering standard for judging claims of self-defense on behalf of third parties).
5. *Ellison v. Brady*, 924 F.2d 872, 878-79 (9th Cir. 1991) (employing reasonable victim/reasonable woman standard); *Rabidue v. Osceola Refining Co.*, 805 F.2d 611, 626 (6th Cir. 1986) (Keith, J., concurring in part, dissenting in part) (urging reasonable victim/reasonable woman standard), *cert. denied*, 481 U.S. 1041 (1987); *Robinson v. Jacksonville Shipyards, Inc.*, 760 F. Supp. 1486, 1524 (M.D. Fla. 1991) (measuring conduct against reaction of reasonable person of victim's sex); *cf. Harris v. Forklift Sys. Inc.*, No. 3-89-0557, 1991 WL 487444, at *6-*8 (M.D. Tenn. Feb. 4, 1991) (stating standard is reasonable person, yet measuring plaintiff's conduct against other female employees), *ajfd*, 976 F.2d 733 (6th Cir. 1992), *rev'd*, 114 S. Ct. 367 (1993). One commentator has noted that there is a trend in the judiciary to adopt the reasonable woman standard. See Eric J.

Wallach & Alyse L. Jacobson, "'Reasonable Woman' Test Catches On," *NAT'L L.J.*, July 6, 1992, at 21, 26 (reviewing various Title VII sexual harassment claims).

6. See *Ellison*, 924 F.2d at 878-79 (acknowledging women may be more sensitive to sexual behavior because they are disproportionately victims of sexual assault); *Yates v. Avco Corp.*, 819 F.2d 630, 637 & n.2 (6th Cir. 1987) (noting different conduct may offend men and women); see also *Rabidue*, 805 F.2d at 636 (Keith, J., concurring in part, dissenting in part) (arguing reasonable person standard would ingrain aggressors' views of reasonable behavior).

7. See Kingsley R. Browne, "Title VII as Censorship: Hostile-Environment Harassment and the First Amendment," 52 *Ohio State L.J.* 481, 510-31 (1991) (considering First Amendment issues that sexual harassment regulation implicates); Marcy Strauss, "Sexist Speech in the Workplace," 25 *Harvard Civil Rights—Civil Liberties L. REV.* 1, 17-33 (1990) (analyzing First Amendment protection of sexist speech in workplace); see also *Robinson*, 760 F. Supp. at 1534-37 (concluding state interest in opening workplaces to women outweighs any free speech rights).

8. Catharine A. MacKinnon, *Feminism Unmodified: Discourses on Life and Law* 115 (1987) [hereinafter MacKinnon, *Feminism Unmodified*]; *see* Andrea Dworkin, *Pornography: Men Possessing Women* (1981) (analyzing pornography as expression of male domination and female subjugation).

9. Professor MacKinnon and Andrea Dworkin spearheaded efforts to enact anti-pornography ordinances in Minneapolis, Minnesota and Indianapolis, Indiana. See Andrea Dworkin & Catharine MacKinnon, *Pornography and Civil Rights: A New Day For Women's Equality* 60-66 (1988); Catharine MacKinnon, *Only Words* 90-97 (1993) [hereinafter MacKinnon, *Only Words*] (discussing antipornography ordinance and decision invalidating it). Indianapolis, Ind., Code § 16-3(q) (1984).

10. See *American Booksellers Ass'n v. Hudnut*, 771 F.2d 323, 331-32 (7th Cir. 1985) (concluding ordinance unconstitutional because it regulated expression on basis of content, establishing an approved viewpoint), *aff'd mem.*, 475 U.S. 1001 (1986).

11. See *R.A.V. v. City of St. Paul*, 112 S. Ct. 2538, 2547-48 (1992) (concluding that although city may prohibit "fighting words" generally, it may not prohibit racially-biased "fighting words").

12. See Brief of Amicus Curiae for Feminists for Free Expression at 22-

25, *Harris v. Forklift Sys, Inc.*, 114 S. Ct. 367 (1993) (No. 92-1168) (arguing that defining harassment broadly to include centerfold pictures and sexist jokes violates First Amendments); *cf.* Nan D. Hunter and Sylvia A. Law, Brief Amicus Curiae of Feminist Anticensorship Task Force et al., in *American Booksellers Association v. Hudnut*, in *Feminist Jurisprudence* 467, 472-77 (Patricia Smith, ed., 1993) (arguing ordinance prohibiting pornography unconstitutionally discriminated on basis of sex and gender stereotypes).

13. See Bettina B. Plevan, "Harris Won't End Harassment Questions," *Nat'l L.J.*, Dec. 6, 1993, at 19 (noting Supreme Court had opportunity in *Harris* to resolve standard in sexual harassment claims).

14. *Harris v. Forklift Sys., Inc.*, 114 S. Ct. 367, 370 (1993).

15. *Id.* at 371.

16. By "intersubjective" I mean the capacity for mutual understanding, or shared knowledge, or an understanding of the perspectives of others. See generally Abraham Kaplan, *The Conduct of Inquiry: Methodology for Behavioral Science* 127-28 (1964) (explaining behavioral science construct of "intersubjectivity").

17. Strauss, *supra* note 7, at 1-2 (footnotes omitted); *see also* Catharine MacKinnon, *Sexual Harassment of Working Women* 29-55 (1979) [hereinafter MacKinnon, *Sexual Harassment*] (recounting various women's experiences with sexual harassment).

18. *Harris v. Forklift Sys., Inc.*, No. 3-89-0557, 1991 WL 487444, at *3 (M.D. Tenn. Feb. 4, 1991), *aff'd*, 976 F.2d 733 (6th Cir. 1992), *rev'd*, 114 S. Ct. 367 (1993).

19. Robert C. Ford & Frank S. McLaughlin, "Sexual Harassment at Work," *Bus. Horizons*, Nov.-Dec. 1988, at 14, 17; *see also* Susan Crawford, "A Wink Here, a Leer There: It's Costly," *N.Y. Times*, Mar. 28, 1993, at F17 (reporting 50% to 85% of female employees are sexually harassed during careers, 15% in given year).

20. Michele Galen et al. "Sexual Harassment Out of the Shadows: The Thomas Hearings Force Business To Confront an Ugly Reality," *Bus. Wk.*, Oct. 28, 1991, at 30, 31; see also Crawford, *supra* note 20, at F17 (noting sexual harassment claims have been filed at 90% of Fortune 500 Companies).

21. See U.S. Merit Systems Protection Board Office of Policy and Evaluation, *Sexual Harassment in the Federal Government; An Update 16* (1988).

22. Id.

23. See David E. Terpstra, "Who Gets Sexually Harassed? Knowing How to Educate and Control Your Work Environment," *Personnel Admin.*, Mar. 1989, at 84, 85 (noting survey finding that women filed 94% of sexual harassment charges submitted to Illinois EEOC).

24. See Cynthia G. Bowman, "Street Harassment and the Informal Ghettoization of Women," 106 *Harvard L. Rev.* 517, 522-34 (1993) (discussing common ways women are sexually harassed on the street); Melinda Henneberger & Michel Marriott, "For Some, Youthful Courting Has Become a Game of Abuse," *N.Y. Times*, July II, 1993, at Al (reporting disturbingly high .prevalence of high schoolers engaging in sexual harassment to gain peer acceptance).

25. See Crawford, *supra* note 20, at F17 (reporting 1988 study's findings that sexual harassment causes $6.7 million loss to average large company).

26. 29 C.F.R. § 1604.11(a) (1993) (footnote omitted); see also *infra* notes 38-60 and accompanying text (discussing case law interpretation of standards employed to adjudicate sexual harassment claims).

27. Strauss, *supra* note 7, at 7.

28. See Strauss, *supra* note 7, at 8-9 (acknowledging difficulty of ascertaining what speech is degrading and by whose perspective courts should judge this).

29. 42 U.S.C. § 2000e-2 (1988 & Supp. Ill 1992).

30. See 110 Cong. Rec. 2577-84 (1986).

31. MacKinnon, *Sexual Harassment*, *supra* note 18, at 4.

32. MacKinnon, *Sexual Harassment*, *supra* note 18, at 1.

33. See MacKinnon, *Sexual Harassment, supra* note 18, at 32, 40 (describing these two forms of sexual harassment).

34. See MacKinnon, *Sexual Harassment*, *supra* note 18, at 106-27 (arguing Equal Protection Clause mandates equal treatment of men and women and Title VII requires nondiscriminatory treatment). See generally MacKinnon, *Feminism Unmodified, supra* note 8, at 206-13 (asserting Constitution excludes women; attacking First Amendment "absolutism" that protects pornography); MacKinnon, *Only Words, supra* note 9, at 50-53, 60-68; Catharine MacKinnon, *Towards a Feminist Theory of the State* 219-34 (1989) [hereinafter MacKinnon, *Feminist Theory*] (concluding sex discrimination laws are fundamentally flawed because they are shaped by men and measure women by male standard).

35. *See* MacKinnon, *Sexual Harassment, supra* note 18, at 208-13 (arguing sexual harassment limits women's employment opportunities); *cf.*

MacKinnon, *Feminist Theory, supra* note 34, at 241-43 (asserting sexual equality laws have been defined by men and therefore fail to recognize many inequalities).

36. 29 C.F.R. § 1604.1 l(a) (1993).
37. *Id.* § 1604.11(b). The EEOC indicated that a determination of sexual harassment would be resolved by looking "at the record as a whole and at the totality of the circumstances, such as the nature of the sexual advances and the context in which the alleged incidents occurred."
38. 477 U.S. 57 (1986).
39. *Id.* at 66.
40. *Id.* at 73. The plaintiff also testified that the supervisor sexually harassed other women, although she was not permitted to present all the evidence available to support this allegation. *Id.* at 60-61.
41. *Id.* at 64.
42. *Id.* at 66-67 (quoting *Henson v. City of Dundee*, 682 F.2d 897, 902 (11th Cir. 1982)).
43. *Meritor Sav. Bank, FSB v. Vinson*, 477 U.S. 57, 67 (1986).
44. *Id.* (alteration in original) (quoting *Henson*, 682 F.2d at 902).
45. *Id.* at 69.
46. *See id.* (noting lack of per se rules).
47. *Id.* at 72.
48. *Meritor Sav. Bank, FSB v. Vinson*, 477 U.S. 57, 72 (1986).
49. *Id.* at 74-75 (Marshall, J., dissenting).
50. *Id.* at 76-77.
51. 798 F.2d 210 (7th Cir. 1986).
52. *Id.* at 211.
53. *Id.* at 211-12.
54. *Id* at 212.
55. See id. (supervisor informed plaintiff that two brake jobs per day was insufficient). The supervisor stated that he "didn't want to pay a woman $7 an hour when he could get a man to do three brake jobs for that." *Id.*
56. See *Scott v. Sears, Roebuck & Co.*, 798 F.2d 210, 212-14 (7th Cir. 1986) (applying principles from *Meritor* and upholding summary judgment for employer).
57. *Id.* at 214.
58. *Id.* at 213-14.
59. *Id.*
60. *Id.* at 212-14

61. 805 F.2d 611 (6th Cir. 1986), *cert. denied,* 481 U.S. 1041 (1986).
62. See *id.* at 620 (stating plaintiff must demonstrate reasonable person in same circumstances would be affected).
63. *Id.* at 614.
64. *Id.* at 615.
65. *Id.* at 619-20. This five-part analysis has been employed by many courts in sexual harassment claims under Title VII.
66. *Rabidue v. Osceola Refining Co.,* 805 F.2d 611, 620 (6th Cir. 1986) (emphasis added), *cert. denied,* 481 U.S. 1041 (1987).
67. *Id.*
68. *Id.*
69. *Id.* at 621-23.
70. *Id.* at 621.
71. 881 F.2d 412 (7th Cir. 1989).
72. *Id.* at 419.
73. *Id.* at 416-17.
74. *Id.* at 417, 420.
75. *Id.* at 419-20.
76. *Brooms v. Regal Tube Co.,* 881 F.2d 412, 419-20 (7th Cir. 1989).
77. *Rabidue v. Osceola Refining Co.,* 805 F.2d 611, 626 (6th Cir. 1986) (Keith, J., dissenting), *cert. denied,* 481 U.S. 1041 (1987). Specifically, Judge Keith stated: Nor do I agree with the majority holding that a court considering hostile environment claims should adopt the perspective of the reasonable person's reaction to a similar environment. In my view, the reasonable person perspective fails to account for the wide divergence between most women's views of appropriate sexual conduct and those of men.... Moreover, unless the outlook of the reasonable woman is adopted, the defendants as well as the courts are permitted to sustain ingrained notions of reasonable behavior fashioned by the offenders, in this case, men. *Id.* (citations omitted).
78. *Id.*
79. *Id.*
80. See *Yates v. Avco Corp.,* 819 F.2d 630, 636-37 & n.2 (6th Cir. 1987) (holding standard should be reasonable person of victim's gender because different behavior offends men and women).
81. 760 F. Supp. 1486 (M.D. Fla. 1991).
82. *id.* at 1491.
83. See *id.* at 1494-99 (providing detailed description of comments made to plaintiff and pictures posted at worksite).

84. *Id.* at 1496.

85. *Id.*

86. *Robinson v. Jacksonville Shipyards*, 760 F. Supp. 1486, 1490 (M.D. Fla. 1991).

87. *Id.* at 1522-24 (quoting *Meritor Sav. Bank, FSB v. Vinson*, 477 U.S. 57, 67 (1986)); See *also supra* text accompanying note 65 (detailing similar five-part analysis set out in *Rabidue*).

88. *Robinson,* 760 F. Supp. at 1524. The court specified that: The objective standard asks whether a reasonable person of Robinson's sex, that is, a reasonable woman, would perceive that an abusive work environment had been created.... A reasonable woman would find the working environment at JSI was abusive. This conclusion reaches the totality of the circumstances, including the sexual remarks, the sexual jokes, the sexually oriented pictures of woman, and the nonsexual rejection of women by coworkers. *Id.*

89. See *id.* at 1524-27 (rejecting *Rabidue's* "social context" argument).

90. *Id.* at 1526.

91. 924 F.2d 872 (9th Cir. 1991).

92. *Id.* at 877-79.

93. *Id.* at 874.

94. Ellison requested the IRS to transfer her or the coworker. *Id.*

95. *Id.* at 875.

96. *Ellison v. Brady*, 924 F.2d 872, 878 (9th Cir. 1991).

97. *Id.*

98. *Id.* The court further stated: [W]e believe that in evaluating the severity and pervasiveness of sexual harassment, we should focus on the perspective of the victim. If we only examined whether a reasonable person would engage in allegedly harassing conduct, we would run the risk of reinforcing the prevailing level of discrimination. Harassers could continue to harass merely because a particular discriminatory practice was common ...*Id.* (citations omitted).

99. See *id.* at 878-79 (noting women may find behavior offensive that men believe is harmless).

100.See *id.* at 879 & n.ll (noting if alleged victim is male, court should use reasonable man standard).

101.*Id.* at 878-79.

102.*Ellison v. Brady*, 924 F.2d 872, 878-79 (9th Cir. 1991).

103.*See* generally Carol Gilligan, *In a Different Voice* (1982) (reporting and analyzing research regarding how women view relationships, morality, and decision making differently than men).

104.See *id.* at 159-71 (reporting men view themselves independently and separately whereas women concentrate on interdependence and view themselves in context of relationships).

105.See Suzanna Sherry, "Civic Virtue and the Feminine Voice in Constitutional Adjudication," 72 *Virginia Law Review* 543, 592-613 (1986) (contrasting O'Connor's opinions with male justices' and concluding she is more likely to impose individual responsibility to community).

106.See Susan Behuniak-Long, "Justice Sandra Day O'Connor and the Power of Maternal Legal Thinking," 54 *Rev. Pol.* 417, 426-37 (1992) (describing "feminine jurisprudence" and concluding O'Connor's opinions reflect these characteristics).

107.See Sherry, *supra* 105, at 563-79 (asserting American law has been defined by male liberalism, which is individualistic and values autonomy).

108.See Oayle Binon, "Toward a Feminist Regrounding of Constitutional Law," 72 *Soc. Sci. Q.* 207, 212-19 (1991) (arguing that women's sense of interrelatedness and community influences feminist constitutional analysis); Joan C. Williams, "Deconstructing Gender," 87 *Mich. L. Rev.* 797, 803-06 (1989) (describing modern feminist philosophy as embracing certain aspects of stereotype of women). See generally Kathryn Abrams, "Gender Discrimination and the Transformation of Workplace Norms," 42 *Vand. L. Rev.* 1183, 1186-97 (1989) (arguing women must challenge male norms which dominate workplaces because men structured them); Nancy S. Ehrenreich, "Pluralist Myths and Powerless Men: The Ideology of Reasonableness in Sexual Harassment Law," 99 *Yale L.J.* 1177, 1210-14 (1990) (discussing reasonable person icon and concluding it excludes many segments of American society, particularly women); Carol Sanger, "The Reasonable Woman and the Ordinary Man," 65 *S. Cal. L. Rev.* 1411,1411-17 (1992) (examining how reasonable woman standard will affect sexual harassment in the workplace).

109.See generally Mary F. Belensky et al., *Women's Ways of Knowing: The Development of Self, Voice, and Mind* (1986) (studying how women acquire and process knowledge and concluding male-dominated institutions do not cultivate women); Genevieve Lloyd, *The Man of Reason: "Male" and "Female" in Western Philosophy* 1-9 (2d ed. 1991) (discussing equivocation of rational with male and irrational with female in modem western philosophy).

110.See generally Nancy Chodorow, *The Reproduction of Mothering: Psychoanalysis and the Sociology of Gender* (1978) (examining women's role within family and noting differences in relationships of mother-daughter and mother-son); Sondra Farganis, *Social Reconstruction of the Feminine Character* (1986) (sociological and historical examination of "feminine" characteristics); Sandra Harding, *Whose Science? Whose Knowledge? Thinking from Women's Lives* (1991) (discussing various feminist theories and examining intersection with western science, knowledge, and social relations); Evelyn F. Keller, *A Feeling for the Organism: The Life and Work of Barbara McClintock* (1983) (biography of female scientist who played important role in creation of study of genetics); Nel Noddings, *Caring: A Feminine Approach to Ethics & Moral Education* (1984) (studying the "ethic of caring" and noting differences in how men and women approach ethics and morality); Sara Ruddick, "Maternal Thinking," in *Mothering: Essays in Feminist Theory* 213, 213-27 (Joyce Trebilcot ed., 1983) (explaining motherhood shapes women's thought processes, particularly the responsibility to preserve, foster, and shape their children); Sara Ruddick, "Preservative Love and Military Destruction: Some Reflections on Mothering and Peace," in: *Mothering: Essays in Feminist Theory* 231, 231-59 (Joyce Trebilcot ed., 1983) (exploring extent to which motherhood tends to make women more pacifistic and anti-militaristic than men).

111.See Judith A. Baer, *Women in American Law: The Struggle Toward Equality From the New Deal to the Present* (1991) (tracing women's modem efforts to influence and participate in patriarchal legal system).

112.See MacKinnon, *Feminist Theory, supra* note 34, at 237-49 (examining formulation of law from male perspective, excluding women); Katherine O'Donovan, "Before and After: The Impact of Feminism on the Academic Discipline of Law," in *Men's Studies Modified: The Impact of Feminism on the Academic Disciplines* 175, 176 (Dale Spender ed., 1981) (reasoning women do not enjoy legal rights because they were historically in private domain, unregulated by law).

113.See MacKinnon, *Feminism Unmodified, supra* note 8, at 105, 116 (concluding incorporation of women's experience into the law will fundamentally change the law).

114.See O'Donovan, *supra* note 112, at 176 (discussing reasons law does not treat men and women equally).

115.See MacKinnon, *Feminist Theory, supra* note 34, at 220-21 (asserting that although women are different than men, they are measured against men).

116. *Ellison v. Brady*, 924 F.2d 872, 879 (9th Cir. 1991) (noting women share common views regarding sexual abuse, rape, and harassment).

117. *Rabidue v. Oseola Refining Co.*, 805 F.2d 611, 622-23 (6th Cir. 1986), cert. denied, 481 U.S. 1041 (1987).

118. *Robinson v. Jacksonville Shipyards*, 760 F. Supp. 1486, 1524-25 (M.D. Fla. 1991).

119. See *Yates v. AVCO Corp.*, 819 F.2d 630, 637 (6th Cir. 1987) (stating constructive discharge because of sexual harassment should be judged by reasonable woman standard); *Stingley v. Arizona*, 796 F. Supp. 424, 428 (D. Ariz. 1992) (hostile environment should be judged on basis of reasonable person of victim's race of sex); *Smolsky v. Consolidated Rail Corp.*, 780 F. Supp. 283, 294-95 (E.D. Pa. 1991) (employing reasonable woman standard to sexual harassment claim); *Harris v. Forklift Sys., Inc.*, No. 3-89-0557, 1991 WL 487444, at *5 (M.D. Tenn. Feb. 4, 1991), aff'd, 976 F.2d 733 (6th Cir. 1992), rev'd, 114 S. Ct. 367 (1993); *Austen v. Hawaii*, 759 F. Supp. 612, 628 (D. Haw. 1991) (employing reasonable woman standard for sex discrimination claim), ajfd, 967 F.2d 583 (9th Cir. 1992); *Radtke v. Everett*, 189 Mich. App. 346, 353-54, 471 N.W.2d 660, 664 (1991) (adopting reasonable woman standard for sexual harassment claim), ajfd in part, rev'd in part, 442 Mich. 368, 501 N.W.2d 155 (1993); *Muench v. Township of Haddon*, 255 N.J. Super. 288, 299, 605 A.2d 242, 248 (App. Div. 1992) (evaluating sexual harassment claim by whether reasonable woman would consider conduct created hostile environment); cf. *Carrillo v. Ward Co.*, 770 F. Supp. 815, 822 (S.D.N.Y. 1991) (quoting reasonable woman standard from *Ellison* in context of allegation of unconstitutional sex discrimination); *Harris v. International Paper Co.*, 765 F. Supp. 1509, 1515 (D. Me. 1991) (adopting reasonable African-American standard for racial discrimination claim); *T.L. v. Toys 'R' Us, Inc.*, 255 N.J. Super. 616, 637-38, 605 A.2d 1125, 1137 (App. Div. 1992) (adopting reasonable woman standard to evaluate sexual harassment claims state law counterpart to Title VII), modified and ajfd, 132 N.J. 587, 626 A.2d 445 (1993); *State ex rel. Hughes v. City of Albuquerque*, 113 N.M. 209, 214, 824 P.2d 349, 354 (Ct. App. 1991) (using reasonable woman standard to evaluate claim of municipal employee discharged for sexual harassment). The *Austen* court stated that "[t]he perspective of a reasonable woman is justified because 'a sex-blind reasonable person standard tends to be male-biased and

tends to systematically ignore the experiences of women.' " *Austen,*
759 F. Supp. at 628 (quoting *Ellison,* 924 F.2d at 879). The *Radtke* court
adopted the reasonable woman standard, contending that: [W]e
believe that in a sexual harassment case involving a woman, the
proper perspective to view the offensive conduct from is that of the
"reasonable woman," not that of the "reasonable person." Thus, the
severity or pervasiveness of the conduct should be viewed from the
perspective of the victim, not that of a hypothetical employee
irrespective of gender. We believe that a standard which views
harassing conduct from the "reasonable person" perspective has the
tendency to be male-biased and runs the risk of reinforcing the
prevailing level of discrimination which the state Civil Rights Act
and title VII were designed to eliminate. In such a case, harassers
could continue to discriminate merely because such harassment was
the norm at the workplace. *Radtke,* 189 Mich. App. at 353-54, 471
N.W.2d at 664 (footnotes omitted) (citations omitted). The *Stingley*
court reasoned that a reasonable woman "standard is designed to
accommodate the different ways men and women may view similar
behavior," *Stingley,* 796 F. Supp. at 428.

120. *Harris v. Forklift Sys., Inc.,* No. 3-89-0557, 1991 WL 487444, at *8 (M.D.
Tenn. Feb. 4, 1991) (finding plaintiff failed to prove sexual
harassment created hostile environment), *affd,* 976 F.2d 733 (6th Cir.
1992), *rev'd,* 114 S. Ct. 367 (1993).

121. *Id.* at *7.

122. *Id.*

123. *Id.* Although the Supreme Court of the United States reversed the
district court's decision on the basis that proof of psychological
injuries is not necessary to prove a hostile environment, the Court
failed to address the reasonable person/woman/victim standard.
Harris v. Forklift Systems, Inc., 114 S. Ct. 367, 371 (1993).

124. *See Meritor Sav. Bank, FSB v. Vinson,* 477 U.S. 57, 67 (1986) (holding
sexual harassment that creates a hostile or abusive environment is
actionable under Title VII).

125. See generally Paul Feyerabend, *Farewell to Reason* (1987); Michel
Foucault, *The Order of Things: An Archeology of the Human Sciences*
(1973); David Harvey, *The Condition of Posmodernity: An Enquiry into
the Origins of Cultural Change* (1989).

126. Although not a postmodernist, Catharine MacKinnon argues that the
law embodies a male and patriarchal view of the law that excludes
and discriminates against women. MacKinnon, *Feminist Theory, supra*

note 34, at 237-49. Similarly, Andrea Dworkin describes pornography as a genre of male power, suggesting that it, along with other legal instruments of power, are used to exclude women from political power in our society. Dworkin, *supra* note 8, at 24-25.

127. *Ellison v. Brady*, 924 F.2d 872, 879 n.ll (9th Cir. 1991).

128. *Id.*

129. *Harris v. Forklift Sys., Inc.*, No. 3-89-0557, 1991 WL 487444, at *8 (M.D. Tenn. Feb. 4, 1991), aff'd, 976 F.2d 733 (6th Cir. 1992), *rev'd*, 114 S. Ct. 367 (1993).

130. 765 F. Supp. 1509 (D. Me. 1991).

131. *Id.* at 1515.

132. 796 F. Supp. 424 (D. Ariz. 1992).

133. *Id.* at 428-29 (citations omitted) (footnote omitted).

134. Hans-Georg Gadamer describes the "hermeneutic problem" of individuals being trapped by their own prejudices and horizons and, hence, unable to transcend them and place themselves in another perspective. Hans-Georg Gadamer, *Truth and Method* 274-341 (1982).

135. See *infra* notes 148-154 and accompanying text (discussing impact of reasonable woman standard).

136. See *supra* notes 119-135 and accompanying text (discussing evolving reasonable victim standard).

137. See *Sanger, supra* note 108, at 1415 (arguing reasonable woman standard necessary to secure women's equal access in workplace (quoting *Radtke v. Everett*, 189 Mich. App. 346, 354, 471 N.W.2d 660, 664 (1991))).

138. See *supra* notes 18-25 and accompanying text (discussing recent surveys showing prevalence of workplace sexual harassment).

139. See MacKinnon, *Feminism Unmodified, supra* note 8, at 107 (noting sexual harassment follows and transcends male hierarchy as males harass their female coworkers and superiors).

140. See MacKinnon, *Feminism Unmodified supra* note 8, at 105, 116 (challenging women to define sexual harassment law).

141. See MacKinnon, *Feminism Unmodified, supra* note 8, at 104 (urging women to use power of the law to assert self-determination).

142. See Strauss, *supra* note 7, at 22-29 (acknowledging argument that sexist speech is constitutionally protected free speech.)

143. *Cf. Feiner v. New York*, 340 U.S. 315, 320-21 (1951) (affirming right of state to suppress speech when it rises to level of incitement to riot).

144. See Michael Saltman, *The Demise of the 'Reasonable Man'* 1-10 (1991) (tracing the evolution of reasonable man standard in American law);

Abrams, *supra* note 108, at 1210-15 (discussing need to ascertain which claims result from purely idiosyncratic reactions).

145.See Brief of Amicus Curiae for Feminists for Free Expression at 8-9, *Harris v. Forklift Sys., Inc.*, 114 S. Ct. 367 (1993) (No. 92-1169).

146.See Note, "Pornography, Equality, and a Discrimination-Free Workplace: A Comparative Perspective," 106 *Harvard L. Rev.* 1075, 1090-91 (1993) (noting women frequently forced to employee's claim that male coworkers harassed him because conduct did not result in antimale environment). The purported harassment in *Goluszek* included male coworkers showing him pictures of nude women, offering to secure sex for him, and physically touching him. *Id.* At 1453-54. In this case, the court concluded that the conduct did not violate Title VII even though Goluszek may have been harassed because of his gender. *Id.* at 1456. The court reasoned that Title VII was intended to prevent exploitation of a power imbalance resulting in discrimination against a less powerful group. *Id.* Since Goluszek was a male in a male-dominated workplace, the court concluded that Title VII was not designed to reach such conduct. *Id.* A similar type of action by male colleagues towards women would be deemed a Title VII violation. *See* Browne, *supra* note 7, at 497-98 (asserting court would have found harassment had *Goluszek* plaintiff been female).

147.See *Robinson v. Jacksonville Shipyards, Inc.*, 760 F. Supp. 1486, 1535 (M.D. Fla. 1991) (concluding sexist speech can constitutionally be prohibited because women employees are captive audience). Similarly, the Supreme Court has upheld limits on speech to protect a captured audience. See *Frisby v. Schultz*, 487 U.S. 474, 487-88 (1988) (upholding ordinance limiting residential picketing directed at unwilling viewers); *Lehman v. City of Shaker Heights*, 418 U.S. 298, 304 (1974) (plurality) (upholding municipality's refusal to allow political advertising on transit system).

148.See Jeanne L. Schroeder, "Abduction from the Seraglio: Feminist Methodologies and the Logic of Imagination," 10 *Texas Law Review* 115, 143 (1991) (presenting argument that law reflects male perspective, therefore, law does not recognize certain injuries that women uniquely experience).

149.See *Goluszek v. Smith*, 697 F. Supp. 1452, 1456 (N.D. Ill. 1988).

150.*Harris v. Forklift Sys., Inc.*, No. 3-89-0557, 1991 WL 487444, at *5 (M.D. Tenn. Feb. 4, 1991) (dismissing plaintiff's Title VII claims), *affd*, 976 F.2d 733 (6th Cir. 1992), *rev'd*, 114 S. Ct. 367 (1993). One cannot be sure that the use of an alternative standard continually results in reaching a particular decision.

151. See Ehrenreich, *supra* note 108, at 1217 (asserting reasonable woman standard is neither inherently neutral nor fair).

152. See Susan Estrich, "Sex at Work," 43 *Stanford Law Review* 813, 845-46 (1991) (arguing reasonable woman is an idealized "superwoman" who behaves like a man).

153. See *J.E.B. v. Alabama ex re!. T.B.*, 128 L. Ed. 2d 89, 97 (1994) (holding Equal Protection Clause prohibits exercise of peremptory challenges on basis of gender); *Edmonson v. Leesville Concrete Co.*, Ill S. Ct. 2077, 2080 (1991) (holding racial criteria for peremptory challenges in civil trials violates Equal Protection Clause); *Powers v. Ohio*, III S. Ct. 1364, 1370 (1991) (holding Equal Protection Clause prohibits prosecutor's use of peremptory challenge on basis of race); *Batson v. Kentucky*, 476 U.S. 79, 86-88 (1986) (finding racial discrimination in selection of jurors harms accused, juror, and community).

154. A related argument against the reasonable victim standard is that it may preclude a fair trial. For example, if the perspective of the victim is definitive, then whatever the victim says is offensive and hostile is in fact offensive and hostile, and there is no method by which an alleged aggressor can win a case except by claiming that the victim is extra-sensitive or the victim's sensibilities are wrong or not the same as a reasonable victim of this victim's characteristics. Proving any of this would clearly be difficult, if not impossible.

155. See *Brooms v. Regal Tube Co.*, 881 F.2d 412, 417 (7th Cir. 1989) (manager showed black female employee photograph depicting interracial sodomy).

156. See *Moore v. Hughes Helicopters, Inc.*, 708 F.2d 475, 480 (9th Cir. 1983) (upholding determination that black female could not adequately represent class of all black or all female employees); *Payne v. Travenol Labs., Inc.*, 673 F.2d 798, 810-12 (5th Cir.) (considering black female's ability to represent class of black workers and class of female employees), *cert. denied*, 459 U.S. 1038 (1982); *Degraffenreid v. General Motors Assembly Div.*, 413 F. Supp. 142, 143 (E.D, Mo. 1976) (rejecting assertion black women are protected category; reasoning plaintiffs must prove sex and/or race discrimination), *aff'd in part, rev'd in part*, 558 F.2d 480 (8th Cir. 1977); see also Kimberle Crenshaw, "Demarginalizing the Intersection of Race and Sex: A Black Feminist Critique of Antidiscrimination Doctrine, Feminist Theory, and Antiracist Politics," 1989 *U. Chi. Legal F.* 139, 141-52 (examining cases

refusing to certify black women as a class; concluding black women are marginalized).

157.See Patricia A. Cain, "Feminist Jurisprudence: Grounding the Theories," 4 *Berkely Women's L.J.* 191, 210-14 (1989-90) (explaining because part of lesbians' lives is outside the patriarchal system, their feminist experience differs).

158.See Deborah L. Rhode, "Feminism and the State," 107 *Harvard Law Review* 1181, 1182-83 (noting race, ethnicity, sexual orientation, and class tend to divide women and complicates attempts to formulate unifed definition of feminism).

159.See Immanuel Kant, *Critique of Pure Reason* 93 (Norman K. Smith trans., 1968) ("Thoughts without content are empty, intuitions without concepts are blind.").

160.See Browne, *supra* note 7, at 502 (asserting EEOC definition of sexual harassment provides insufficient guidance of what expression Title VII prohibits).

161.Cf. Estrich, *supra* note 152, at 846 (arguing reasonable woman standard requires women to react like men); Note, "Sexual Harassment Claims of Abusive Environment Under Title VII," 91 *Harvard Law Review* 1449, 1459 (1984) (arguing even hypersensitive victim should recover if she notified employer she was offended yet conduct continued).

162.See Strauss, *supra* note 7, at 21-33 (presenting various theories under which sexist speech would be afforded constitutional protection).

163.Browne, *supra* note 7, at 500-02.

164.Indianapolis, Ind., Code § 16-3(q) (1984).

165.*American Booksellers Ass'n v. Hudnut*, 771 F.2d 323, 331-32 (7th Cir. 1985) (finding pornography is not a category of constitutionally unprotected expression), *aff'd mem.*, 475 U.S. 1001 (1986).

166.See Heather L. Hanson, Note, "The Fourth Amendment in the Workplace: Are We Really Being Reasonable?," 79 *VA. L. Rev.* 243, 246-47 (1993) (criticizing court's unwillingness to protect employees' privacy rights); Jane E. Bahls, "Checking up on Workers," 78 *Nation's Bus.*, Dec. 1990, at 29, 30 (discussing employer's exposure to liability for privacy invasion in investigating employers); Jennifer L. Laabs, "Surveillance: Tool or Trap?," 71 *Personnel J.*, June 1992, at 96, 96-98 (discussing methods of electronically monitoring employee performance); Ellen Bravo, "Mistrust and Manipulation: Electronic Monitoring of the American Workforce," *USA Today*, May 1991, at 46, 47 (citing statistics concerning monitoring activities of employers).

167.See Baer, *supra* note III, at 1-18 (explaining patriarchal legal system and its protective legislation).

168.Brief of Amicus Curiae for Feminists for Free Expression at 5, *Harris v. Forklift Sys.*, Inc., 114 S. Ct. 367 (1993) (No. 92-1168).

169.See *Robinson v. Jacksonville Shipyards, Inc.*, 760 F. Supp. 1486, 1535 (M.D. Fla. 1991) (recognizing women employees as captive audience at worksite).

170.See *id.* at 1524 (balance of men and women in workforce relevant in assessing severity and pervasiveness of harassment).

171.See *Collin v. Smith*, 447 F. Supp. 676, 686 (N.D. III.) (permitting Nazis to express their political philosophy in predominantly Jewish community), af*fd*, 578 F.2d 1197 (7th Cir.), *cert. denied*, 439 U.S. 916 (1978).

172.See John S. Mill, "On Liberty," in *Essential Works of John Stuart Mill* 300-01 (Max Lemer ed,, Bantam Books 1965).

173.See *United States v. O'Brien*, 391 U.S. 367, 377 (1968) (discussing requirement that regulation of speech be narrowly tailored to serve important or substantial state interests).

174.*Id.*

175.See Brief of Amicus Curiae for Feminists for Free Expression at 6-7, *Harris v. Forklift Sys., Inc.*, 114 S. Ct. 367 (1993) (No. 92-1168) (urging contraction of hostile environment scope and focus on harmfulness of conduct).

176.See Note, *supra* note 146, at 1091-92 (stressing focus should be on victim's reaction not on whether conduct was unusual).

177.See Estrich, *supra* note 152, at 858 (arguing women should not bejudged against "abstract idealized standard").

178.See Strauss, *supra* note 7, at 7 (describing four categories of sexist speech).

179.See *Beauhamais v. Illinois*, 343 U.S. 250, 263-64 (1952) (holding state may prohibit speech that libels particular racial group); *Chaplinsky v. New Hampshire*, 315 U.S. 568, 572 (1942) (holding state may ban speech that imposes injury or tends to incite breach of peace). But see *Cohen v. California*, 403 U.S. 15, 20 (1971) (limiting *Chaplinsky* by holding speech must be directed at individual not group); *New York Times Co. v. Sullivan*, 376 U.S. 254, 279-83 (1964) (undermining *Beauhamais* by finding libel may be constitutionally protected); Strauss, *supra* note 7, at 20-21 (acknowledging group libel and *Chaplinsky* probably insufficient basis for banning sexist speech).

180.See Strauss, *supra* note 7, at 4-5 (recommending balancing test rather than categorical exclusion of sexist speech). A balancing of interests test in Title VII adjudication may, however, weigh employee speech rights against the judge's own values. See Browne, *supra* note 7, at 538-39 (noting risk decision maker will judge speech against own values).

181.*Cf.* Estrich, *supra* note 152, at 858-59.

182.For discussions on how to assess the adequacy of participation to ensure meaningful input into political decision-making, see Lani Guinier, *The Tyranny of the Majority: Fundamental Fairness in Representative Democracy* 93-94 (1994); Hanna F. Pitkin, *The Concept of Representation* 209-40 (1967); David A. Schultz, *Property, Power, and American Democracy* 192-94 (1992).

183.See MacKinnon, *Sexual Harassment, supra* note 18, 1,4,215 (concluding harassment result of sexual inequalities on job).

184.For a general discussion of the value and importance of workplace democracy, see Bennett Harrison & Barry Bluestone, *The Great U-Turn: Corporate Restructuring and the Polarizing of America* 184-86 (1988) (discussing importance of workplace democracy); Len Krimerman & Frank Lindenfeld, Eds., *When Workers Decide: Workplace Democracy Takes Root in North America* (1992) (analyzing various models of worker democracy); Robert E. Lane, *The Market Experience* 235-313 (1991) (arguing workplace satisfaction should replace consumption as primary motivational focus).

185.Jurgen Habermas, Knowledge and Human Interests (Jeremy J. Shapiro, trans., 1971); Jorgen Habermas *The Structural Transformation of the Public Sphere* (Thomas Burger, trans., 1989); Jurgen Habermas, *1 Theory of Communicative Action: Reason and the Rationalization of Society* (Thomas McCarthy, trans., 1981); Jurgen Habermas, *2 Theory of Communicative Action: Lifeworld and System: A Critique of Functionalist Reason* (Thomas McCarthy, trans., 1987).

Part 4
Appendix

Selected Bibliography

Books

Baxter, Ralph and Lynne Hermle. *Sexual Harassment in the Work Place: A Guide to the Law*. New York: Executive Enterprises Publications, 1989.

Crichton, Michael. *Disclosure*. New York: Knopf, 1994.

Dziech , Billie Wright. *The Lecherous Professor: Sexual Harassment on Campus*. Champaign: University of Illinois Press, 1990.

Forell, Caroline A. and Donna M. Matthews. *A Law of Her Own: The Reasonable Woman as a Measure of Man*. New York: New York University Press, 1999.

Gates, Henry Louis. *Speaking of Race, Speaking of Sex*. New York: New York University Press, 1994.

Gredes, Louise (editor). *Sexual Harassment (Current Controversies Series)*. San Diego: Greenhaven Press, 1999.

Hartel, Lynda Jones and Helena M. VonVille. *Sexual Harassment: A Selected, Annotated Bibliography*. Westport, CT: Greenwood Publishing Group, 1995.

Hill, Anita. *Speaking Truth to Power*. Norman, OK: University of Oklahoma Press, 1997.

Hill, Anita (editor) and Emma Coleman Jordan (Editor). *Race, Gender, and Power in America : The Legacy of the Hill-Thomas Hearings*. New York: Oxford University Press, 1995.

Lemoncheck, Linda (Editor) and James P. Sterba (Editor). *Sexual Harassment : Issues and Answers*. New York: Oxford University Press, 2001.

Levy, Anne and Michele Antoinette Paludi. *Workplace Sexual Harassment*. Upper Saddle River, NJ: Prentice Hall, 1996.

Lindemann, Barbara and David Kadue. *Primer on Sexual Harassment*. Washington, D.C.: BNA Books, 1992.

———. *Sexual Harassment in Employment Law*. Washington, D. C.: BNA Books, 1992.

———. *Sexual Harassment in Employment Law : 1999 Cumulative Supplement*. Washington, D. C.: BNA Books, 1999.

MacKinnon, Catharine. *Feminism Unmodified: Discourses on Life and Law*. Cambridge, MA: Harvard University Press, 1987.

———. *Only Words*. Cambridge, MA: Harvard University Press, 1993.

———. *Sexual Harassment of Working Women: A Case of Sex Discrimination*. New Haven, CT: Yale University Press, 1979.

———. *Toward a Feminist Theory of the State*. Cambridge, MA: Harvard University Press, 1989.

Mayer, Jane and Jill Abramson. *Strange Justice : The Selling of Clarence Thomas*. New York: Houghton Mifflin Company, 1994.

Miller, Anita (editor). *The Complete Transcripts of the Clarence Thomas-Anita Hill Hearings: October 11, 12, 13, 1991.* Chicago: Academy Chicago Publishers, 1994.

Mink, Gwendolyn. *Hostile Environment : The Political Betrayal of Sexually Harassed Women.* Ithaca, NY: Cornell University Press, 2000.

Paludi, Michelle and Richard Barickman. *Academic and Work Place Sexual Harassment.* Albany, NY: SUNY Press, 1991.

Patai, Daphne. *Heterophobia : Sexual Harassment and the Future of Feminism.* Lanham, MD: Rowman & Littlefield, 1998.

Phelps, Timothy M. and Helen Winternitz. *Capitol Games: The Inside Story of Clarence Thomas, Anita Hill, and a Supreme Court Nomination.* New York: Hyperion Press, 1992.

Roiphe, Katie. *The Morning After : Sex, Fear, and Feminism.* New York: Little Brown & Company, 1994.

Rosen, Jeffrey. *The Unwanted Gaze: The Destruction of Privacy in America.* New York: Random House, 2001.

Sandler, Bernice R. (editor) and Robert J. Shoop (editor). *Sexual Harassment on Campus: A Guide for Administrators, Faculty, and Students.* New York: Allyn & Bacon, 1996.

Schneider, Elizabeth. *Battered Women and Feminist Lawmaking.* New Haven, CT: Yale University Press, 2000.

Smitherman, Geneva (editor). *African American Women Speak Out on Anita Hill-Clarence Thomas.* Dertoit: Wayne State University Press, 1995.

Stein, Laura W. (editor). *Sexual Harassment in America.* Westport, CT: Greenwood Publishing Group, 1999.

Strossen, Nadine. *Defending Pornography : Free Speech, Sex, and the Fight for Women's Rights.* New York: New York University Press, 1999.

Weizer, Paul. *The Supreme Court and Sexual Harassment.* Lanham, MD: Lexington Books, 2000.

Articles

Alexander, Kamla. "A Modest Proposal: The "Reasonable Victim" Standard and Alaska Employers' Affirmative Defense to Vicarious Liability for Sexual Harassment." *Alaska Law Review,* 17 (December, 2000): 297- 324.

Ator, Jennifer J. "Same-Sex Sexual Harassment After Oncale v. Sundowner Offshore Services, Inc.: Overcoming the History of Judicial Discrimination in Light of the "Common Sense" Standard." *American University Journal of Gender and* Law, 6 (Summer, 1998): 583-615.

Baldrate, Brian C. "Agency Law and the Supreme Court's Compromise on 'Hostile Environment' Sexual Harassment in *Burlington Industries, Inc. v. Ellerth* and *Faragher v. City of Boca Raton." Connecticut Law* Review, 31 (Spring, 1999): 1149-1177.

Balkan, J.M. "Free Speech and Hostile Environments." *Columbia University Law Review,* 99 (December 1999): 2295-2318.

Bernstein, David E. "Sex Discrimination Laws Versus Civil Liberties." *University of Chicago Legal Forum,* 1999 (1999): 133-197.

Browne, Kingsley. "Title VII as Censorship: Hostile Environment Harassment and the First Amendment." *Ohio State Law Journal*, 52 (Spring, 1991): 481-550.

Buchanan, Paul and Courtney W. Wiswall. "The Evolving Understanding of Workplace Harassment and Employer Liability: Implications of Recent Supreme Court Decisions Under Title VII." *Wake Forest Law Review*, 34 (Spring, 1999): 55-69.

Burns Jr.,James A. "Sexual Harassment as Free Speech." *Employee Relations Law Journal*, 17, 4 (Spring 1992): 693-701.

Candido, Amy H. 1997, "A Right to Talk Dirty?: Academic Freedom Values and Sexual Harassment in the University Classroom." *University of Chicago Law School Roundtable*, 4 (1997): 85- 126.

Clark, Charles. "On Sexual Harassment." *CQ Researcher* (August 1991): 538-559.

Clougherty, Lydia, D. "Feminist Legal Methods and the First Amendment Defense to Sexual Harassment Liability." *Nebraska Law Review*, 75 (1996): 1-24.

Davis, Paul A. "What Is Sex? Heterosexual-Male-on-Male Sexual Harassment Actions After *Oncale v. Sundowner Offshore Services, Inc.*" 71 *Southern California Law Review*, 71 (September, 1998): 1341-1376.

Eddy, Margery Corbin. "Finding the Appropriate Standard for Employer Liability in Title VII Retaliation Cases: An Examination of the Applicability of Sexual Harassment Paradigms." 63 *Albany Law Review*, (1999): 361-378.

Epstein, Deborah. "Can a 'Dumb Ass Woman' Achieve Equality in the Workplace? Running the Gauntlet of Hostile Environment Harassing Speech." *Georgetown Law Review*, 84 (1996): 399-452.

Estlund, Cynthia. "Freedom of Speech in the Workplace and the Problem of Discriminatory Harassment." *Texas Law Review*, 75 (1997): 687-707.

Fallon, Jr., Richard H. "Sexual Harassment, Content Neutrality, and the First Amendment Dog That Didn't Bark." 1994 *Supreme Court Review*, 1-44.

Foster, Laura. "A Modified Approach to Claims of Sexual Harassment Under Title IX: Finding Protection Against Peer Sexual Harassment." *University of Cincinnati Law Review*, 67 (1999): 1229-1267.

Flemling, Gerturud M. & Richard A. Posner. "Status, Signaling and the Law, with Particular Application to Sexual Harassment" *University of Pennsylvania Law Review*, 147 (May 1999): 1069-1109.

Graham, Amy K. "*Gebser v. Lago Vista Independent School District*: The Supreme Court's Determination That Children Deserve Less Protection than Adults from Sexual Harassment." *Loyola University of Chicago Law Journal*, 30 (1999): 551-599.

Greve, Michael, B. "Sexual Harassment: Telling the Other Victim's Story." *Northern Kentucky Law Review*, 23 (1996): 523-539.

Hames, David. "Examining the Relationship Between Title VII's Sexual Harassment Prohibitions and the First Amendment's Free Speech Provisions: Is There a Conflict?" *Labor Law Journal*, (March 1995): 175-181.

Harris, Anne-Marie and Kenneth B. Grooms. "A New Lesson Plan for Educational Institutions: Expanded Rules Governing Liability Under Title IX of the Education Amendments of 1972 for Student and Faculty Sexual Harassment." *American University Journal of Gender, Social Policy, and Law* 8 (2000): 575-631.

Houghton, Kim. "Internet Pornography in the Library: Can the Public Library Employer Be Liable for Third-Party Sexual Harassment When a Client Displays Internet Pornography to Staff?" *Brooklyn Law Review*, 65 (1999): 827-880.

Hunt, Valerie B. "*Faragher v. Boca Raton*: Employer Liability in Hostile Environment Sexual Harassment Cases—Ignorance Is No Longer Bliss." *Arkansas Law Review*, 52 (1999): 479-497.

Jean, Shelby. "Peer Sexual Harassment Since *Oncale* and *Davis*: Taking Sex Out of Sexual Harassment." *Detroit College Law Review*, 2000 (Summer, 2000): 485-510.

Juliano, Ann and Stewart J. Schwab. "The Sweep of Sexual Harassment Cases." *Cornell Law Review*, 86 (March, 2001): 548-595.

Kaesebier, Tara. "Employer Liability in Supervisor Sexual Harassment Cases: The Supreme Court Finally Speaks." *Arizona State Law Journal*, 31 (Spring, 1999): 203-229.

Karner, Jessica. "Political Speech, Sexual Harassment, and a Captive Work Force." *California Law Review*, 83 (March 1995): 637-673.

Kelsey, Lisa M. "Kids with the Kissies and Schools with the Jitters: Finding a Reasonable Solution to the Problem of Student-to-Student Sexual Harassment in Elementary Schools." *Boston University Public Interest Law Journal,* 8 (Fall, 1998): 119-146.

Kreisberg, Jill. "Employers and Employees Beware: The Duties Imposed by the Recent Supreme Court Decisions and Their Impact on Sexual Harassment Law." *Cardoza Women's Law Journal,* 6 (1999): 153-180.

Kruse, Brian S. "Strike One--You're Out! Cautious Employers Lose Under New Sexual Harassment Law: *Faragher v. City of Boca Raton." Nebraska Law Review,* 78 (1999): 444-469.

Lawton, Anne. "The Emperor's New Clothes: How the Academy Deals with Sexual Harassment." *Yale Journal of Law and Feminism,* 11 (1999): 75-153.

Lussier, Deb. "*Oncale v. Sundowner Offshore Services Inc.* and the Future of Title VII Sexual Harassment Jurisprudence." *Boston College Law Review,* 39 (July, 1998): 937-963.

Nash, Maureen O. "Student on Student Sexual Harassment: If Schools Are Liable, What About the Parents?" *Creighton Law Review,* 31 (June, 1998): 1131-1153.

Oppenheimer, David B. "Workplace Harassment and the First Amendment: A Reply to Professor Volokh." *Berkeley Journal of Employment & Labor Law,* 17 (1996): 320-331.

Overman, Tracey Williams. "Employment Discrimination Law— Title VII and Same-Sex Sexual Harassment—Closing the Great Divide: What to Do in a Same-Sex Sexual Harassment Case: *Oncale v. Sundowner Offshore Services, Inc." University of Arkansas Little Rock Law Review,* 21 (Winter, 1999): 323-351.

Peirce, Ellen R. "Reconciling Sexual Harassment Sanctions and Free Speech Rights in the Workplace." *Virginia Journal of Social Policy and Law,* 4 (Fall, 1996): 127-204.

Pontes, Audra. "Peer Sexual Harassment: Has Title IX Gone Too Far?" *Emory Law Journal,* 47 (Winter, 1998): 341-373.

Rauch, Jonathan. "Cover Story, Offices and Gentlemen." *The New Republic* (June 23, 1997,): 22-28.

Rosen, Jeff. "Court Watch: Reasonable Women." *The New Republic* (November 1, 1993): 12.

Ruark, Kimberly S. "Damned If You Do, Damned If You Don't? Employers' Challenges in Conducting Sexual Harassment Investigations." *Georgia State University Law Review,* 17 (Winter, 2000): 575-605.

Sangree, Suzanne. "Title VII Prohibitions Against Hostile Environment Sexual Harassment and the First Amendment: No Collision in Sight." *Rutgers University Law Review,* 47 (Winter 1995): 461-561.

Scalia, Eugene. "The Strange Career of Quid Pro Quo Sexual Harassment." *Harvard Journal of Law and Public Policy,* 21 (Spring, 1998): 307-322.

Schultz, David. "From Reasonable Man to Unreasonable Victim." *Suffolk University Law Review,* 27 (1995): 717-748.

Schultz, Vicki. "Reconceptualizing Sexual Harassment." *Yale Law Journal,* 107 (April, 1998): 1683-1730.

Stone-Harris, Regina L. "Same-SexHarassment: The Next Step in the Evolution of Sexual Harassment Law Under Title VII." *St. Mary's Law Journal,* 28 (1996,): 269-312.

Storrow, Richard F. "Same-Sex Sexual Harassment Claims After *Oncale*: Defining the Boundaries of Actionable Conduct." *American University Law Review,* 47 (February, 1998): 677-744.

Strossen, Nadine. "Regulating Workplace Sexual Harassment and Upholding the First Amendment –Avoiding a Collision." *Villanova Law Review,* 37 (1992): 757- 804.

Sutton, Richard D. "Suits About Nothing: Does the Seinfeld Case Indicate That Businesses Need to Reconsider the Rights of Employees Accused of Sexual Harassment?" *University of Pennsylvania Journal of Labor and Employment Law,* 2 (Fall, 1999): 345-368.

Volokh, Eugene. "What Speech Does "Hostile Work Environment" Harassment Law Restrict?" *Georgetown Law Journal,* 85 (1997): 627- 653.

———. "Freedom of Speech and Appellate Review in Work Place Harassment Cases." *Northwestern Law Review,* 90, 3, (1996): 1009-1031.

———."Freedom of Speech in Cyberspace from the Listener's Perspective." *U. Chicago Legal Forum* 377 (1996): 414-21.

———. "Thinking Ahead About Freedom of Speech and Hostile Work Environment Harassment." 17 *Berkeley Journal of Employment & Labor Law,* 17 (1996): 305-333.

———. "Freedom of Speech and Work Place Harassment." *UCLA Law Review,* 39 (1992): 1791-1872.

Welsh, Diane M. "Limiting Liability Through Education: Do School Districts Have a Responsibility to Teach Students

About Peer Sexual Harassment?" *American University Journal of Gender and Law*, 6 (Fall, 1997): 165-199.

Williams, C. Scott. "Schools, Peer Sexual Harassment, Title IX, and *Davis v. Monroe County Board of Education.*" *Baylor Law Review*, 51 (Fall, 1999): 1087-1111.

Wood, Casey J. "Inviting Sexual Harassment: The Absurdity of the Welcomeness Requirement in Sexual Harassment Law." *Brandeis Law Journal*, 38 (Winter, 2000): 423-438.

Woodward, Lisa M. "Collision in the Classroom: Is Academic Freedom a License for Sexual Harassment." *Capital University Law Review*, 27 (1999): 667-715.

Zalesne, Deborah. "Sexual Harassment Law: Has It Gone Too Far, or Has the Media?" *Temple Politics and Civil Rights Law Review*, 8 (Spring, 1999): 351-377.

Title VII, Civil Rights Act of 1964

Pub. L. 88-352, 78 Stat. 253 42 U.S.C. 2000e

Unlawful Employment Practices

SEC. 2000e-2. [Section 703]

(a) It shall be an unlawful employment practice for an employer—

(1) to fail or refuse to hire or to discharge any individual, or otherwise to discriminate against any individual with respect to his compensation, terms, conditions, or privileges of employment, because of such individual's race, color, religion, sex, or national origin; or

(2) to limit, segregate, or classify his employees or applicants for employment in any way which would deprive or tend to deprive any individual of employment opportunities or otherwise adversely affect his status as an employee, because of such individual's race, color, religion, sex, or national origin.

(b) It shall be an unlawful employment practice for an employment agency to fail or refuse to refer for employment, or otherwise to discriminate against, any individual because of his race, color, religion, sex, or national origin, or to classify or refer for employment any individual on the basis of his race, color, religion, sex, or national origin.

Enforcement Guidance: Vicarious Employer Liability for Unlawful Harassment by Supervisors

The U.S. Equal Employment Opportunity Commission
EEOC Notice 915.002 Issued 6/18/99

Introduction

In *Burlington Industries, Inc. v. Ellerth*, 118 S. Ct. 2257 (1998), and *Faragher v. City of Boca Raton*, 118 S. Ct. 2275 (1998), the Supreme Court made clear that employers are subject to vicarious liability for unlawful harassment by supervisors. The standard of liability set forth in these decisions is premised on two principles: 1) an employer is responsible for the acts of its supervisors, and 2) employers should be encouraged to prevent harassment and employees should be encouraged to avoid or limit the harm from harassment. In order to accommodate these principles, the Court held that an employer is always liable for a supervisor's harassment if it culminates in a tangible employment action. However, if it does not, the employer may be able to avoid liability or limit damages by establishing an affirmative defense that includes two necessary elements:

> (a) the employer exercised reasonable care to prevent and correct promptly any harassing behavior, and
> (b) the employee unreasonably failed to take advantage of any preventive or corrective opportunities provided by the employer or to avoid harm otherwise.

While the *Faragher* and *Ellerth* decisions addressed sexual harassment, the Court's analysis drew upon standards set forth in cases involving harassment on other protected bases. Moreover, the Commission has always taken the position that the same basic standards apply to all types of prohibited harassment. Thus, the standard of liability set forth in the decisions applies to all forms of unlawful harassment.

Harassment remains a pervasive problem in American workplaces. The number of harassment charges filed with the EEOC and state fair employment practices agencies has risen significantly in recent years. For example, the number of sexual harassment charges has increased from 6,883 in fiscal year 1991 to 15,618 in fiscal year 1998. The number of racial harassment charges rose from 4,910 to 9,908 charges in the same time period.

While the anti-discrimination statutes seek to remedy discrimination, their primary purpose is to prevent violations. The Supreme Court, in *Faragher* and *Ellerth*, relied on Commission guidance which has long advised employers to take all necessary steps to prevent harassment. The new affirmative defense gives credit for such preventive efforts by an employer, thereby "implement[ing] clear statutory policy and complement[ing] the Government's Title VII enforcement efforts."

The question of liability arises only after there is a determination that unlawful harassment occurred. Harassment does not violate federal law unless it involves discriminatory treatment on the basis of race, color, sex, religion, national origin, age of 40 or older, disability, or protected activity under the anti-discrimination statutes. Furthermore, the anti-discrimination statutes are not a "general civility code." Thus federal law does not prohibit simple teasing, offhand comments, or isolated incidents that are not "extremely serious." Rather, the conduct must be "so objectively offensive as to alter the 'conditions' of the victim's employment." The conditions of employment are altered only if the harassment culminated in a tangible employment action or was sufficiently severe or pervasive to create a hostile work environment. Existing Commission guidance on the standards for determining whether challenged conduct rises to the level of unlawful harassment remains in effect.

This document supersedes previous Commission guidance on the issue of vicarious liability for harassment by supervisors. The

Commission's long-standing guidance on employer liability for harassment by co-workers remains in effect—an employer is liable if it knew or should have known of the misconduct, unless it can show that it took immediate and appropriate corrective action. The standard is the same in the case of non-employees, but the employer's control over such individuals' misconduct is considered.

The Vicarious Liability Rule Applies to Unlawful Harassment on All Covered Bases

The rule in *Ellerth* and *Faragher* regarding vicarious liability applies to harassment by supervisors based on race, color, sex (whether or not of a sexual nature), religion, national origin, protected activity, age, or disability. Thus, employers should establish anti-harassment policies and complaint procedures covering all forms of unlawful harassment.

Who Qualifies as a Supervisor?

Harasser in Supervisory Chain of Command

An employer is subject to vicarious liability for unlawful harassment if the harassment was committed by "a supervisor with immediate (or successively higher) authority over the employee." Thus, it is critical to determine whether the person who engaged in unlawful harassment had supervisory authority over the complainant.

The federal employment discrimination statutes do not contain or define the term "supervisor." The statutes make employers liable for the discriminatory acts of their "agents," and supervisors are agents of their employers. However, agency principles "may not be transferable in all their particulars" to the federal employment discrimination statutes. The determination of whether an individual has sufficient authority to qualify as a "supervisor" for purposes of vicarious liability cannot be resolved by a purely mechanical application of agency law. Rather, the purposes of the anti-discrimination statutes and the reasoning of the Supreme Court decisions on harassment must be considered.

The Supreme Court, in *Faragher* and *Ellerth*, reasoned that vicarious liability for supervisor harassment is appropriate because supervisors are aided in such misconduct by the authority that the employers delegated to them. Therefore, that authority must be of a sufficient magnitude so as to assist the harasser explicitly or implicitly in carrying out the harassment. The determination as to whether a harasser had such authority is based on his or her job function rather than job title (e.g., "team leader") and must be based on the specific facts.

An individual qualifies as an employee's "supervisor" if: the individual has authority to undertake or recommend tangible employment decisions affecting the employee; or the individual has authority to direct the employee's daily work activities.

Authority to Undertake or Recommend Tangible Employment Actions

An individual qualifies as an employee's "supervisor" if he or she is authorized to undertake tangible employment decisions affecting the employee. "Tangible employment decisions" are decisions that significantly change another employee's employment status. (For a detailed explanation of what constitutes a tangible employment action, see subsection IV(B), below.) Such actions include, but are not limited to, hiring, firing, promoting, demoting, and reassigning the employee. As the Supreme Court stated, "[t]angible employment actions fall within the special province of the supervisor."

An individual whose job responsibilities include the authority to recommend tangible job decisions affecting an employee qualifies as his or her supervisor even if the individual does not have the final say. As the Supreme Court recognized in *Ellerth*, a tangible employment decision "may be subject to review by higher level supervisors." As long as the individual's recommendation is given substantial weight by the final decisionmaker(s), that individual meets the definition of supervisor.

Authority to Direct Employee's Daily Work Activities

An individual who is authorized to direct another employee's day-to-day work activities qualifies as his or her supervisor even if that individual does not have the authority to undertake or recommend tangible job decisions. Such an individual's ability to commit harassment is enhanced by his or her authority to increase the employee's workload or assign undesirable tasks, and hence it is appropriate to consider such a person a "supervisor" when determining whether the employer is vicariously liable.

In *Faragher*, one of the harassers was authorized to hire, supervise, counsel, and discipline lifeguards, while the other harasser was responsible for making the lifeguards' daily work assignments and supervising their work and fitness training. There was no question that the Court viewed them both as "supervisors," even though one of them apparently lacked authority regarding tangible job decisions.

An individual who is temporarily authorized to direct another employee's daily work activities qualifies as his or her "supervisor" during that time period. Accordingly, the employer would be subject to vicarious liability if that individual commits unlawful harassment of a subordinate while serving as his or her supervisor.

On the other hand, someone who merely relays other officials' instructions regarding work assignments and reports back to those officials does not have true supervisory authority. Furthermore, someone who directs only a limited number of tasks or assignments would not qualify as a "supervisor." For example, an individual whose delegated authority is confined to coordinating a work project of limited scope is not a "supervisor."

Harasser Outside Supervisory Chain of Command

In some circumstances, an employer may be subject to vicarious liability for harassment by a supervisor who does not have actual authority over the employee. Such a result is appropriate if the employee reasonably believed that the harasser had such power. The employee might have such a belief because, for example, the chains of command are unclear. Alternatively, the employee might reasonably believe that a harasser with broad delegated powers has the ability to significantly influence employment decisions affecting him or her even if the harasser is outside the employee's chain of command.

If the harasser had no actual supervisory power over the employee, and the employee did not reasonably believe that the harasser had such authority, then the standard of liability for co-worker harassment applies.

Harassment by Supervisor That Results in a Tangible Employment Action

Standard of Liability

An employer is always liable for harassment by a supervisor on a prohibited basis that culminates in a tangible employment action. No affirmative defense is available in such cases. The Supreme Court recognized that this result is appropriate because an employer acts through its supervisors, and a supervisor's undertaking of a tangible employment action constitutes an act of the employer.

Definition of "Tangible Employment Action"

A tangible employment action is "a significant change in employment status." Unfulfilled threats are insufficient. Characteristics of a tangible employment action are:

it requires an official act of the enterprise;
it usually is documented in official company records;
it may be subject to review by higher level supervisors; and
it often requires the formal approval of the enterprise and use of
its internal processes.

A tangible employment action usually inflicts direct economic harm. A tangible employment action, in most instances, can only be caused by a supervisor or other person acting with the authority of the company.

Examples of tangible employment actions include:
hiring and firing; promotion and failure to promote; demotion; undesirable reassignment; a decision causing a significant change in benefits; compensation decisions; and work assignment.

Any employment action qualifies as "tangible" if it results in a significant change in employment status. For example, significantly changing an individual's duties in his or her existing job constitutes a tangible employment action regardless of whether the individual retains the same salary and benefits. Similarly, altering an individual's duties in a way that blocks his or her opportunity for promotion or salary increases also constitutes a tangible employment action.

On the other hand, an employment action does not reach the threshold of "tangible" if it results in only an insignificant change in the complainant's employment status. For example, altering an individual's job title does not qualify as a tangible employment action if there is no change in salary, benefits, duties, or prestige, and the only effect is a bruised ego. However, if there is a significant change in the status of the position because the new title is less prestigious and thereby effectively constitutes a demotion, a tangible employment action would be found.

If a supervisor undertakes or recommends a tangible job action based on a subordinate's response to unwelcome sexual demands, the employer is liable and cannot raise the affirmative defense. The result is the same whether the employee rejects the demands and is subjected to an adverse tangible employment action or submits to the demands and consequently obtains a tangible job benefit. Such harassment previously would have been characterized as "quid pro quo." It would be a perverse result if the employer is foreclosed from raising the affirmative defense if its supervisor denies a tangible job benefit based on an employee's rejection of unwelcome sexual demands, but can raise the defense if its supervisor grants a tangible job benefit based on submission to such demands. The Commission rejects such an analysis. In both those situations the supervisor undertakes a tangible employment action on a discriminatory basis. The Supreme Court stated that there must be a significant change in employment status; it did not require that the change be adverse in order to qualify as tangible.

If a challenged employment action is not "tangible," it may still be considered, along with other evidence, as part of a hostile environment claim that is subject to the affirmative defense. In *Ellerth*, the Court concluded that there was no tangible employment action because the supervisor never carried out his threats of job harm. *Ellerth* could still proceed with her claim of harassment, but the claim was properly "categorized as a hostile work environment claim which requires a showing of severe or pervasive conduct." 118 S. Ct. at 2265.

Link Between Harassment and Tangible Employment Action

When harassment culminates in a tangible employment action, the employer cannot raise the affirmative defense. This sort of claim is analyzed like any other case in which a challenged employment action is alleged to be discriminatory. If the employer produces evidence of a non-discriminatory explanation for the tangible employment action, a determination must be made whether that explanation is a pretext designed to hide a discriminatory motive.

For example, if an employee alleged that she was demoted because she refused her supervisor's sexual advances, a determination would have to be made whether the demotion was because of her response to the advances, and hence because of her sex. Similarly, if an employee alleges that he was discharged after being subjected to severe or pervasive harassment by his supervisor based on his national origin, a determination would have to be made whether the discharge was because of the employee's national origin.

A strong inference of discrimination will arise whenever a harassing supervisor undertakes or has significant input into a tangible employment action affecting the victim, because it can be "assume[d] that the harasser...could not act as an objective, non-discriminatory decisionmaker with respect to the plaintiff." However, if the employer produces evidence of a non-discriminatory reason for the action, the employee will have to prove that the asserted reason was a pretext designed to hide the true discriminatory motive.

If it is determined that the tangible action was based on a discriminatory reason linked to the preceding harassment, relief could be sought for the entire pattern of misconduct culminating in the tangible employment action, and no affirmative defense is available. However, the harassment preceding the tangible employment action must be severe or pervasive in order to be actionable. If the tangible employment action was based on a non-discriminatory motive, then the employer would have an opportunity to raise the affirmative defense to a claim based on the preceding harassment.

Harassment by Supervisor That Does Not Result in a Tangible Employment Action

Standard of Liability

When harassment by a supervisor creates an unlawful hostile environment but does not result in a tangible employment action, the employer can raise an affirmative defense to liability or damages, which it must prove by a preponderance of the evidence. The defense consists of two necessary elements:

> (a) the employer exercised reasonable care to prevent and correct promptly any harassment; and
> (b) the employee unreasonably failed to take advantage of any preventive or corrective opportunities provided by the employer or to avoid harm otherwise.

Effect of Standard

If an employer can prove that it discharged its duty of reasonable care and that the employee could have avoided all of the harm but unreasonably failed to do so, the employer will avoid all liability for unlawful harassment. For example, if an employee was subjected to a pattern of disability-based harassment that created an unlawful hostile environment, but the employee unreasonably failed to complain to management before she suffered emotional harm and the employer exercised reasonable care to prevent and promptly correct the harassment, then the employer will avoid all liability.

If an employer cannot prove that it discharged its duty of reasonable care and that the employee unreasonably failed to avoid the harm, the employer will be liable. For example, if unlawful harassment by a supervisor occurred and the employer failed to exercise reasonable care to prevent it, the employer will be liable even if the employee unreasonably failed to complain to management or even if the employer took prompt and appropriate corrective action when it gained notice.

In most circumstances, if employers and employees discharge their respective duties of reasonable care, unlawful harassment will be prevented and there will be no reason to consider questions of liability. An effective complaint procedure "encourages employees to report harassing conduct before it becomes severe or pervasive," and if an employee promptly utilizes that procedure, the employer can usually stop the harassment before actionable harm occurs.

In some circumstances, however, unlawful harassment will occur and harm will result despite the exercise of requisite legal care by the employer and employee. For example, if an employee's supervisor directed frequent, egregious racial epithets at him that caused emotional harm virtually from the outset, and the employee promptly complained, corrective action by the employer could prevent further harm but might not correct the actionable harm that the employee already had suffered. Alternatively, if an employee complained about harassment before it became severe or pervasive, remedial measures undertaken by the employer might fail to stop the harassment before it reaches an actionable level, even if those measures are reasonably calculated to halt it. In these circumstances, the employer will be liable because the defense requires proof that it exercised reasonable legal care and that the employee unreasonably failed to avoid the harm. While a notice-based negligence standard would absolve the employer of liability, the standard set forth in *Ellerth* and *Faragher* does not. As the Court explained, vicarious liability sets a "more stringent standard" for the employer than the "minimum standard" of negligence theory.

While this result may seem harsh to a law abiding employer, it is consistent with liability standards under the anti-discrimination statutes which generally make employers responsible for the discriminatory acts of their supervisors. If, for example, a supervisor rejects a candidate for promotion because of national origin-based bias, the employer will be liable regardless of whether the employee complained to higher management and regardless of whether higher management had any knowledge about the supervisor's motivation. Harassment is the only type of discrimination carried out by a supervisor for which an employer can avoid liability, and that limitation must be construed narrowly. The employer will be shielded from liability for harassment by a supervisor only if it proves that it exercised reasonable care in preventing and correcting the harassment and that the employee unreasonably failed to avoid all of the harm. If both parties exercise reasonable care, the defense will fail.

In some cases, an employer will be unable to avoid liability completely, but may be able to establish the affirmative defense as a means to limit damages. The defense only limits damages where the employee reasonably could have avoided some but not all of the harm from the harassment. In the example above, in which the supervisor used frequent, egregious racial epithets, an unreasonable delay by the employee in complaining could limit damages but not eliminate liability entirely. This is because a reasonably prompt complaint would have reduced, but not eliminated, the actionable harm.

First Prong of Affirmative Defense: Employer's Duty to Exercise Reasonable Care

The first prong of the affirmative defense requires a showing by the employer that it undertook reasonable care to prevent and promptly correct harassment. Such reasonable care generally requires an employer to establish, disseminate, and enforce an anti-harassment policy and complaint procedure and to take other reasonable steps to prevent and correct harassment. The steps described below are not mandatory requirements—whether or not an employer can prove that it exercised reasonable care depends on the particular factual circumstances and, in some cases, the nature of the employer's workforce. Small employers may be able to effectively prevent and correct harassment through informal means, while larger employers may have to institute more formal mechanisms.

There are no "safe harbors" for employers based on the written content of policies and procedures. Even the best policy and complaint procedure will not alone satisfy the burden of proving reasonable care if, in the particular circumstances of a claim, the employer failed to implement its process effectively. If, for example, the employer has an adequate policy and complaint procedure and properly responded to an employee's complaint of harassment, but management ignored previous complaints by other employees about the same harasser, then the employer has not exercised reasonable care in preventing the harassment. Similarly, if the employer has an adequate policy and complaint procedure but an official failed to carry out his or her responsibility to conduct an effective investigation of a harassment complaint, the employer has not discharged its duty to exercise reasonable care. Alternatively, lack of a formal policy and complaint procedure will not defeat the defense if the employer exercised sufficient care through other means.

Policy and Complaint Procedure

It generally is necessary for employers to establish, publicize, and enforce anti-harassment policies and complaint procedures. As the Supreme Court stated, "Title VII is designed to encourage the creation of anti-harassment policies and effective grievance mechanisms." *Ellerth*, 118 S. Ct. at 2270

An employer should provide every employee with a copy of the policy and complaint procedure, and redistribute it periodically. The policy and complaint procedure should be written in a way that will be understood by all employees in the employer's workforce. Other measures to ensure effective dissemination of the policy and complaint procedure include posting them in central locations and incorporating them into employee handbooks. If feasible, the employer should provide training to all employees to ensure that they understand their rights and responsibilities.

An employer's policy should make clear that it will not tolerate harassment based on sex (with or without sexual conduct), race, color, religion, national origin, age, disability, and protected activity (i.e., opposition to prohibited discrimination or participation in the statutory complaint process). This prohibition should cover harassment by anyone in the workplace— supervisors, co-workers, or non-employees. Management should convey the seriousness of the prohibition. One way to do that is for the mandate to "come from the top," i.e., from upper management.

The policy should encourage employees to report harassment before it becomes severe or pervasive. While isolated incidents of harassment generally do not violate federal law, a pattern of such incidents may be unlawful. Therefore, to discharge its duty of preventive care, the employer must make clear to employees that it will stop harassment before it rises to the level of a violation of federal law.

Questions to Ask the Complainant:

Who, what, when, where, and how: Who committed the alleged harassment? What exactly occurred or was said? When did it occur and is it still ongoing? Where did it occur? How often did it occur? How did it affect you?

How did you react? What response did you make when the incident(s) occurred or afterwards?

How did the harassment affect you? Has your job been affected in any way?

Are there any persons who have relevant information? Was anyone present when the alleged harassment occurred? Did you tell anyone about it? Did anyone see you immediately after episodes of alleged harassment?

Did the person who harassed you harass anyone else? Do you know whether anyone complained about harassment by that person?

Are there any notes, physical evidence, or other documentation regarding the incident(s)?

How would you like to see the situation resolved?

Do you know of any other relevant information?

Questions to Ask the Alleged Harasser:

What is your response to the allegations?

If the harasser claims that the allegations are false, ask why the complainant might lie.

Are there any persons who have relevant information?

Are there any notes, physical evidence, or other documentation regarding the incident(s)?

Do you know of any other relevant information?

Questions to Ask Third Parties:

What did you see or hear? When did this occur? Describe the alleged harasser's behavior toward the complainant and toward others in the workplace.

What did the complainant tell you? When did s/he tell you this?

Do you know of any other relevant information?

Are there other persons who have relevant information?

Credibility Determinations

If there are conflicting versions of relevant events, the employer will have to weigh each party's credibility. Credibility assessments can be critical in determining whether the alleged harassment in fact occurred. Factors to consider include:

Inherent plausibility: Is the testimony believable on its face? Does it make sense?

Demeanor: Did the person seem to be telling the truth or lying?

Motive to falsify: Did the person have a reason to lie?

Corroboration: Is there witness testimony (such as testimony by eye-witnesses, people who saw the person soon after the alleged incidents, or people who discussed the incidents with him or her at around the time that they occurred) or physical evidence (such as written documentation) that corroborates the party's testimony?

Past record: Did the alleged harasser have a history of similar behavior in the past?

None of the above factors are determinative as to credibility. For example, the fact that there are no eye-witnesses to the alleged harassment by no means necessarily defeats the complainant's credibility, since harassment often occurs behind closed doors. Furthermore, the fact that the alleged harasser engaged in similar behavior in the past does not necessarily mean that he or she did so again.

Reaching a Determination

Once all of the evidence is in, interviews are finalized, and credibility issues are resolved, management should make a determination as to whether harassment occurred. That determination could be made by the investigator, or by a management official who reviews the investigator's report. The parties should be informed of the determination.

In some circumstances, it may be difficult for management to reach a determination because of direct contradictions between the parties and a lack of documentary or eye-witness corroboration. In such cases, a credibility assessment may form the basis for a determination, based on factors such as those set forth above.

If no determination can be made because the evidence is inconclusive, the employer should still undertake further preventive measures, such as training and monitoring.

Assurance of Immediate and Appropriate Corrective Action

An employer should make clear that it will undertake immediate and appropriate corrective action, including discipline, whenever it determines that harassment has occurred in violation of the employer's policy. Management should inform both parties about these measures.

Remedial measures should be designed to stop the harassment, correct its effects on the employee, and ensure that the harassment does not recur. These remedial measures need not be those that the employee requests or prefers, as long as they are effective.

In determining disciplinary measures, management should keep in mind that the employer could be found liable if the harassment does not stop. At the same time, management may have concerns that overly punitive measures may subject the employer to claims such as wrongful discharge, and may simply be inappropriate.

To balance the competing concerns, disciplinary measures should be proportional to the seriousness of the offense. If the harassment was minor, such as a small number of "off-color" remarks by an individual with no prior history of similar misconduct, then counseling and an oral warning might be all that is necessary. On the other hand, if the harassment was severe or persistent, then suspension or discharge may be appropriate.

Remedial measures should not adversely affect the complainant. Thus, for example, if it is necessary to separate the parties, then the harasser should be transferred (unless the complainant prefers otherwise). Remedial responses that penalize the complainant could constitute unlawful retaliation and are not effective in correcting the harassment.

Remedial measures also should correct the effects of the harassment. Such measures should be designed to put the employee in the position s/he would have been in had the misconduct not occurred.

Examples of Measures to Stop the Harassment and Ensure That It Does Not Recur:

- oral or written warning or reprimand;
- transfer or reassignment;
- demotion;
- reduction of wages;
- suspension;
- discharge;
- training or counseling of harasser to ensure that s/he understands why his or her conduct violated the employer's anti-harassment policy; and monitoring of harasser to ensure that harassment stops.

Examples of Measures to Correct the Effects of the Harassment:

- restoration of leave taken because of the harassment;
- expungement of negative evaluation(s) in employee's personnel file that arose from the harassment;
- reinstatement;
- apology by the harasser;
- monitoring treatment of employee to ensure that s/he is not subjected to retaliation by the harasser or others in the work place because of the complaint; and
- correction of any other harm caused by the harassment (e.g., compensation for losses).

Conclusion

The Supreme Court's rulings in *Ellerth* and *Faragher* create an incentive for employers to implement and enforce strong policies prohibiting harassment and effective complaint procedures. The rulings also create an incentive for employees to alert management about harassment before it becomes severe and pervasive. If employers and employees undertake these steps, unlawful harassment can often be prevented, thereby effectuating an important goal of the anti-discrimination statutes.

Sexual Harassment Guidelines

The U.S. Equal Employment Opportunity Commission
EEOC Notice Number N-915-050, Issued 3/19/90

This document provides guidance on defining sexual harassment and establishing employer liability in light of recent cases.

Section 703(a)(1) of Title VII, 42 U.S.C. § 2000e-2(a) provides:

It shall be an unlawful employment practice for an employer

> ...to fail or refuse to hire or to discharge any individual, or otherwise to discriminate against any individual with respect to his compensation, terms conditions or privileges of employment, because of such individual's race, color, religion, sex, or national origin[.]

In 1980 the Commission issued guidelines declaring sexual harassment a violation of Section 703 of Title VII, establishing criteria for determining when unwelcome conduct of a sexual nature constitutes sexual harassment, defining the circumstances under which an employer may be held liable, and suggesting affirmative steps an employer should take to prevent sexual harassment. See Section 1604.11 of the Guidelines on Discrimination Because of Sex, 29 C.F.R. § 1604.11 ("Guidelines"). The Commission has applied the Guidelines in its enforcement litigation, and many lower courts have relied on the Guidelines.

The issue of whether sexual harassment violates Title VII reached the Supreme Court in 1986 in *Meritor Savings Bank v. Vinson*, 106 S. Ct. 2399 (1986). The Court affirmed the basic premises of the Guidelines as well as the Commission's definition. The purpose of this document is to provide guidance on the following issues in light of the developing law after *Vinson*:

- determining whether sexual conduct is "un-welcome";
- evaluating evidence of harassment;
- determining whether a work environment is sexually "hostile";
- holding employers liable for sexual harassment by supervisors; and
- evaluating preventive and remedial action taken in response to claims of sexual harassment.

Background

Definition

Title VII does not proscribe all conduct of a sexual nature in the workplace. Thus it is crucial to clearly define sexual harassment: only unwelcome sexual conduct that is a term or condition of employment constitutes a violation. 29 C.F.R. § 1604.11(a). The EEOC's Guidelines define two types of sexual harassment: "quid pro quo" and "hostile environment." The Guidelines provide that "unwelcome" sexual conduct constitutes sexual harassment when "submission to such conduct is made either explicitly or implicitly a term or condition of an individual's employment," 29 C.F.R § 1604.11 (a) (1). "Quid pro quo harassment" occurs when "submission to or rejection of such conduct by an individual is used as the basis for employment decisions affecting such individual," 29 C.F.R § 1604.11(a)(2). 29 C.F.R. § 1604.11(a)(3). The Supreme Court's decision in *Vinson* established that both types of sexual harassment are actionable under section 703 of Title VII of the Civil Rights Act of 1964, 42 U.S.C. § 2000e-2(a), as forms of sex discrimination.

Although "quid pro quo" and "hostile environment" harassment are theoretically distinct claims, the line between the two is not always clear, and the two forms of harassment often occur together. For example, an employee's tangible job conditions are affected when a sexually hostile work environment results in her constructive discharge. Similarly, a supervisor who makes sexual advances toward a subordinate employee may communicate an implicit threat to adversely affect her job status if she does not comply. "Hostile environment" harassment may acquire characteristics of "quid pro quo" harassment if the offending supervisor abuses his authority over employment decisions to force the victim to endure or participate in the sexual conduct. Sexual harassment may culminate in a retaliatory discharge if a victim tells the harasser or her employer she will no longer submit to the harassment, and is then fired in retaliation for this protest. Under these circumstances it would be appropriate to conclude that both harassment and retaliation in violation of section 704(a) of Title VII have occurred.

Distinguishing between the two types of harassment is necessary when determining the employer's liability. But while categorizing sexual harassment as "quid pro quo," "hostile environment," or both is useful analytically these distinctions should not limit the Commission's investigations, which generally should consider all available evidence and testimony under all possibly applicable theories.

Supreme Court's Decision in Vinson

Meritor Savings Bank v. Vinson posed three questions for the Supreme Court:
(1) Does unwelcome sexual behavior that creates a hostile working environment constitute employment discrimination on the basis of sex?
(2) Can a Title VII violation be shown when the district court found that any sexual relationship that existed between the plaintiff and her supervisor was a "voluntary one"? and
(3) Is an employer strictly liable for an offensive working environment created by a supervisor's sexual advances when the

employer does not know of, and could not reasonably have known of, the supervisor's misconduct?

1) Facts—The plaintiff had alleged that her supervisor constantly subjected her to sexual harassment both during and after business hours, on and off the employer's premises; she alleged that he forced her to have sexual intercourse with him on numerous occasions, fondled her in front of other employees, followed her into the women's restroom and exposed himself to her, and even raped her on several occasions. She alleged that she submitted for fear of jeopardizing her employment. She testified, however, that this conduct had ceased almost a year before she first complained in any way, by filing a Title VII suit, her EEOC charge was filed later. The supervisor and the employer denied all of her allegations and claimed they were fabricated in response to a work dispute.

2) Lower Courts' Decisions—After trial, the district court found the plaintiff was not the victim of sexual harassment and was not required to grant sexual favors as a condition of employment or promotion. *Vinson v. Taylor*, 22 EPD 30,708 (D.D.C. 1980). Without resolving the conflicting testimony, the district court found that if a sexual relationship had existed between plaintiff and her supervisor, it was "a voluntary one...having nothing to do with her continued employment." The district court nonetheless went on to hold that the employer was not liable for its supervisor's actions because it had no notice of the alleged sexual harassment; although the employer had a policy against discrimination and an internal grievance procedure, the plaintiff had never lodged a complaint.

The court of appeals reversed and remanded, holding the lower court should have considered whether the evidence established a violation under the "hostile environment" theory. *Vinson v. Taylor*, 753 F.2d 141, denial of rehearing en banc, 760 F.2d 1330, (D.C. Cir. 1985). The court ruled that a victim's "voluntary" submission to sexual advances has "no materiality whatsover" to the proper inquiry: whether "toleration of sexual harassment [was] a condition of her employment." The court further held that an employer is absolutely liable for sexual harassment committed by a supervisory employee, regardless of whether the employer actually knew or reasonably could have known of the misconduct, or would have disapproved of and stopped the misconduct if aware of it.

3) Supreme Court's Opinion—The Supreme Court agreed that the case should be remanded for consideration under the "hostile environment" theory and held that the proper inquiry focuses on the "unwelcomeness" of the conduct rather than the "voluntariness" of the victim's participation. But the Court held that the court of appeals erred in concluding that employers are always automatically liable for sexual harassment by their supervisory employees.

a) "Hostile Environment" Violates Title VII—The Court rejected the employer's contention that Title VII prohibits only discrimination that causes "economic" or "tangible" injury: "Title VII affords employees the right to work in an environment free from discriminatory intimidation, ridicule, and insult whether based on sex, race, religion, or national origin." 106 S. Ct. at 2405. Relying on the EEOC's Guidelines definition of harassment, the court held that a plaintiff may establish a violation of Title VII "by proving that discrimination based on sex has created a hostile or abusive work environment." Id. The Court quoted the Eleventh Circuit's decision in *Henson v. City of Dundee*, 682 F.2d 897 (11th Cir. 1982, 106 S. Ct. at 2406):

> Sexual harassment which creates a hostile or offensive environment for members of one sex is every bit the arbitrary barrier to sexual equality at the workplace that racial harassment is to racial equality. Surely, a requirement that a man or woman run a gauntlet of sexual abuse in return for the privilege of being allowed to work and made a living can be as demeaning and disconcerting as the harshest of racial epithets.

The Court further held that for harassment to violates Title VII, it must be "sufficiently severe or pervasive 'to alter the conditions of [the victim's] employment and create an abusive working environment.'" Id. (quoting *Henson*, 682 F.2d at 904).

b) Conduct Must Be "Unwelcome"—Citing the EEOC's Guidelines, the Court said the gravamen of a sexual harassment claim is that the alleged sexual advances were "unwelcome." 106 S. Ct. at 2406. Therefore, "the fact that sex-related conduct was 'voluntary,' in the sense that the complainant was not forced to participate against her will, is not a defense to a sexual harassment suit brought under Title VII...The correct inquiry is whether [the victim] by her conduct indicated that the alleged sexual advances were unwelcome, not whether her actual participation in sexual intercourse was voluntary." Id. Evidence of a complainant's sexually provocative speech or dress may be relevant in determining whether she found particular advances unwelcome, but should be admitted with caution in light of the potential for unfair prejudice, the Court held.

c) Employer Liability Established Under Agency Principles—On the questions of employer liability in "hostile environment" cases, the Court agreed with EEOC's position that agency principles should be used for guidance. While declining to issue a "definitive rule on employer liability," the Court did reject both the court of appeals' rule of automatic liability for the actions of supervisors and the employer's position that notice is always required. 106 S. Ct. at 2408- 09.

The following sections of this document provide guidance on the issues addressed in *Vinson* and subsequent cases.

Guidance

Determining Whether Sexual Conduct Is Unwelcome

Sexual harassment is "unwelcome...verbal or physical conduct of a sexual nature...." 29 C.F.R. § 1604.11(a). Because sexual attraction may often play a role in the day-to-day social exchange between employees, "the distinction between invited, uninvited-but-welcome, offensive- but-tolerated, and flatly rejected" sexual advances may well be difficult to discern. *Barnes v. Costle*, 561 F.2d 983 (D.C. Cir. 1977) (MacKinnon J., concurring). But this distinction is essential because sexual conduct becomes unlawful only when it is unwelcome. The Eleventh Circuit provided a general definition of "unwelcome conduct" in *Henson v. City of Dundee*, 682 F.2d at 903: the challenged conduct must be unwelcome "in the sense that the employee did not solicit or incite it, and in the sense that the employee regarded the conduct as undesirable or offensive."

When confronted with conflicting evidence as to welcomeness, the Commission looks "at the record as a whole and at the totality of circumstances...." 29 C.F.R. § 1604.11(b), evaluating each situation on a case-by-case basis. When there is some indication of welcomeness or when the credibility of the parties is at issue, the charging party's claim will be considerably strengthened if she made a contemporaneous complaint or protest. Particularly when the alleged harasser may have some reason (e.g., prior consensual relationship) to believe that the advances will be welcomed, it is important for the victim to communicate that the conduct is unwelcome. Generally, victims are well-advised to assert their right to a workplace free from sexual harassment. This may stop the harassment before it becomes more serious. A contemporaneous complaint or protest may also provide persuasive evidence that the sexual harassment in fact occurred as alleged. Thus, in investigating sexual harassment charges, it is important to develop detailed evidence of the circumstances and nature of any such complaints or protests, whether to the alleged harasser, higher management, co-workers or others.

While a complaint or protest is helpful to charging party's case, it is not a necessary element of the claim. Indeed, the Commission recognizes that victims may fear repercussions from complaining about the harassment and that such fear may explain a delay in opposing the conduct. If the victim failed to complain or delayed in complaining, the investigation must ascertain why. The relevance of whether the victim has complained varies depending upon "the nature of the sexual advances and the context in which the alleged incidents occurred." 29 C.F.R. § 1604.11(b).

Example—Charging Party (CP) alleges that her supervisor subjected her to unwelcome sexual advances that created a hostile work environment. The investigation into her charge discloses that her supervisor began making intermittent sexual advances to her in June, 1987, but she did not complain to management about the harassment. After the harassment continued and worsened, she filed a charge with EEOC in June, 1988. There is no evidence CP welcomed the advances. CP states that she feared that complaining about the harassment would cause her to lose her job. She also states that she initially believed she could resolve the situation herself, but as the harassment became more frequent and severe, she said she realized that intervention by EEOC was necessary. The investigator determines CP is credible and concludes that the delay in complaining does not undercut CP's claim.

When welcomeness is at issue, the investigation should determine whether the victim's conduct is consistent, or inconsistent, with her assertion that the sexual conduct is unwelcome.

In *Vinson*, the Supreme Court made clear that voluntary submission to sexual conduct will not necessarily defeat a claim of sexual harassment. The correct inquiry "is whether [the employee] by her conduct indicated that the alleged sexual advances were unwelcome, not whether her actual participation in sexual intercourse was voluntary."

In some cases the courts and the Commission have considered whether the complainant welcomed the sexual conduct by acting in a sexually aggressive manner, using sexually-oriented language, or soliciting the sexual conduct. Thus, in *Gan v. Kepro Circuit Systems*, 27 EPD 32,379 (E.D. Mo. 1982), the plaintiff regularly used vulgar language, initiated sexually-oriented conversations with her co-workers, asked male employees about their marital sex lives and whether they engaged in extramarital affairs, and discussed her own sexual encounters. In rejecting the plaintiff's claim of "hostile environment" harassment, the court found that any propositions or sexual remarks by co-workers were "prompted by her own sexual aggressiveness and her own sexually-explicit conversations" And in *Vinson*, the Supreme Court held that testimony about the plaintiff's provocative dress and publicly expressed sexual fantasies is not per se inadmissible, but the trial court should carefully weigh its relevance against the potential for unfair prejudice. 106 S. Ct. at 2407.

Conversely, occasional use of sexually explicit language does not necessarily negate a claim that sexual conduct was unwelcome. Although a charging party's use of sexual terms or off-color jokes may suggest that sexual comments by others in that situation were not unwelcome, more extreme and abusive or persistent comments or a physical assault will not be excused, nor would "quid pro quo" harassment be allowed.

Any past conduct of the charging party that is offered to show "welcomeness" must relate to the alleged harasser. In *Swentek v. US AIR, Inc.*, 830 F.2d 552, 557 (4th Cir. 1987), the Fourth Circuit held the district court wrongly concluded that the plaintiff's own past conduct and use of foul language showed that "she was the kind of person who could not be offended by such comments and therefore welcomed them generally, " even though she had told the harasser to leave her alone. Emphasizing that the proper inquiry is "whether plaintiff welcomed the particular conduct in question from the alleged harasser," the court of appeals held that "Plaintiff's use of foul language or sexual innuendo in a consensual setting does not waive 'her legal protections against unwelcome harassment.'" 830 F.2d at 557 (quoting *Katz v. Dole*, 709 F.2d 251 (4th Cir. 1983)). Thus, evidence concerning a charging party's general character and past behavior toward others has limited, if any, probative value and does not substitute for a careful examination of her behavior toward the alleged harasser.

A more difficult situation occurs when an employee first willingly participates in conduct of a sexual nature but then ceases to participate and claims that any continued sexual conduct has created a hostile work environment. Here the employee has the burden of showing that any further sexual conduct is unwelcome, work-related harassment. The employee must clearly notify the alleged harasser that his conduct is no longer welcome. If the conduct still continues, her failure to bring the matter to the attention of higher management or the EEOC is evidence, though not dispositive, that any continued conduct is, in fact, welcome or unrelated to work. In any case, however, her refusal to submit to the sexual conduct cannot be the basis for denying her an employment benefit or opportunity; that would constituted a "quid pro quo" violation.

Evaluating Evidence of Sexual Harassment

The Commission recognizes that sexual conduct may be private and unacknowledged, with no eye-witnesses. Even sexual conduct that occurs openly in the workplace may appear to be consensual. Thus the resolution of a sexual harassment claim often depends on the credibility of the parties. The investigator should question the charging party and the alleged harasser in detail. The Commission's investigation also should search thoroughly for corroborative evidence of any nature. Supervisory and managerial employees, as well as co-workers, should be asked about their knowledge of the alleged harassment.

In appropriate cases, the Commission may make a finding of harassment based solely on the credibility of the victim's allegation. As with any other charge of discrimination, a victim's account must be sufficiently detailed and internally consistent so as to be plausible, and lack of corroborative evidence where such evidence logically should exist would undermine the allegation. By the same token, a general denial by the alleged harasser will carry little weight when it is contradicted by other evidence.

Of course, the Commission recognizes that a charging party may not be able to identify witnesses to the alleged conduct itself. But testimony may be obtained from persons who observed the charging party's demeanor immediately after an alleged incident of harassment. Persons with whom she discussed the incident—

such as co-workers, a doctor or a counselor—should be interviewed. Other employees should be asked if they noticed changes in charging party's behavior at work or in the alleged harasser's treatment of charging party. As stated earlier, a contemporaneous complaint by the victim would be persuasive evidence both that the conduct occurred and that it was unwelcome. So too is evidence that other employees were sexually harassed by the same person.

The investigator should determine whether the employer was aware of any other instances of harassment and if so what was the response. Where appropriate the Commission will expand the case to include class claims.

Example—Charging Party (CP) alleges that her supervisor made unwelcome sexual advances toward her on frequent occasions while they were alone in his office. The supervisor denies this allegation. No one witnessed the alleged advances. CP's inability to produce eyewitnesses to the harassment does not defeat her claim. The resolution will depend on the credibility of her allegations versus that of her supervisor's. Corroborating, credible evidence will establish her claim. For example, three co-workers state that CP looked distraught on several occasions after leaving the supervisor's office, and that she informed them on those occasions that he had sexually propositioned and touched her. In addition, the evidence shows that CP had complained to the general manager of the office about the incidents soon after they occurred. The corroborating witness testimony and her complaint to higher management would be sufficient to establish her claim. Her allegations would be further buttressed if other employees testified that the supervisor propositioned them as well.

If the investigation exhausts all possibilities for obtaining corroborative evidence, but finds none, the Commission may make a cause finding based solely on a reasoned decision to credit the charging party's testimony.

In a "quid pro quo" case, a finding that the employer's asserted reasons for its adverse action against the charging party are pretextual will usually establish a violation. The investigation should determine the validity of the employer's reasons for the charging party's termination. If they are pretextual and if the sexual harassment occurred, then it should be inferred that the charging party was terminated for rejecting the employer's sexual advances, as she claims. Moreover, if the termination occurred because the victim complained, it would be appropriate to find, in addition, a violation of section 704(a).

Determining Whether a Work Environment Is "Hostile"

The Supreme Court said in *Vinson* that for sexual harassment to violate Title VII, it must be "sufficiently severe or pervasive 'to alter the conditions of [the victim's] employment and create an abusive working environment.'" 106 S. Ct. at 2406 (quoting *Henson v. City of Dundee*, 682 F.2d at 904. Since "hostile environment' harassment takes a variety of forms, many factors may affect this determination, including: (1) whether the conduct was verbal or physical, or both; (2) how frequently it was repeated; (3) whether the conduct was hostile and patently offensive; (4) whether the alleged harasser was a co-worker or a supervisor; (5) whether the others joined in perpetrating the harassment; and (6) whether the harassment was directed at more than one individual.

In determining whether unwelcome sexual conduct rises to the level of a "hostile environment" in violation of Title VII, the central inquiry is whether the conduct "unreasonably interfer[es] with an individual's work performance" or creates "an intimidating, hostile, or offensive working environment." 29 C.F.R. § 1604.11(a)(3). Thus, sexual flirtation or innuendo, even vulgar language that is trivial or merely annoying, would probably not establish a hostile environment.

1) Standard for Evaluating Harassment—In determining whether harassment is sufficiently severe or pervasive to create a hostile environment, the harasser's conduct should be evaluated from the objective standpoint of a "reasonable person." Title VII does not

serve "as a vehicle for vindicating the petty slights suffered by the hypersensitive." *Zabkowicz v. West Bend Co.*, 589 F. Supp. 780 (E.D. Wis. 1984). See also *Ross v. Comsat*, 759 F.2d 355 (4th Cir. 1985). Thus, if the challenged conduct would not substantially affect the work environment of a reasonable person, no violation should be found.

Example—Charging Party alleges that her coworker made repeated unwelcome sexual advances toward her. An investigation discloses that the alleged "advances" consisted of invitations to join a group of employees who regularly socialized at dinner after work. The coworker's invitations, viewed in that context and from the perspective of a reasonable person, would not have created a hostile environment and therefore did not constitute sexual harassment.

A "reasonable person" standard also should be applied to be more basic determination of whether challenged conduct is of a sexual nature. Thus, in the above example, a reasonable person would not consider the co-worker's invitations sexual in nature, and on that basis as well no violation would be found.

This objective standard should not be applied in a vacuum, however. Consideration should be given to the context in which the alleged harassment took place. As the Sixth Circuit has stated, the trier of fact must "adopt the perspective of a reasonable person's reaction to a similar environment under similar or like circumstances." *Highlander v. K.F.C.National Management Co.* 805 F.2d 644 (6th Cir. 1986).

The reasonable person standard should consider the victim's perspective and not stereotyped notions of acceptable behavior. For example, the Commission believes that a workplace in which sexual slurs, displays of "girlie" pictures, and other offensive conduct abound can constitute a hostile work environment even if many people deem it to be harmless or insignificant. *Cf. Rabidue v. Osceola Refining Co.*, 805 F.2d 611 (6th Cir. 1986) (Keith, C.J., dissenting), cert. denied, 107 S. Ct. 1983 (1987). *Lipsett v. University of Puerto Rico*, 864 F.2d 881 (1st Cir. 1988).

2) Isolated Instances of Harassment—Unless the conduct is quite severe, a single incident or isolated incidents of offensive sexual conduct or remarks generally do not create an abusive environment. As the Court noted in *Vinson*, "mere utterance of an ethnic or racial epithet which engenders offensive feelings in an employee would not affect the conditions of employment to a sufficiently significant degree to violate Title VII." 106 S.Ct. at 2406 (quoting *Rogers v. EEOC*, 454 F.2d 234 (5th Cir. 1971), cert. denied, 406 U.S. 957 (1972)). A "hostile environment" claim generally requires a showing of a pattern of offensive conduct. In contrast, in "quid pro quo" cases a single sexual advance may constitute harassment if it is linked to the granting or denial of employment benefits.

But a single, unusually severe incident of harassment may be sufficient to constitute a Title VII violation; the more severe the harassment, the less need to show a repetitive series of incidents. This is particularly true when the harassment is physical. Thus, in *Barrett v. Omaha National Bank*, 584 F. Supp, 22 (D. Neb. 1983), aff'd, 726 F.2d 424 (8th Cir. 1984), one incident constituted actionable sexual harassment. The harasser talked to the plaintiff about sexual activities and touched her in an offensive manner while they were inside a vehicle from which she could not escape.
The Commission will presume that the unwelcome, intentional touching of a charging party's intimate body areas is sufficiently offensive to alter the condition of her working environment and constitute a violation of Title VII. More so than in the case of verbal advances or remarks, a single unwelcome physical advance can seriously poison the victim's working environment. If an employee's supervisor sexually touches that employee, the Commission normally would find a violation. In such situations, it is the employer's burden to demonstrate that the unwelcome conduct was not sufficiently severe to create a hostile work environment.

When the victim is the target of both verbal and non-intimate physical conduct, the hostility of the environment is exacerbated and a violation is more likely to be found. Similarly, incidents of sexual harassment directed at other employees in addition to the charging party are relevant to a showing of hostile work environment. *Hall v. Gus Construction Co.*, 842 F.2d 1010 (8th Cir. 1988); *Hicks v. Gates Rubber Co.*, 833 F.2d 1406 (10th Cir. 1987); *Jones v. Flagship International*, 793 F.2d 714 (5th Cir. 1986), cert. denied, 107 S. Ct. 952 (1987).

3) Non-physical Harassment—When the alleged harassment consists of verbal conduct, the investigation should ascertain the nature, frequency, context, and intended target of the remarks. Questions to be explored might include:

- Did the alleged harasser single out the charging party?
- Did the charging party participate?
- What was the relationship between the charging party and the alleged harasser(s)?
- Were the remarks hostile and derogatory?

No one factor alone determines whether particular conduct violates Title VII. As the Guidelines emphasize, the Commission will evaluate the totality of the circumstances. In general, a woman does not forfeit her right to be free from sexual harassment by choosing to work in an atmosphere that has traditionally included vulgar, anti-female language. However, in *Rabidue v. Osceola Refining Co.*, 805 F.2d 611, 41 EPD ¶ 36,643 (6th Cir. 1986), cert. denied, 107 S. Ct. 1983 (1987), the Sixth Circuit rejected the plaintiff's claim of harassment in such a situation.

One of the factors the court found relevant was "the lexicon of obscenity that pervaded the environment of the workplace both before and after the plaintiff's introduction into its environs, coupled with the reasonable expectations of the plaintiff upon voluntarily entering that environment." 805 F.2d at 620. Quoting the district court, the majority noted that in some work environments, "`humor and language are rough hewn and vulgar. Sexual jokes, sexual conversations, and girlie magazines may abound. Title VII was not meant to—or can—change this.`" Id. At 620-21. The court also considered the sexual remarks and poster at issue to have a "de minimus effect on the plaintiff's work environment when considered in the context of a society that condones and publicly features and commercially exploits open displays of written and pictorial erotica at the newsstands, on prime-time television, at the cinema, and in other public places." Id. at 622.

The Commission believes these factors rarely will be relevant and agrees with the dissent in *Rabidue* that a woman does not assume the risk of harassment by voluntarily entering an abusive, anti-female environment. "Title VII's precise purpose is to prevent such behavior and attitudes from poisoning the work environment of classes protected under the Act." 805 F.2d at 626 (Keith, J., dissenting in part and concurring in part). Thus, in a decision disagreeing with *Rabidue*, a district court found that a hostile environment was established by the presence of pornographic magazines in the workplace and vulgar employee comments concerning them; offensive sexual comments made to and about plaintiff and other female employees by her supervisor; sexually oriented pictures in a company-sponsored movie and slide presentation; sexually oriented pictures and calendars in the workplace; and offensive touching of plaintiff by a co-worker. *Barbetta v. Chemlawn Services Corp.* 669 F. Supp. 569 (W.D.N.Y. 1987). The court held that the proliferation of pornography and demeaning comments, if sufficiently continuous and pervasive "may be found to create an atmosphere in which women are viewed as men's sexual playthings rather than as their equal coworkers." *Barbetta*, 669 F. Supp. At 573. The Commission agrees that, depending on the totality of circumstances, such an atmosphere may violate Title VII. See also *Waltman v. International Paper Co.*, 875 F.2d 468 (5th Cir. 1989), in which the 5th Circuit endorsed the Commission's position in its amicus brief that evidence of ongoing sexual graffiti in the workplace, not all of which was directed at the plaintiff, was relevant to her claim of harassment. *Bennett v. Coroon & Black Corp.*, 845 F.2d 104 (5th Cir. 1988) (the posting of obscene cartoons in an office men's room bearing the plaintiff's name and depicting her engaged in crude and deviant sexual activities could create a hostile work environment).

4) Sex-based Harassment—Although the Guidelines specifically address conduct that is sexual in nature, the Commission notes that sex-based harassment—that is, harassment not involving sexual activity or language—may also give rise to Title VII liability (just as in the case of harassment based on race, national origin or religion) if it is "sufficiently patterned or pervasive" and directed at employees because of their sex. *Hicks v. Gates Rubber Co.*, 833 F.2d at 1416; *McKinney v. Dole*, 765 F.2d 1129 (D.C. Cir. 1985).

Acts of physical aggression, intimidation, hostility or unequal treatment based on sex may be combined with incidents of sexual harassment to establish the existence of discriminatory terms and conditions of employment. *Hall v. Gus Construction Co.*, 842 F.2d 1014; *Hicks v. Gates Rubber Co.*, 833 F. 2d at 1416.

5) Constructive Discharge—Claims of "hostile environment" sexual harassment often are coupled with claims of constructive discharge. If constructive discharge due to a hostile environment is proven, the claim will also become one of "quid pro quo" harassment. It is the position of the Commission and a majority of courts that an employer is liable for constructive discharge when it imposes intolerable working conditions in violation of Title VII when those conditions foreseeably would compel a reasonable employee to quit, whether or not the employer specifically intended to force the victim's resignation. See *Derr v. Gulf Oil Corp.*, 796 F.2d 340 (10th Cir. 1986); *Goss v. Exxon Office Systems Co.*, 747 F.2d 885 (3d Cir. 1984); *Nolan v. Cleland*, 686 F.2d 806 (9th Cir. 1982); *Held v. Gulf Oil Co.*, 684 F.2d 427 (6th Cir. 1982); *Clark v. Marsh*, 655 F.2d 1168 (D.C. Cir. 1981); *Bourque v. Powell Electrical Manufacturing Co.*, 617 F.2d 61 (5th cir. 1980); Commission Decision 84-1, CCH EEOC Decision 6839. However, the Fourth Circuit requires proof that the employer imposed the intolerable conditions with the intent of forcing the victim to leave. See *EEOC v. Federal Reserve Bank of Richmond*, 698 F.2d 633 (4th Cir. 1983). But this case is not a sexual harassment case and the Commission

believes it is distinguishable because specific intent is not likely to be present in "hostile environment" cases.

An important factor to consider is whether the employer had an effective internal grievance procedure. The Commission argued in its *Vinson* brief that if an employee knows that effective avenues of complaint and redress are available, then the availability of such avenues itself becomes a part of the work environment and overcomes, to the degree it is effective, the hostility of the work environment. As Justice Marshall noted in his opinion in *Vinson*, "Where a complainant without good reason bypassed an internal complaint procedure she knew to be effective, a court may be reluctant to find constructive termination...." 106 S.Ct. at 2411 (Marshall, J., concurring in part and dissenting in part). Similarly, the court of appeals in *Dornhecker v. Malibu Grand Prix Corp.*, 828 F.2d 307 (5TH Cir. 1987), held the plaintiff was not constructively discharged after an incident of harassment by a co-worker because she quit immediately, even though the employer told her she would not have to work with him again, and she did not give the employer a fair opportunity to demonstrate it could curb the harasser's conduct.

Preventive and Remedial Action

1) Preventive Action—The EEOC'S Guidelines encourage employers to:

take all steps necessary to prevent sexual harassment from occurring, such as affirmatively raising the subject, expressing strong disapproval, developing appropriate sanctions, informing employees of their right to raise and how to raise the issue of harassment under Title VII, and developing methods to sensitize all concerned.

29 C.F.R. § 1604.11(f). An effective preventive program should include an explicit policy against sexual harassment that is clearly

and regularly communicated to employees and effectively implemented. The employer should affirmatively raise the subject with all supervisory and non-supervisory employees, express strong disapproval, and explain the sanctions for harassment. The employer should also have a procedure for resolving sexual harassment complaints. The procedure should be designed to "encourage victims of harassment to come forward" and should not require a victim to complain first to the offending supervisor. See *Vinson*, 106 S. Ct. at 2408. It should ensure confidentiality as much as possible and provide effective remedies, including protection of victims and witnesses against retaliation.

2) Remedial Action

Since Title VII "affords employees the right to work in an environment free from discriminatory intimidation, ridicule, and insult" (*Vinson*), 106 S. Ct. at 2405), an employer is liable for failing to remedy known hostile or offensive work environments. See, e.g., *Garziano v. E.I. Dupont de Nemours & Co.*, 818 F.2d 380 (5th Cir. 1987) (*Vinson* holds employers have an "affirmative duty to eradicate 'hostile or offensive' work environments"); *Bundy v. Jackson*, 641 F.2d 934 (D.C. Cir. 1981) (employer violated Title VII by failing to investigate and correct sexual harassment despite notice); *Tompkins v. Public Service Electric & Gas Co.*, 568 F.2d 1044 (3d Cir. 1977) (same); *Henson v. City of Dundee*, 682 F.2d 897 (11th Cir. 1982) (same); *Munford v. James T. Barnes & Co.*, 441 F. Supp. 459 (E.D. Mich. 1977) (employer has an affirmative duty to investigate complaints of sexual harassment and to deal appropriately with the offending personnel; "failure to investigate gives tactic support to the discrimination because the absence of sanctions encourages abusive behavior").

When an employer receives a complaint or otherwise learns of alleged sexual harassment in the workplace, the employer should investigate promptly and thoroughly. The employer should take immediate and appropriate corrective action by doing whatever is necessary to end the harassment, make the victim whole by restoring lost employment benefits or opportunities, and prevent the misconduct from recurring. Disciplinary action against the offending supervisor or employee, ranging from reprimand to discharge, may be necessary. Generally, the corrective action should reflect the severity of the conduct. See *Waltman v. International Paper Co.*, 875 F.2d at 479 (appropriateness of remedial action will depend on the severity and persistence of the harassment and the effectiveness of any initial remedial steps). *Dornhecker v. Malibu Grand Prix Corp.*, 828 F.2d 307 (5th Cir. 1987) (the employer's remedy may be "assessed proportionately to the seriousness of the offense"). The employer should make follow-up inquiries to ensure the harassment has not resumed and the victim has not suffered retaliation.

Recent Court decisions illustrate appropriate and inappropriate responses by employers. In *Barrett v. Omaha National Bank*, 726 F.2d 424 (8th Cir. 1984), the victim informed her employer that her co-worker had talked to her about sexual activities and touched her in an offensive manner. Within four days of receiving this information, the employer investigated the charges, reprimanded the guilty employee placed him on probation, and warned him that further misconduct would result in discharge. A second co-worker who had witnessed the harassment was also reprimanded for not intervening on the victim's behalf or reporting the conduct. The court ruled that the employer's response constituted immediate and appropriate corrective action, and on this basis found the employer not liable.

In contrast, in *Yates v. Avco Corp.*, 819 F.2d 630 (6th Cir. 1987), the court found the employer's policy against sexual harassment failed to function effectively. The victim's first-level supervisor had responsibility for reporting and correcting harassment at the company, yet he was the harasser. The employer told the victims not to go to the EEOC. While giving the accused harasser administrative leave pending investigation, the employer made the plaintiffs take sick leave, which was never credited back to them and was recorded in their personnel files as excessive absenteeism without indicating they were absent because of sexual harassment. Similarly, in *Zabkowicz v. West Bend Co.*, 589 F. Supp. 780 (E.D. Wis. 1984), co-workers harassed the plaintiff over a period of nearly four years in a manner the court described as "malevolent" and "outrageous." Despite the plaintiff's numerous complaints, her supervisor took no remedial action other than to hold occasional meetings at which he reminded employees of the company's policy against offensive conduct. The supervisor never conducted an investigation or disciplined any employees until the plaintiff filed an EEOC charge, at which time one of the offending co-workers was discharged and three others were suspended. The court held the employer liable because it failed to take immediate and appropriate corrective action.

When an employer asserts it has taken remedial action, the Commission will investigate to determine whether the action was appropriate and, more important, effective. The EEOC investigator should, of course, conduct an independent investigation of the harassment claim, and the Commission will reach its own conclusion as to whether the law has been violated. If the Commission finds that the harassment has been eliminated, all victims made whole, and preventive measures instituted, the Commission normally will administratively close the charge because of the employer's prompt remedial action.